THE PRESIDENTIAL QUEST

# The presidential quest: candidates and images in American political culture, 1787–1852

M. J. Heale

*Longman*
London and New York

**Longman Group Limited**
*Longman House*
*Burnt Mill, Harlow, Essex, UK*

*Published in the United States of America
by Longman Inc., New York*

© M. J. Heale 1982

*First published 1982*

**British Library Cataloguing in Publication Data**

Heale, M. J.
   The presidential quest
   1. United States – Politics and government
   – 1783–1865
   I. Title
   320.9'73   JK116
   ISBN 0–582–29542–4

**Library of Congress Cataloging in Publication Data**

Heale, M. J.
   The presidential quest.
   Bibliography: p.
   Includes index.
   1. Presidents–United States–Election–
History. I. Title.
JK524.H39   324.973' 05   81–8415
ISBN 0–582–29542–4 (pbk.)   AACR2

Printed in Singapore by
Selector Printing Co Pte Ltd.

# Contents

*For Lesley*

# Preface

American presidential elections command attention in a way un-
equalled by any other regular political event of the Western world.
The outcome of a presidential election is deemed to be of critical
importance, even though foreign observers and many Americans
themselves frequently feel that there is little to choose between the
two major candidates, and even though, once elected, a president
finds his powers to be frustratingly limited. There is something
almost sublime in the spectacle of a great nation, which has declared all its millions of citizens to be equal and allows every adult a
vote, choosing one man to be its ultimate representative, and
perhaps its personification. The drama is magnified by the election
campaigns themselves, by the often unpredictable primary contests,
by the hullabaloo of national nominating conventions, by the
cavortings, manoeuvrings, stumblings and vauntings of the candidates. A presidential election is always conducted before the arc-
lights of the media, and pundits across the world compete with one
another to distil some meaning from the event. If American politics
are dominated by these quadrennial contests, it may only be because they are so widely treated as the primary force in American
political life.

The presidential campaign assumed its most glorious dimension
in the second quarter of the nineteenth century, the so-called age of
Jackson. For Americans, at least, the presidential contest seemed to
arouse even more interest then than it does today. The election
which made Andrew Jackson president witnessed a greater turnout
of the electorate than the election which produced President
Reagan. About half as many Americans again, measured as a proportion of qualified voters, went to the polls in the presidential elec-

tions of the 1840s than in those of the 1970s. It was in these years that the popular campaign developed, accompanied by features which are still considered characteristic of American elections. Presidents came in effect to be elected on the basis of virtually universal (white manhood) suffrage; candidates competed for the electoral votes of each state on a 'winner-take-all' basis; the national political system was ordered by two major, coalitional parties; national nominating conventions made their colourful appearance; the deliberate manufacture of 'images' around the candidates became a major phenomenon; extravagant political rallies, punctuated by fireworks, song, and patriotic rituals, enlivened the campaigns. A few important features, such as primary elections, did not appear until much later, but it can be said that the American presidential campaign was in large part invented in the Jacksonian era.

In the eye of the storm was the presidential candidate himself. He was the subject of the serious debate and the less serious ballyhoo. Much of the distinctive machinery, procedures and ceremonies of presidential campaigns clearly developed in response to the arrival of popular democracy – to the fact that by the 1820s presidents were effectively being elected by popular vote – but tradition enjoined on the candidate a passive role. A curious and anomalous situation was created: in the age of the common man, when the president was said to be the supreme spokesman of the people, presidential candidates were prohibited from presenting themselves directly *to* the people. Hence one reason for the extraordinary developments in American campaigning was that the candidates themselves were obliged to remain mute.

This study seeks to explore the nature of nineteenth century American political culture by examining the emergence of the popular presidential election, focussing particularly on the role of the candidate. The period chosen is that from George Washington's presidency to the dislocations of the 1850s, with a concentration on the life of what is known as 'the second American party system' in the second half of that period. Despite the scholarly attention given to presidential elections, past and present, little has been written about the candidates themselves in nineteenth-century campaigns, what they did and what was done to and for them. By examining how presidents were made between the Revolution and the Civil War, this book seeks to establish a vantage point from which to view a number of related topics, such as the cultural functions of presidential campaigns, the ideology and psychology of republicanism, the nature of the American party system and the characters of the major parties, and the phenomenon of Jacksonian democracy. In short, this book attempts to use the role of the presidential candidate as a means of exposing something of the larger political culture at a formative stage.

A few words of explanation may be in order. The book does not offer a chronological narrative on an election-by-election basis. It was hoped that a more analytical approach would prove more revealing. But not all elections have been treated in the same way. Where a regular party system was clearly in existence it was possible to examine the relevant elections together. Thus Chapters 5 to 9 cover differing aspects of the presidential elections of the second-party system. The elections of 1824 and 1828, however, were each in a sense 'one-off' affairs and have therefore been given chapters of their own. This does not mean that they were necessarily more important than the elections which preceded or followed them; they simply did not fit into a larger party system which could be studied as a whole.

A book which analyses several presidential elections is grappling with an enormous subject and must be selective. The decision to focus on the figure of the presidential candidate should explain some of the lacunae. The important question of who voted for whom, for example, lies outside the scope of this study, though of course has been given considerable attention by other scholars. Vice-presidential and third-party candidates have been favoured with only occasional glances, partly because the obscure and the ephemeral do not lend themselves to the kind of treatment possible for the candidates of major parties, but also because it became evident in the course of writing the book that an analysis of the behaviour of such figures would add little to the subject addressed here.

Perhaps a word should be added about sources. The book is based very largely on primary material, much of it in the form of campaign publications (which have been curiously little-used by other studies of early presidential elections). These effusions were frequently rhetorical and self-serving, but that does not detract from their value as historical documents. Much can be learned about a political culture from the language of that culture, as scholars such as Gordon Wood, Henry Nash Smith and John William Ward have shown. This may be especially true of a political society in which ideology is important, as was the case with the *antebellum* United States. The ways in which men perceive the world around them, and the values and ideas which they hold, condition their behaviour. Personal ambition and private interests play their important part too, of course, but men's public utterances are also instructive guides to the beliefs which shape their actions.

There was something rather messianic in the political convictions which animated public men in the first half of the nineteenth century, and this perhaps served to separate their world from the United States of today. The modern appearance of their political forms and procedures is somewhat misleading in that the society which gave rise to them was anything but modern. In the 1820s, 1830s and 1840s the American Revolution was not long in the past and the Industrial Revolution had yet to take place. Jacksonian America was a pre-industrial society suffused with memories of the Revolution and conscious of the novelty, distinctiveness and fragility of the great experiment in republican government. It was also a deeply divided society, and the divisions could be related at least in part to differing conceptions over how best to nourish, protect and expand the heritage of freedom. Jacksonian America has often been characterized as a highly confident and optimistic society, but it was also a society marked by fear and anxiety. The hope of an ever more splendid future was paralleled by a harrowing fear that the mission in republicanism might somehow go awry. The anxiety which underlay the political discourse of this period was not altogether misplaced. The major parties spoke of their high hopes for the republic, but it was their worst fears that were ultimately fulfilled.

# Acknowledgements

Probably the foremost debt of any writer of history is to those scholars who have written before him. The references at the end of this book are to the immediate sources used and do little to acknowledge the part played by countless other writings in my understanding of American politics in the period between the Revolution and the Civil War. Those familiar with this subject will espy in the following pages the influence of scholars as diverse as, say, J. G. A. Pocock, Richard P. McCormick, and John William Ward, and of many others too. Another kind of debt is owed to those who offered advice and suggestions on the writing of this book: Marcus Cunliffe, Herbert Nicholas, Donald J. Ratcliffe, Robert M. Bliss, Irving Bartlett, Alasdair Kean, Michael Abramson and John A. Thompson helped in this respect. Richard P. McCormick was generous with his time and advice during the early shaping of this work. John Ashworth read the entire manuscript even before it became a typescript and offered many helpful suggestions. Two visits to the United States were indispensable, first a year at Rutgers University made possible by a fellowship from the American Council of Learned Societies, and later several months as a visiting scholar at the Charles Warren Center for Studies in American History at Harvard University, made possible by the courtesy of its director, Donald Fleming, and by a research grant from the University of Lancaster. I would also like to thank the staffs of the Library of Congress, the New York Public Library, the American Antiquarian Society, and of the libraries of Rutgers, Columbia, Princeton, Harvard and Lancaster universities. A debt of gratitude is also owed to Pat Dennison for her accomplished production of the typescript.
M. J. H.

# CHAPTER ONE
# *The Mute Tribune*

One day deep in the winter of 1821–22 a South Carolina congressman deliberated on his recent nomination to the presidency by his state legislature. The honour gratified him, he admitted, but he could not allow it to influence his conduct, for 'the Presidency is not an office to be either solicited or declined'. A premature death a few months later spared William Lowndes from further temptation (as it denied him a larger role in the history books), but for a time his phrase lived on and was cited with approval as presidential elections loomed. He was echoing the sentiment enunciated by Benjamin Franklin many decades before: 'I shall never *ask*, never *refuse*, nor ever *resign* an Office'. Later generations of Americans would find such an attitude baffling, but the citizens of the early republic had come to expect a decorous measure of diffidence from their leading men. No candidate for high office could honourably advance his own fortunes; nor could he honourably refuse office when it was thrust upon him. In this strange land where all the officers of government were the chosen agents of the people, those who discreetly eyed the Chief Magistracy had quietly to await the summons of their fellow countrymen.[1]

Only in a later and very different age would ambitious men announce their own candidacy for the presidency and bustle down the campaign trail, delivering speeches, discussing issues, making pledges and asking for votes. Any modern presidential candidate who sought to remain as aloof from his campaign as, say, Thomas Jefferson or John Adams had from theirs, would be chastised for treating his electoral masters with contempt, for failing to make himself or his views available for public appraisal. But the political culture which had nurtured Jefferson and Adams was not the popular political culture of today. A candidate then had to remain pas-

1

sive – and outwardly uninterested – if he was to escape censure.

There was indeed a singular anomaly in the novel system of government that Americans had established for themselves. They had broken with all precedent in devising a national government all of whose members were the chosen representatives of the people and only the people. Even the executive was not the bastion of some distinct propertied, titled, clerical or military class, but represented the sovereign people as much as any other branch. At least one of the framers of the Constitution had seen the presidency as 'the guardian of the people, even of the lower classes, agst. Legislative tyranny', that is, as a kind of popular tribune whose duty it would be to protect the people's liberties against the depredations of 'the Great & the wealthy' who would inevitably find their way into Congress. Yet if the president was the supreme representative of the people, and if it was his first duty to guard their freedom, he was allowed little communication with his masters. A candidate for that office was enjoined by the political imperatives of the day *not* to address himself to the people, and even as president he could not do so directly. The architects of the American system of government had provided the people with a kind of tribune, but one who was in no small part rendered mute. This was an arrangement which was hardly likely to prove permanent, the exigencies of electoral politics being what they were – and what they were to become – but it did last for a surprisingly long time, and was not even completely undone by the boisterous politicking of the Jacksonian era.[2]

From George Washington to John Quincy Adams most aspirants to the presidential office conducted themselves with the gentlemanly restraint that their era demanded. 'Motives of delicacy have prevented me hitherto from conversing or writing on this subject', observed a fretful Washington during the first presidential campaign, 'whenever I could avoid it with decency.' As befitted the humble farmer that he claimed to be, Washington spent these months quietly at Mount Vernon, riding conscientiously around his farms, juggling unhappily with his insistent debts, occasionally entertaining visitors, and gravely assuring his correspondents – when he referred to the matter at all – that he really did not want to be president. But he never absolutely ruled himself out and no other serious contender emerged. It had long been taken for granted by men in public life that George Washington would be the nation's first president, and across the country electors were chosen on that assumption. Even the general's friends had little need to work on his behalf and the election duly ran its predicted course. 'I am so much affected by this fresh proof of my Country's Esteem and Confidence that silence can best explain my gratitude,' responded Washington when he was formally notified of his new distinction, maintaining his diffidence to the very end. Wrapping himself in as much gloom as he could muster, he proceeded to 'the chair of government . . . accompanied by feelings not unlike those of a culprit who is going to the place of his execution'.[3]

None of his successors could quite equal the degree of reluctance that Washington managed to convey, but then none of them faced as little opposition. Yet for a generation and more presidential aspirants did their best to emulate the general's weighty example. Thomas Jefferson in 1796 was determined not to lift a finger on his own behalf, busying himself instead with the ambitious rebuilding of Monticello and conducting little correspondence. 'The little spice of ambition which I had in my younger days has long since evaporated', he told James Madison in demurring at the suggestion that he should be a candidate, 'and I set still less store by a posthumous than present name.' His rival John Adams used the excuse of his own and his wife's health to request leave from his vice-presidential duties, and he repaired to his farm at Quincy, where he spent the summer and autumn of 1796 raising a barn, husbanding his crops, trying to reform a drunken workman, deliberating on the Christian religion, and on occasion talking to the political friends who visited him. Indeed, he described the summer as 'the freest from Care' of his life: 'My health has been better, the Season fruitful, my farm was conducted. Alass! what may happen to redress all this?' That he desired the presidency there is little doubt, but he was trying to persuade himself otherwise and he took no active part in the campaign. Both Jefferson and Adams were the inescapable candidates of their respective parties in that election, and as such neither needed actively to seek nor formally to accept a nomination. Their friends in Philadelphia (then the seat of the federal government) and through the Union were able to conduct their campaigns without involving them, and Madison indeed deliberately refrained from consulting or even seeing Jefferson at this time so as 'to present him no opportunity of protesting to his friends against being embarked in the contest'. John Adams continued to protest his indifference to the outcome, while Jefferson chivalrously insisted that he must concede to the vice-president in the event of a tie in the electoral college, for 'He has always been my senior, from the commencement of our public life. . . .' So the candidates comported themselves in the presidential election of 1796, maintaining a gracious silence in their respective country retreats as their fellow citizens weighed their fitness for the republic's highest office.[4]

From these early presidential elections there stemmed the tradition of the Mute Tribune. As party warfare sharpened, it is true, presidential candidates began to manoeuvre for electoral advantage, but publicly they presented a posture of indifference, taking no overt part in the campaign, keeping out of the public eye, and protesting to their correspondents their lack of ambition for the presidency. The very act of quitting public life, indeed, in itself could seem suspect. John Adams reacted cynically to a report in 1797 that James Madison was to retire: 'Madison, I suppose, after a retirement of a few years, is to be President or Vice-President. . . . It is marvellous how political plants grow in the shade.' Certainly no one covetous of the presidency dared be seen working his way towards it. 'Should the nation be disposed to call any citizen to that station it would be his duty to accept it. . . . .' observed James Monroe on one occasion. 'I have done nothing to draw the attention of anyone to me in reference to it, nor shall I in future.' It was to be many decades before presidential candidates were permitted to behave as if they wanted to be elected.[5]

But why was it that seekers after high office had to conduct themselves with such circumspection? To some degree, perhaps, the early presidential candidates felt themselves bound to follow the massive example of George Washington, but this does nothing to explain Washington's own show of lugubrious reluctance, and it is insufficient to explain the pervasiveness and persistence of the tradition. Candidates for other offices were also usually expected to abstain from personal campaigning, although in some states the electioneering occasioned by contests for local positions as early as the 1780s and 1790s seriously distressed high-minded citizens. But in general the higher the office the greater the apparent diffidence of the candidates, and not until the middle decades of the nineteenth century – at least in most states – could a candidate openly press his claims for the chief executiveship, either of the state or of the nation. The Mute Tribune, then, was no fortuitous phenomenon. He was the product of the political culture of his day, and his bashful behaviour tells us something about that culture. It was a political culture which was based in no small part on the fear of power.

'To anticipate the future glory of America', wrote a New England cleric in 1773, 'is ravishing and transporting to the mind.' Such expressions of transcendent optimism by members of the revolutionary generation have sometimes blinded scholars to the darker side of the American mind. Pessimism as well as optimism has been a characteristic of the American people, and the Founding Fathers were as subject to anxiety and unease as any group of men. At any rate, the constraints under which politicians operated in the early republic were related ultimately to a measure of distrust in both men and governments. Americans could not be certain that they would live up to the trust that Providence seemed to be thrusting upon them. Perhaps, as Washington said, if 'property was well secured, faith and justice well preserved, a stable government well administered, and confidence restored, the tide of wealth and population would flow to us from every part of the globe, and, with a due sense of the blessings, make us the happiest people on earth'. But even this felicitous vision was dependent on a series of 'ifs', and should any of the conditional circumstances not prevail a far from happy society could result. It could yet be that the American experiment in republican government would not succeed.[6]

One source of pessimism was the grandiose nature of the expectations generated by the American mission. The promise of glory triggered both exuberance and anxiety, great hopes for a more perfect future and great fears lest it be not achieved. In his Farewell Address, George Washington could not only congratulate his countrymen that Heaven had granted them 'the choicest tokens of its beneficence', but also admit to an 'apprehension of danger' resulting from the concern he felt for his fellow citizens, and then list the fatal errors into which they could yet fall. But perhaps a more potent source of unease was the conventional social and political wisdom of the eighteenth century, with its emphasis upon human frailty. A lingering Puritan tradition spoke of the depravity of man and the imminent vengeance of God. Political theorists assumed the inexorable rise and fall of civilizations, and usually related their decline to the moral failings of their citizens. More immediately, the constitutional thought inherited from England warned of the precariousness of liberty and the untrustworthiness of government. Throughout the eighteenth century gloomy Cassandras in both England and America tirelessly lamented the decay and corruption they espied around them.[7]

Decay or corruption could come in a variety of forms. The Country critics of Sir Robert Walpole and the Duke of Newcastle saw it in ministerial patronage, which, they argued, was serving to subvert the balance of England's celebrated constitution. It was the historic function of Parliament, they believed, to preserve the liberty of Englishmen by maintaining a jealous scrutiny over the king's government. If the royal ministers succeeded in attaching Members of Parliament instead to the interest of the Court, whether by places or pensions or other means, as Country spokesmen insisted was happening, then the ultimate result could be tyranny. Liberty depended on preserving the constitution from corruption, and in particular on resisting the encroachments of power. To the Court party, striving to maintain an orderly regime through its own conception of a constitutional balance, the obstreperous antics of its opponents could seem a species of subversion, as ambitious and designing men put their own selfish interests before those of the realm. The rhetorical battles between Court and Country echoed through the American colonies, where oppositionist writings in particular were eagerly imbibed, for their insistent warnings against the corrupt machinations of the Crown's ministers seemed corroborated by the colonial experience. But Americans did not identify corruption solely with the Old Country. Many American clerics were deeply worried by the rapid economic expansion of the colonies in the eighteenth century and fretted lest the desire for wealth and luxury generate an acquisitive spirit which would tear society apart. Lay leaders, too, often felt that the colonial experiments had failed, both by comparison with the ideals of the Founders and with the cultural achievements of contemporary England. The spectre of decline and disaster stalked the public discourse of the so-called Age of Enlightenment.[8]

The pessimistic awareness that societies and constitutions were prone to decay seemed vindicated by the Founding Fathers' reading of history. Like the Greek city-states and like ancient Rome, all nations seemed destined to decline and fall. The favourite classical authors of the period conveyed in particular an image of a sick and tottering Rome. As a generation which had rebelled against the pretensions of the British king, the Founding Fathers judged governments and societies according to their capacity to nourish liberty, and most they found dispiritingly wanting. In their perspective, liberty was forever pitted against power, and it was in the nature of power to expand. History seemed to show that sooner or later a free society would fall victim to tyranny. 'From the conclusion of this war we shall be going down hill,' said Thomas Jefferson in issuing a warning not to delay 'fixing every essential right on a legal basis . . . while our rulers are honest', for 'Our rulers will become corrupt, our people careless' and freedom could be lost. It was their rulers that a free people had most occasion to fear because the greatest concentration of power was in government. 'Fountains of tears have been shed, and rivers of blood have been spilt at the shrine of arbitrary power,' moaned one American revolutionary. 'History both ancient and modern is but a detail of calamities which have been brought upon mankind from this quarter.' In the classical world Greece and Rome had succumbed, more recently Sweden and Poland had been enslaved, and the American revolutionaries had learned, too, that even Englishmen were losing their prized liberty to the voracious depredations of a corrupt administration. The locus of power was ever to be feared. It seemed to Jefferson in 1796 that 'Either force or corruption has been the principle of every modern government. . . .' By cutting themselves off from the Old World, indeed, Jefferson and other Americans hoped that it might fall to them to find the secret of how men might live together successfully in freedom and harmony, but history was not the most reassuring guide.[9]

In some ways the commitment to republicanism served to deepen American apprehensions. Republics were the most notoriously vulnerable of polities. In a monarchy order might be imposed from above, but in a republic, in which all public officials were the agents of the people, from whom all authority derived, order had to flow from below. A republic, by its very nature, rested not on the force of arms or ancient prescriptions; it rested on the support of its citizens, who had voluntarily to surrender their private interests to the public good. Much, therefore, depended on the character of the people and of their leaders. This was at once the strength and weakness of a republic. 'In the very structure . . . of our government, we discern on the one hand the sources of its vigour, and the means of preservation; and on the other the latent, though certain causes of decay . . . ,' went a typical analysis. 'In our republican form of government, where the sovereignty resides in the people, there exists an indispensable necessity, that the people should be wise & enlightened, virtuous & good.' With those qualities the people would be 'prosperous and happy'; to lose them would be to 'invite the lash of the oppressor'. The republics of the past had usually been destroyed not by a foreign foe but by discord and corruption from within. From the very beginning, Americans were enjoined to maintain a wary scrutiny on themselves and on their leaders lest they stray from the republican faith.[10]

The revolutionary generation's reading of history revealed to them clearly enough the disorders to which a free society might succumb. It was imperative, of course, that the people should retain their virtue, that is, their capacity to subordinate their private interests to the public good. Simplicity, frugality and industry helped to keep men honest, but luxury bred corruption, by which seemed to be meant a selfish pursuit of personal pleasure and private gain. As men fell prey to hedonistic vices, they resorted to factious intrigues to advance their own fortunes, to the detriment of social harmony and the common interest, or became criminally indifferent to the public good or the fate of liberty. When 'Private Views, selfish Lusts, and haughty Passions' are 'cloaked over with specious Pretences to public Good', warned a Boston clergyman in an election sermon of 1762, 'we may naturally expect, Tergiversations, Intrigues, and all the artful Labyrinths of Machiavellian Politicks'. It was widely known that towards the end of a society's life wealth and prosperity betrayed men into 'luxury and dissipation, idleness and sensuality' and rendered them incapable 'of preserving or even bearing the blessings of equal liberty'. Too many peoples had in the past lost their freedom as their public virtue degenerated into private vices. A favourite example for American clergymen was the ancient kingdom of Israel, which 'was brought to destruction, because its iniquities were full'.[11]

The eighteenth-century belief that republicanism rested on the virtue of the people has often enough been remarked on by scholars, but less attention has been paid to the accompanying belief that it rested also on the virtue of the rulers. Even under the best forms of government, said Jefferson, 'experience hath shewn, that . . . those entrusted with power have, in time . . . perverted it into tyranny'. No one believed more fervently than the revolutionary generation that power tends to corrupt. A major reason why a loss of public virtue was so dangerous was that it rendered people indifferent to the designs of the leading men or vulnerable to their beguiling ways. Eternal vigilance was necessary if liberty was to be kept safe from the intrigues of the mighty. Republics had too often fallen prey to the ambitions of their great men. The Roman senate under Julius Caesar had 'retained all its ancient formalities but voted always only as Caesar dictated'. 'Every republic at all times', said Alexander Hamilton, 'has its Catilines and its Caesars.' Despite their answerability to the people, even in a republic officials enjoyed a special authority which many found intoxicating. 'The executive power', said a Delaware revolutionary, 'is ever restless, ambitious, and ever grasping at increase of power.' Perhaps even more dangerous to a republic than the corruption of the people was the ambition of its leaders.[12]

The American republic, then, had to be wary of luxury and corruption, intrigue and ambition. To a substantial degree, of course, the framers of the Constitution sought to build into their political system various protections against these vices. The ingenious separation and distribution of powers were meant to frustrate the designs of faction and to limit the authority of individual officers. Titles of nobility were outlawed, thus denying the civil authorities one potential source of bribery. The president and his ministers were debarred from sitting in Congress, and members of Congress were to be prohibited from accepting executive offices. From the radical Whigs of England the American revolutionaries had inherited an abiding distrust, almost a horror, of the power of appointment. It had been executive patronage in that country, Pierce Butler reminded the framers, which 'was the source of the corruption that ruined their Govt'.[13]

But despite the system of checks and balances, which has so fascinated constitutional scholars, there was still a profound concern that disinterested and wise men should assume the great offices of state. Constitutional curbs alone might not suffice to arrest ambition. The holistic assumptions of eighteenth-century political philosophy demanded that virtue should reside in the rulers as well as the ruled. If political society was a single corporate entity, as had traditionally been assumed, it followed that there could be only one public interest, the good of the whole, and it was the duty of the civil authorities to identify and pursue that good. Generations of clergymen had impressed this truth on Americans. '*A good Ruler must be a good man*', Azariah Mather had emphasized in 1725, adding that 'A good Ruler will study the Interest of the Commonwealth, and will not suffer any Private Views to come in Competition therewith: All shall be Sacrificed to subserve the Publick.' Abraham Williams's election sermon of 1762 was peppered with the characteristics that he expected of civil rulers: Skill, Uprightness, Courage, Prudence, Fidelity, Unanimity, Understanding, Knowledge, Capacity, Integrity, Wisdom, Truth, Sincerity, Faithfulness, and not least 'hating Covetousness, not govern'd by private Interests, but truly regarding the public Good'. Over forty years later another clergyman was still insisting on the need for a chief magistrate, 'who, rightly understanding the true interests of the people, will be disposed to devote all his powers and influence in subserviency to the public good'. Such convictions extended far beyond the clergy. Jefferson himself could speak of the need for governors who were 'wise and honest' and 'endowed with genius and virtue'. As the

9

first federal elections were being held under the new Constitution a Pennsylvania newspaper urged the selection of 'men of approved probity and talents', for 'The best government is of no consequence, when it falls to the fatal management of bad ministers and indifferent rulers.'[14]

The framers of the Constitution themselves hoped to bring forward men of wisdom and virtue to lead the republic. They, too, hankered after a harmonious political order, and they continued to assume that civil leaders should ideally determine the public good by rational deliberations among themselves and calmly reach accord, virtuously rising above selfish and partial interests. Because they knew that great men were as subject to temptation as any they carefully divided power, but they also tried to devise a constitution which would tend to raise up the virtuous and talented. 'An auxiliary desideratum for the melioration of the Republican form is such a process of elections as will most certainly extract from the mass of the society the purest and noblest characters which it contains'; wrote Madison before setting out for the constitutional convention at Philadelphia, 'such as will at once feel most strongly the proper motives to pursue the end of their appointment, and be most capable to devise the proper means of attaining it.' Disinterested and enlightened statesmen could help the republic succeed, and the Constitution was designed to recruit them as well as to check them once they were in power. Virtue in the officers of government was in itself a safeguard against the abuse of power.[15]

The replacement of the old Articles of Confederation with the Constitution shifted authority away from the state governments and towards the federal government, a move which was intended in part to increase the political role of the nation's leading men at the expense of 'the local demagogues who will be degraded by it from the importance they now hold'. In a sense, the uprightness and skill of those who could be expected to take command of the national administration were meant to function as a kind of counterpoise to the selfishness and ambition of the lesser men who had made their way into state politics. In a constituency thus enlarged, at any rate, only notables might expect to win the support necessary to carry them to high office. 'In the nature of things, nine times in ten', complained a critic of the small size of the House of Representatives, 'men of the elevated classes in the community only can be chosen.' If the people at large should elect the president, argued Gouverneur Morris, 'they will never fail to prefer some man of distinguished character, or services; some man . . . of continental repu-

tation'. The screening devices introduced into the process for election to the Senate and the presidency were also meant to ensure that
only the worthiest men reached those eminences. Certainly the
presiding officer of the Philadelphia Convention was convinced that
the republic's well-being rested in part on the character of its leading men. 'It is my most earnest wish that none but the most disinterested, able and virtuous men may be appointed to either house of
Congress': wrote Washington during the first federal elections, 'because, I think, the tranquility and happiness of this Country will
depend essentially upon that circumstance.'[16]

The Founding Fathers' views of history and politics were eloquently illustrated in their creation of the presidency. Their recent
experience with state and national politics had persuaded them that
the virtual abolition of the executive branch was no answer to the
admitted perils of concentrated power, and they were determined to
create a chief executive possessed of some energy and authority.
But the danger of executive tyranny would be averted both by the
constitutional constraints placed on the president and by ensuring
that only the most disinterested of statesmen reached that office.
Thus would the United States be saved from the unhappy fate
which had overtaken earlier republics. The presidency had to be in-
sulated from the corruption, intrigue and ambition which could
otherwise wreck the great experiment in liberty. Hence, not only
was the president required to secure approval for any legislative
measures from both houses of Congress (and ultimately in cases of
questionable constitutionality from the Supreme Court). He was
also required to obtain the consent of the Senate for most of his
appointments, and he was prohibited from appointing members of
Congress to executive posts. This was one of the few issues on
which the constitutional convention was in virtual unanimity. Its
members knew too well the England that Sir Lewis Namier was
later to rediscover.

Safeguards against corruption were also written into the method
of election. The constitutional convention eventually decided
against the legislative appointment of the president because it was
'Certain', in Madison's words, that such an arrangement 'would be
attended with intrigues and contentions'. The manoeuvrings of the
cabals in the English Parliament around the office of prime minister
were cited as evidence of the dangers of such a system. To avoid
such intrigue the selection of the president was best placed outside
Congress, and it was decided to rest the responsibility with a separate electoral college, from which senators and congressmen were

explicitly excluded. 'Nothing was more to be desired than that every practicable obstacle should be opposed to cabal, intrigue, and corruption', observed Alexander Hamilton, explaining why the election was not vested in 'any pre-existing bodies of men' which could be tampered with, but in special electors chosen 'for the temporary and sole purpose of making the appointment'. Further, each state's electors were to assemble and vote separately, in the hope that 'this detached and divided situation' would serve to protect them from 'heats and ferments' and make it difficult for them to cabal or to be corrupted. The electors themselves were to be chosen as the state legislature determined, perhaps by the people or by the legislature itself, but it was hoped that they, too, would be wise and experienced men, 'capable of analysing the qualities adapted to the station'.[17]

The whole process of electing a president, then, was designed to avert the destructive diseases of intrigue, cabal and corruption, or what a later age might call electioneering. It was also designed to facilitate the elevation of the best men to that office. This would be an additional safeguard against subversion. 'The process of election affords a moral certainty that the office of President will never fall to the lot of any man who is not in an eminent degree endowed with the requisite qualification,' wrote a confident Alexander Hamilton. Perhaps 'the little arts of popularity' could make a man a state governor, but it would require more than that 'to establish him in the esteem and confidence of the whole Union....' (Again, the deficiencies of state politicians were to be remedied by rectitude at the top.) There was a 'constant probability', indeed, of seeing 'the station filled by characters pre-eminent for ability and virtue'. James Madison expressed a similar view to the constitutional convention. The republic was to be protected from the designs of ambitious men both by measures to render intrigue harmless and by restricting access to the Chief Magistracy to those who would scorn to serve themselves before their country.[18]

In thus seeking to make the federal government safe from intrigue, corruption and self-serving ambition, the framers tried to ensure that no one could win control of it via a political campaign. The Constitution itself carried forward to later generations their convictions that the president – above all others – should be virtuous and that the office – above all others – should not actively be sought. The peculiar system of indirect elections which grew out of those beliefs, it was thought in the days when political parties as coherent national bodies were quite unknown and apparently unimaginable, would put the federal government in the hands of men of experience, standing and integrity. The Founding Fathers had learned from history that societies and constitutions were subject to decay, and that republics in particular were often destroyed from within, by corruption and contention among the people and by the voracious ambition of those in authority. They thus attempted to create a system of government which would prove resistant to these ills, and not least an executive which would be denied the traditional instruments of corruption and would be commanded by trustworthy men. Indeed, the president would have been accorded even less authority, wrote one delegate after the constitutional convention, 'had not many of the members cast their eyes toward General Washington as President; and shaped their Ideas of the Powers to be given a President, by their opinions of his Virtue'. After the views that Washington had heard expressed at the convention it is hardly surprising that he was so loathe to be thought covetous of the presidency.[19]

The extreme diffidence exhibited by actual and potential contenders for the presidency in the early years of the republic was thus a product both of their own convictions and predilections and of the political values and practices of the day. Power itself was seen as the very antithesis of liberty, a necessary evil which had to be forever constrained, and the love of it was held to be infinitely corrupting. To the eighteenth-century mind, politics was a degraded profession, its very practitioners being among the most likely agents of a country's destruction. In this society, to have appeared too eager to be president would have exposed candidates to accusations of ambition, that self-serving ruthlessness which had transformed other republics into tyrannies. To have been too associated with a partisan campaign for the presidency would have exposed them to accusations of intrigue, of fermenting divisions within the body politic which could prove fatal. And, of course, a contender could not without embarrassment point to his own qualities. Men were to be chosen for this distinguished position for their character, experience and virtue, and a candidate could hardly draw attention to his own virtue without rendering it suspect. These considerations, indeed, virtually paralysed the earliest contenders for the presidency, who seem to have had an almost pathological obsession not to be thought manoeuvring for that prize. Both Washington and Jefferson, at the ages of 56 and 53 respectively, presented themselves as being too advanced in years for the position, casting themselves as exhausted old men in retirement. Washington reminded his admirers of 'my advanced age' and insisted that 'The growing infirmities of age and the increasing love of retirement, daily confirm my decided predilection for domestic life . . . .' Jefferson in 1795 tried to wave aside Madison's overtures regarding the presidency, claiming that his own 'retirement from office . . . high or low' was 'without exception', and citing as further reasons his poor health and his age which required him to put his affairs in order. 'The question', he concluded, 'is forever closed with me . . . .' John Adams at 65 during the election of 1800 perhaps had more reason to quote his 'age, infirmities, family misfortunes' as well as the intolerable behaviour of his enemies as reasons which made him 'too indifferent to whatever can happen'. These men clearly felt the need to disavow even the shadow of ambition, obliging their correspondents to overcome their protestations by insisting that when the public called them into service they could not decently refuse.[20]

Washington, indeed, felt miserably committed by his earlier protestations of his desire only for retirement. He feared that 'the world and Posterity' would accuse him of '*inconsistency* and *ambition*' if he now re-entered public life. Hovering somewhere at the back of his mind seems to have been a certain unease that he should be thought to possess monarchical intentions. There had after all been some sporadic talk in the dark days of the Articles of Confederation of the possibility or even desirability of establishing a king, and Patrick Henry was by no means alone in believing that the Constitution 'squints towards monarchy'. George Mason was unhappy with the projected presidency for 'as it now stands, he may continue in office for life; or, in other words, it will be an elective monarchy'. In an early and wisely-abandoned draft of his inaugural address, Washington even offered a bizarre renunciation of dynastic ambitions: 'In the next place, it will be recollected that the Divine Providence hath not seen fit that my blood should be transmitted or my name perpetuated by the endearing, though sometimes seducing, channel of immediate offspring. I have no child for whom I could wish to make a provision – no family to build in greatness upon my country's ruins.' This awful suspicion, that the republic in creating a president might inadvertently have spawned a king, never quite disappeared from the public discourse of the early republic. The celebrated titles debate in Congress in 1789, when John Adams and Richard Henry Lee advocated that the president be accorded some such title as His Highness or His High Mightiness, served to feed suspicions that some of America's leading men were dissatisfied with republican simplicity. Adams, indeed, was prepared privately to describe the government of the United States as 'to all intents and purposes an Elective tho' limited Monarchy'. It sometimes seemed a small step from the elective to the hereditary, as Washington's discomfort showed. It was even urged on behalf of Jefferson's pretensions to the presidency that he had only fathered daughters. John Adams could make no such claim, and one Republican libel against him during the campaign of 1800 is worth retelling in the words of his biographer:

The story was told and believed that Adams had planned to marry one of his sons to a daughter of George III and thus start an American dynasty which would reunite the country with Great Britain. Before his death Washington, so the tale went, hearing of this enormity, had gone to Adams, dressed in a white uniform, to plead with him but the President had been adamant. The General had gone a second time dressed in black and renewed his arguments. When the president still refused to abandon his scheme Washington had visited him a third time dressed in his Revolutionary uniform and threatened to run him through with his sword if he did not renounce the project. Only then had Adams given up his cherished ambition to become King.[21]

If the story was indeed believed it was in part because many regarded the presidency itself as a dangerous – if necessary – invention. A republic had always to fear the possibility of subversion from within, not least by the restless ambition of those in possession of power. As James Monroe put it, 'the human character is not perfect', and while he himself had 'boundless confidence' in George Washington's virtues, nonetheless 'if he partakes of those qualities which we have too much reason to believe are almost inseparable from the frail nature of our being, the people of America will perhaps be lost'. If even Washington could arouse such misgivings, what hope had lesser men? Behind the president there often seemed to lurk the shadow of Caesar. Fears of executive usurpation were often graphically exaggerated for partisan reasons, yet the fugitive suspicion that the president was invested with a dangerous degree of power and that he could yet transform the republic into a monarchy lingered on. Jefferson himself, after all, could privately describe the Federalists of the 1790s as 'an Anglican, monarchical, and aristocratical party', and this conviction that the Federalist administration was thus subverting the republic helped to create and consolidate the Republican party. Federalists, too, were not slow to spot a dangerous potential in the executive once the Republicans were in power. In 1803 Uriah Tracy told the Senate that 'the President is vested with powers vastly extensive and important', powers indeed which would 'excite the avarice and ambition of the human

15

heart'. The president of the United States, thought the Chief Justice of Michigan Territory, 'during the term for which he is elected, is invested with the prerogatives of a monarch'. It needed only 'the imbecility, or vice' of but one incumbent, and 'the toils and the labors of preceding generations may be prostrated in dust'. Senator Hillhouse in 1808 thought that presidential power was such as to imperil the survival of the country's freedom; the fault, he contended, lay in 'setting the people to choose a King'. The perception of the presidency as a worrisomely weak link in the republic's constitutional arrangements, as an office which an unscrupulous ambition could use to direct the republic even down the fell road of monarchy, served to encourage candidates to approach their goal with the most exemplary diffidence.[22]

Fortunately, perhaps, for the sanity of presidential aspirants, the advent of party warfare in some measure helped to establish their legitimacy. Thomas Jefferson late in 1796 indicated a wish to defer to Adams in the event of a tie between them, and early in 1797 he was prepared to consider allowing Adams to be re-elected unopposed, if he could be induced 'to administer the government on its true principles, and to relinquish his bias to an English constitution...'. A few years later Jefferson was considerably less self-effacing. In contrast to his behaviour in 1795–97, he worked energetically if discreetly to promote his own election in 1800, convinced that the cause of liberty required the rejection of Federalism. As before, he remained at Monticello, but he now engaged in quite extensive political if private correspondence designed to advance the Republican cause. Early in 1799 he encouraged the distribution of handbills and pamphlets relating to the XYZ affair and the Alien and Sedition Acts, enjoining on one correspondent the instruction 'Do not let my name appear in the matter.' He remained as wedded to the idea of retirement as ever, he assured Monroe, but 'if anything supersedes this propensity, it is merely the desire to see this government brought back to its republican principles'.[23]

At no time did Jefferson communicate directly with the public during the 1800 campaign, and his famous letter to Elbridge Gerry was the closest he came to associating himself with a 'platform'. Describing it as 'a profession of my political faith', Jefferson offered Gerry a summary of his political views, which were essentially those later laid out in his inaugural address. Nonetheless Jefferson did not sign the letter, he sent it by private hand, and he made clear that it was 'a confidential communication' never to leave Gerry's possession 'or be suffered in any wise to commit my name'. Gerry was a prominent Massachusetts figure and a moderate Federalist who was at odds with others in his party, and Jefferson presumably hoped to sway him to his own cause. (Gerry did subsequently stand as the Republican candidate for governor in 1800.) Yet Jefferson's electioneering here was limited in the extreme. Its object was Gerry himself, and Jefferson made no attempt to have his principles disseminated more publicly.[24]

But measures as well as men were now being weighed in presidential elections. The party system had in large part originated in a fundamental division among the nation's leading men over how best to further the cause of republican government. In the early years of the republic, when the success of the country's political system was far from assured, each party tended to see its rival as engaged in activities subversive of the national interest. If to Jefferson the Federalists were an aristocratic and monarchical party whose real unpatriotic intent was 'to draw over us the substance . . . of the British government', to the Federalist chief Alexander Hamilton the views of the Republican leaders were 'subversive of the principles of good government and dangerous to the union, peace and happiness of the Country'. To each party its own measures represented the true patriot cause, and in this perspective a party's presidential candidate could justify a measure of covert electioneering to himself. In his letter to Gerry, Jefferson was not so much serving his own interests – at least in his own eyes – as his country's. He was identifying those principles upon which he believed the very fate of the republic rested. The emergence of party competition, then, in some degree removed the focus of the campaign away from the character of the presidential candidate and towards the measures for which he and his party stood. (The emergence of party organization and of self-appointed campaign directors like John Beckley and Aaron Burr, of course, also meant that party propaganda could be disseminated without the aid of the candidate.) The advent of party enabled a candidate to appear as a supporter of a patriot cause rather than as a self-interested office-seeker. It gave his candidacy – and his discreet electioneering – some legitimacy.[25]

The electioneering of the presidential hopefuls long remained discreet. John Adams denied any real desire for the presidency during his two campaigns and affected to be indifferent as to the outcome, though he did nothing to restrain the promotional activities of his friends. He was in fact deeply distrustful of elections and liked to keep a safe distance from campaigns. 'Corruption in Elections', he told Jefferson in 1796, 'has heretofore destroyed all Elective Governments.' He himself had no intention of introducing 'the foul fiend on the Stage'. Yet like his rival he evidently regarded his own elevation as the best guarantee of the safety of republican institutions. Madison too, snug in the role of heir-apparent, remained aloof from the campaigns which were waged in his (and his party's) name. His less well-positioned rivals were somewhat less circumspect. James Monroe, for example, did cautiously manoeuvre for electoral support in 1808. The Republican ideologue John Randolph and the so-called Tertium Quids had broken with the Jefferson administration because it seemed to lean too far towards Federalism and they were unhappy about Madison's succession. Monroe for his part had been piqued by the administration's decision to reject a treaty he had drawn up with England. Encouraged by Randolph and other opponents of the administration, he wrote a few discreet letters to potential supporters and also a long defence of his negotiations with England, 'an electioneering book' in John Quincy Adams's phrase, while insisting that he was but 'a distant and inactive spectator of the mov'ment'. When the Republican party did finally determine to support Monroe in 1816 and 1820 he was able to live up to that boast more successfully. One editor said that he had been elected with 'less bustle and *national* confusion than belongs to a Westminster election for a member of Parliament in England'. John Quincy Adams also kept a fastidious distance from his electioneering friends. 'Upon the foundation of public service alone must I stand;' he insisted to himself, 'and when the nation shall be called to judge of that, by the result, whatever it may be, I must abide.'[26]

It was indeed 'public service' which qualified men for the presidency. After George Washington's retirement the sceptre invariably fell on either the vice-president or the secretary of state (usually the latter), until Andrew Jackson's disruptive election in 1828. In a day when parties were still deprecated and personal canvassing was deemed unacceptable, a candidate had formally to be judged by his public character and past services. In 1792 Monroe counselled Madison against the notion of substituting Aaron Burr for George Clinton as the Republican vice-presidential candidate, for Burr had arrived too recently 'upon the public theatre'. 'Some person of more advanc'd life and longer standing in publick trust sho'd be selected for it', he continued, 'and particularly one who in consequence of such service had given unequivocal proofs of what his prin-

ciples really were.' This indeed was the advantage of service, for it
enabled a person to mark 'a line of conduct so decisively that you
might tell what he would be hereafter by what he had been heretofore'. Such doubts about according preference to mere politicians
over long-serving statesmen were reinforced by the peculiar election
of 1800, when Aaron Burr as the Republican vice-presidential
candidate secured as many votes in the electoral college as Thomas
Jefferson. Burr had visited New England during the campaign, in
what was widely regarded as an electioneering trip, and his subsequent refusal to withdraw in Jefferson's favour when the election
was thrown into the House of Representatives confirmed his image
among both Federalists and Republicans as a scheming, self-serving
and dangerous politician. Alexander Hamilton spoke of him as 'an
embryo-Caesar'. The tie in the electoral college dismayed John
Adams. 'All the old patriots, all the splendid talents, the long experience', he cried, had been superseded by 'this dextrous gentleman.' Even worse: 'What a discouragement to all virtuous exertion
& what an encouragement to party intrigue and corruption.' The
hopes of the Founding Fathers that the presidency would fall on
men of stature and integrity seemed already to be in jeopardy. In
1812 another bold New York Republican, De Witt Clinton, made
his own break with the administration to run for the presidency and
this precipitated another round of lamentations and pointed remarks
about ambition and corruption. It may be that the failure of the
Burr and Clinton campaigns helped the old values to survive a little
longer. For the time being, at any rate, a party was still expected to
choose its candidate on the grounds of his public character and past
services.[27]

If it was up to the public (perhaps as mediated through party) to
call a man into service, it was also incumbent on him to acquiesce.
The Speaker of the Virginia legislature once told Thomas Jefferson
that 'good and able men had better govern than be governed, since
tis possible, indeed highly probable, that if the able and good withdraw themselves from society, the venal and ignorant will succeed'.
*Noblesse oblige* would make possible an aristocracy of talents and
avert rule by petty demagogues and electioneering politicians.
'There is a debt of service due from every man to his country,' Jefferson himself told Edward Rutledge, 'proportioned to the bounties
which nature and fortune have measured to him.' A New Hampshire politician aggrieved at least some of his constituents during
the first federal elections when he refused to serve as congressman
after having been elected, and was told that he had been 'egregious-

ly deficient in point of politeness', because when the people had so honoured him it was 'highly indelicate to reject their favors'. When a new election had to be held 'so displeased' were the people that many did not vote 'and any person of the least address or interest might have been elected'. A respect for the wishes of the sovereign people, a personal indebtedness to his country, and the need for talent in the public employ, meant that a man should not wantonly refuse office, least of all the presidency. If a candidate could not actively seek the presidency, this convenient doctrine at least made it possible for him to accept the honour when it came his way. The early republic was still a leader-oriented political culture (particularly perhaps at federal rather than local level), in which gentlemen of standing gravely accepted office as a duty incumbent upon them.[28]

A variety of conditions conspired to perpetuate the example of the Mute Tribune. There was the pressure of tradition itself, the expectation that gentlemen did not canvass votes. In the Anglo-American political world of the eighteenth century legislative seats had often been uncontested, rendering campaigning superfluous. The candidate for a local office might still 'treat' his constituents, but if he had no rivals this could hardly be seen as corruption. The limited functions of eighteenth-century governments also militated against the practice of electioneering. Governments were expected to maintain law and order, encourage commerce and treat with foreign powers, but little else. In an age when governments had few positive duties to perform or policies to pursue issue-oriented contests were hardly likely to occur. Until the coming of party, at any rate, a candidate could not present himself as the champion of a particular programme. In a sense, *he* was the issue – his public character and standing. Where government was minimal it was not measures but good administrators who were needed. This kind of traditional political culture, of course, was already being eroded by the time that the American presidency was being contested, but the values and expectations inherited from the past were slow to fade away. As long as they persisted personal campaigning by a candidate could only seem self-serving, and as such could tend only to discredit him.

Further, electoral conditions in the early republic rendered popular electioneering in some degree redundant, as the framers of the Constitution had intended. In these years political authority tended to centre on the state legislatures, where party caucuses selected candidates for office. In many states the legislature retained to itself the power of appointing the presidential electors, so that the role of the people in the election was indirect. In the election of 1800, for example, the electors were chosen by the legislature in as many as ten of the sixteen states, and in 1812 nine of the eighteen states still used the legislative system. In these conditions, candidates were more likely to make discreet advances to local notables than to campaign before the public at large, and much electioneering did go on in the state capitols. (The legislatures had themselves to be elected, of course, and a looming presidential campaign could touch the popular electorate at that point, though even then such elections could be manipulated by a skilful political leader, as Aaron Burr demonstrated in New York in 1800.) The congressional caucus system, whereby a party's representatives in Congress chose its presidential candidate, also tended to deflect attention away from the larger arena and towards the leading men. Those who aspired to the presidency, then, had relatively little inducement to take their cause directly to the people, and to have done so might have upset the powerful men in Congress and in the state legislatures. The electoral environment itself tended to reflect and perpetuate the patrician assumptions of old, and in its turn served to enjoin passivity on presidential contenders.

A candidate for president in the early republic found himself surrounded by a host of electoral, social, ideological and psychological constraints. The Mute Tribune was a product of a variety of forces. The patrician assumption that the duties of government fell naturally on gentlemen; the sprawling nature of the country with its as yet primitive facilities for transportation and communication; electoral arrangements which militated against a direct appeal to the people; all these influenced the nature of presidential campaigns. But ultimately the diffidence of the early candidates was a reflection of eighteenth-century assumptions about the frailty of men and institutions. 'Yes, sir, *"man is man"*,' sighed a Connecticut Federalist, 'and the melancholy truth that he is always imperfect and frequently wicked, induces us to fear his power....' The influence of pessimism in American political history has never been sufficiently appreciated. The imperfection of man was especially to be feared in republics, for history was replete with examples of societies which had lost their freedom when the people had succumbed to corruption and their rulers to ambition. It was the ambition of those in authority which was particularly to be feared, for theirs was the power that was poised against liberty. The framers of the Constitution introduced various checks on executive power, but they were never quite sure that these would suffice, and they tried also to devise a system which would recruit disinterested statesmen to the highest office. If there was a possiblility, however remote, of the president making himself into a kind of king, by whatever designation, it was vital that the office should be held by men of the strictest rectitude. Little wonder that presidential candidates shrank from proclaiming themselves, for to have done so would have been to display that ambition which had once prostrated Rome. And this historical lesson seemed vindicated when Bonaparte emerged from the ruins of the French republic to crown himself emperor.[29]

This generation's suspicion of power, particularly of executive power, not only imposed paralysing constraints on those who eyed the presidency. It also tended to weaken the presidency itself. For a variety of reasons, presidential authority tended to decline once George Washington had ceased to lend it his august presence, and particularly after Jefferson lost political control of Congress in 1808. Presidents Madison, Monroe and John Quincy Adams all in part owed their elevation to the White House either to the congressional caucus or to the House of Representatives, and they continued to find political influence exercised by party chieftains in Congress. The presidency for a time seemed to be turning into a constitutional figurehead, and it was at least conceivable that American politics at the national level would develop in a way not unlike the system of parliamentary government evolving in Britain. This decline in the political authority of the presidency made the office no less alluring to able men, but it did nothing to persuade them to abandon the stance of the Mute Tribune. The office itself was falling victim to those pressures and attitudes which so inhibited those who sought it.

If the American experiment in republicanism was not yet secured, it behoved the president above all to distance himself from the destructive ways associated with self-serving demagogues and scheming politicians. He had to protect himself against those pervasive suspicions of ambition, intrigue and corruption which this political culture so abundantly nurtured. It was the highest duty of the president to protect the liberties of the people, and he could only do this by curbing his own enjoyment of power and conducting himself with as much self-effacement as he could muster. Or so it seemed to presidents and presidential candidates in the early republic.

# CHAPTER TWO
# *Changing the rules*

In 1808, as Jefferson's second term neared its end and the parties prepared themselves for battle, Senator James Hillhouse of Connecticut inveighed against the electioneering associated with choosing a president: 'The evil is increasing, and will increase, until it shall terminate in civil war and despotism.' Hillhouse was a Federalist, but Republicans were often no more reassuring, particularly during the so-called Era of Good Feelings. The presidential election, echoed the future Jacksonian Senator Mahlon Dickerson in 1819, 'is probably the rock upon which our liberties are to be wrecked'. A few years later a correspondent of the influential *Richmond Enquirer* described the presidential contest as 'the severest trial to which our invaluable constitution can be exposed'. Subsequent events did little to abate this unease. As Andrew Jackson was being elected to the presidency in 1828 an apprehensive Boston editor feared that unless a stop were put to the kind of campaigning which had appeared 'the most revered institutions of society will be dissolved, and give place to a state of anarchy and civil war'.[1]

Not everyone viewed presidential elections with such alarm, of course, but for many they constituted the most unsound part of the American system of politics. There was perhaps even more disquiet expressed over the presidential election in the 1810s and 1820s than there had been earlier. As the revolutionary era itself receded into the past, Americans seemed to become more anxious than ever that the nation should not stray from the path laid down by its Founders. In much the same way as the transition from the Bible Commonwealth of the Puritans to a more secular society had been accompanied by the jeremiads of the clergy, so the emergence of the republic from the charge of the patriarchs was greeted with as

23

much fear as hope. 'The sterling virtues of the Revolution are silently passing away', said George McDuffie early in 1826, 'and the period is not distant when there will be no living monument to remind us of those glorious days of trial.' A few months later John Adams and Thomas Jefferson departed this world on the fiftieth anniversary of Independence, another reminder to their fellow countrymen that the republic was passing into untried hands. It was open to question whether the new generation of political leaders could resist the temptations which so beset those in public life.[2]

Fears of the destructive political effects of corruption and division were as strong as ever. The growth of commerce, for example, while welcomed by many Americans, produced an unease in others that prosperity and luxury might undermine the moral basis of American life. The Panic of 1819, and the subsequent economic distress, confirmed for some the delusive nature of the lure of riches and deepened a nostalgia for the pastoral republic of Jefferson's day. With growing socioeconomic tensions went deepening sectional divisions. The crisis over the admission of the slave state of Missouri to the Union in 1819–20 was peaceably resolved, but only after the implacable nature of sectional jealousies had become evident to all. The great trek of the American population westwards in these years added new dimensions to the sectional balance, while the trend towards universal suffrage, at least for white men, made politicians even more vulnerable to popular pressures. In short, the political environment in which presidential campaigns had to be fought out was itself being transformed. The election of a president seemed even more hazardous when conducted in the midst of disconcerting change.

Perhaps, too, the interregnum of the Era of Good Feelings perversely served to deepen apprehensions over the baneful consequences of competition for the presidency. For a brief moment the harmonious, party-free republic dreamed of by the Founding Fathers had been almost within reach. There had not been an epic battle for the presidency since 1800. Jefferson had won an easy re-election in 1804, and Madison had succeeded four years later with little difficulty (although his re-election in 1812 had presented a greater challenge), while James Monroe was elected virtually unopposed in both 1816 and 1820. Those who welcomed the disappearance of party warfare were distressed by every sign of political discord, and even before the end of Monroe's first term their ardent hope for tranquillity was being eroded by the widespread prediction of a revival of the contest for the presidency. The bitter struggle to succeed Monroe rekindled all the old fears about the divisiveness of party and faction, fears which were now intertwined with anxieties over the consequences for the republic of such unsettling phenomena as commercial growth, democratic change and sectional hostility. The republic had always been regarded as a rather fragile construction, and it was now even less evident that it was able to withstand the convulsions of a presidential election, with all the opportunities thus afforded for intrigue, conspiracy and unbridled ambition.

Much of the unease about the changing nature of American society and politics, then, came to be focussed on the central political event, the presidential election. This evoked discussions of the fate of the republic as nothing else did. As its foremost leader, the president was the primary personal symbol of his country, and his election irresistibly directed attention to the national purpose and destiny. It seemed imperative that the election itself should be properly regulated, though to many Americans this was patently not the case. 'It is demanded by the honor of our country', demanded William Gaston in 1816, 'that some remedy should be devised to cure the shameful disorders which are obtruded upon our view, on the approach of every Presidential election.' Such was the dissatisfaction with the prevailing method of electing a president, indeed, that these years witnessed countless attempts to change the process. In Congress, in the state legislatures, in newspapers, in pamphlets and in private correspondence, members of the political community endlessly discussed the ills associated with presidential elections and the ways in which they might be eliminated. There was little agreement on either diagnosis or remedy, but the discussions themselves are testimony to the widespread belief among these Americans that the position of the presidential election within the American political system was in urgent need of reassessment.[3]

The attempts to change the rules of the presidential game gave rise to a large number of proposed amendments to the Constitution. In the two decades between the end of Jefferson's administration and the beginning of Jackson's, over 200 proposed constitutional amendments were formally submitted to Congress, and about half of them – easily the largest single group – concerned Section II, that dealing with the election and powers of the president. Some of these proposals were the result of partisan resentments and ambitions. New England Federalists, for example, had grown restive under the long dominance of the Virginia dynasty and some favoured a constitutional amendment to limit the presidency to one term and to deny it to the same state twice in succession. But the importance of these protracted constitutional discussions lies not in what motivated them, for they were prompted by a wide range of concerns, nor in what they accomplished, which was little, but in what they suggest about the politics of the age. These discussions reveal the political world as perceived by this generation of Americans, particularly the place of the presidency within it, and help to explain why the electoral environment ultimately assumed the shape that it did. Like their fathers before them, the politicians of this era also saw the presidency as a distressingly weak line in the country's political framework. Presidential elections, and the presidency itself, they feared, contained the potential to prostrate the republic.[4]

The proposed amendments to the Constitution were themselves highly varied. It seemed as if almost every congressman and newspaper editor had his own pet proposal. The ideas canvassed included limiting the presidency to one term, prohibiting members of Congress from accepting executive appointments during a given period after a presidential election, electing the president directly by the people, and taking from the House of Representatives its existing power to determine elections unresolved by the electoral college. On occasion it was even suggested that the president should be chosen by lot! The most seriously debated proposal in these years was that presidential electors throughout the Union should be chosen by districts. The Constitution had left it to each state legislature to determine how a state's electors were to be selected, with the exasperating consequence that there was no uniformity. In some states electors were chosen by the legislature itself, a convenient method for legislative caucuses but vulnerable to the criticism of being undemocratic. Nine of the nineteen states used this system in the election of 1816. Other states used the so-called general ticket system. This allowed a vote by the people, who chose between statewide tickets of proposed electors, the winning ticket taking *all* the electoral votes of the state. Seven states used the general ticket in 1816. It had the advantage of popular participation, but could be assailed on the grounds that it tended to obliterate minorities – a party which predominated in, say, forty per cent of the counties in a state could be left with no electoral votes.

In 1816 three states used another method, the district system, in which a state was divided into districts with the people in each district voting for one (or more) presidential elector. This was widely conceded to be the most democratic system, providing a reasonably accurate gauge of local sentiments, but its political deficiency was that it allowed a state's electoral votes to be split, thus reducing its weight in the election. In 1812, for example, Maryland virtually neutralized itself by casting six electoral votes for one candidate and five for his rival. The result was that few states were prepared to use the district system unless all others did so too – hence the support for a constitutional amendment which would impose a uniform district system on all states. It was the very lack of uniformity which irked some politicians, not to mention the tiresome inconsistency, for states frequently changed from one system to another. 'Different rules prevail in the Same state at different times, and in the different States at the same time', complained one congressman, 'all liable to be changed according to the varying views and fluctuating fortunes of political parties.' From this perspective any system, provided that it was uniform and permanent, was to be preferred to the existing electoral chaos. In no small measure the future course of presidential politics and the strategies of presidential campaigns would be determined by whichever system prevailed.[5]

The renewed constitutional discussions arose in part from frustration with the existing capricious arrangements, in part from the resentments of groups who felt that the arrangements discriminated against them, and in part from a belief that unless the arrangements were reformed the republic would be in jeopardy. Haunting the rhetoric of this period was the vision of a political society in decline. No less than their revolutionary forebears, this generation of Americans also distrusted both men and governments. The old theory that republics were liable to be destroyed through a combination of the laxity of their people and the unbridled ambition of their rulers, indeed, had recently been given substance by the example of France, where Napolean Bonaparte had given himself a crown. The United States itself had gone to war with Britain in 1812 in part to demonstrate the vitality of republican government, though its continued strength and prosperity, it seemed to some, could also presage an erosion of public morality. The time would come, warned one gloomy Old Republican in 1819, when 'luxury and corruption' would banish 'republican virtue' from the country. When that happened there would be no effective check on those in government, and an ambitious president would use his powers to secure his own indefinite re-election. 'The broad road to monarchy is left open by those who formed our Constitution, by neglect or by design', he repeated in 1823, when offering a constitutional amendment to restrict presidents to two terms.[6]

Fears of corruption, then, remained as potent as ever, fears of the

corruptibility of presidents, politicians and people alike. In the wake
of the election of 1812 John Adams repeated his old view 'that
Mankind have not yet discovered any remedy against irresistable
[sic] Corruption in Elections to Offices of great Power and Profit,
but making them hereditary'. Those in political life in general,
warned George McDuffie in the 1820s, were less likely to resist
temptation than in the simpler days of their fathers: 'Never was
there, in any country, such rapid advances in luxury and refine-
ment, with all their associated frailties.' Indeed, men in political life
in particular were vulnerable to temptation. With the growth of
democracy and the necessity for a continued homage to popular
sovereignty, perhaps, editors and politicians were less inclined to
find fault with the people. 'If any part of our Government be pure,
be incorruptible, I assert that it is the People,' asserted Congressman Michael Hoffmann of New York. 'If any body of men, under
the Constitution, be above suspicion, and beyond the reach of corruption, it is the voters in the respective States.' George McDuffie
came to a similar conclusion, recognizing (as had its framers) that
the Constitution was harnessed to the people's self-interest: 'The
People are essentially patriotic. With them, selfishness itself is public virtue. By the laws of moral necessity, they are obliged to will
their own happiness.' In an increasingly democratic age, the real
threat to the republic would lie not so much in the waywardness of
the people as in the weaknesses of the politicians.[7]

In their discussions on the constitutional amendments, the members of the political community espied various forms of weakness
and corruption in one another. With the departure of the worthies
of the Revolution, complained the *Albany Argus* in 1824, 'personal
and local partialities, with a whole train of interests and feelings, are
largely and perhaps unreasonably indulged'. One form of weakness
was a surrender to sectional prejudices. 'Of all the species of division', sighed Representative Israel Pickens in 1816, 'none is so truly
to be deprecated as that of a geographical character.' This was one
of the objections to the legislative and general ticket modes of
choosing presidential electors, for both enabled a state to wield its
electoral votes as a single bloc and served to encourage the centri-
fugal pressures which were already threatening the Union. The district system, which would break up the states into smaller units,
was repeatedly offered as a panacea for sectionalism. More bizarre
remedies followed in the wake of the Missouri Crisis, when the
spectre of disunion had hovered unnervingly close. A correspondent
of the *Washington Gazette* urged in February 1822 that the North,

the West, the South and the East be allowed to take it in turns to furnish a president, and a few months later a constitutional amendment to oblige the presidency to rotate among the four sections was introduced into the House of Representatives by Thomas Montgomery of Kentucky. The growth of sectional rivalries created the widespread expectation that presidential elections would normally be contests between several candidates, and would therefore be regularly thrown into the House. To avoid this, suggested one anonymous pamphleteer, the final choice should instead be made by lot: 'The time may come when this will be the only pacific mode of settling the pretensions of rival candidates, and the conflicting claims of emulous and jealous sections.' Such solutions were not taken seriously, but the fact that they should be advanced at all, particularly in competition with the more rational remedy of the district system, is itself instructive. Sectionalism was ceasing to be seen as a transitory phenomenon; increasingly the United States was perceived to be divided into distinct and permanent geographical blocs. This was one reason why the revival of the contest for the presidency was viewed with such apprehension.[8]

If politicians seemed increasingly to be putting their section's interest ahead of that of the Union, they were also surrendering to factional interest. Despite a generation and more of party activity, many Americans continued to look on parties with the deepest distaste, especially when their objective was the presidency. 'Party of all kinds, in its excess, is . . . the bane of our institutions . . . ,' complained Edward Everett. Although the great ideological disputes of the first American party system were now in the past, factional and party conflict persisted, leading some to believe that the responsibility must in part lie with the country's political institutions. President Monroe himself believed that parties were a consequence of defective government. Others regarded them as a consequence of defective electoral arrangements, and nowhere were the defects more glaring than in presidential elections. Under the legislative system of choosing electors, Thomas Hart Benton complained, the votes which were rightfully the people's were bartered in the legislature, which was the scene of constant caballing, while under the general ticket system power fell to the leaders who managed elections. 'The People are called upon to vote a ticket, . . . containing 15, 24, or 36 names – to vote for, to *choose* persons, of whom they may never have heard before . . .', said another congressman of the general ticket system. 'What temptation and opportunity is presented . . . for intrigue and management.' The congressional caucus,

29

too, was assailed as a centralizing device, a procedure which tended to promote parties led by self-appointed managers who arrogated power to themselves. The power assumed by members of Congress to nominate a president, Rufus King warned starkly at the height of the furore over the caucus in the 1824 campaign, 'was placing the complete control of the Government into the hands of a party'. Again the favourite remedy was the district system: the more decentralized the electoral arrangements the more difficult it would be for congressional leaders to call the tune.[9]

By the 1820s both parties and caucuses had their defenders, but what is interesting is the extent to which these phenomena were still seen as corrupt alliances which furthered the interests of their own members while defying the will of the people. The framers of the Constitution had tried to create a governmental system which would afford but limited scope to what they called faction and intrigue, particularly as far as the presidency was concerned (for the office had been designed in part as a counterpoise to local factionalism), but the proliferation of those evils showed that the republic had not been sufficiently protected against them. In this perspective American public life was already experiencing a degeneration. 'It can hardly be doubted that the influence of organized faction, for a given period', lamented a conservative New Yorker, 'would be more injurious to the moral character of the nation than a war of the same duration.'[10]

But the most chilling warnings of political corruption were made in relation to the presidency itself. Many saw a fatal combination in the easy morality of the nation's ordinary politicians and the desperate ambition of her great men. 'The time will come', warned Thomes Hart Benton in 1824, 'when the American President, like the Roman Emperors, will select his successor, take him by the hand, exhibit him to the people, place him upon the heights and eminences in the Republic..., make him the channel of all favor, and draw the whole tribe of parasites and office hunters to the feet of the favorite.' Benton admittedly was then the supporter of a presidential candidate who did not have the favour of the administration, but his remarks echoed those others were making. A principal threat to liberty, Americans had always understood, lay in the power of the executive. Despite the almost crippling constraints placed upon the president in this period, his powers of patronage were still widely held to be a dangerous flaw in the American system of government. By unscrupulous use of his appointing power a president might gradually extend his own tenure, eventually to life, and the nation would find itself with a hereditary monarchy. This extravagant vision not infrequently obtruded into the constitutional discussions of these years, when senators could be heard conjuring the awful warning of Augustus Caesar. George McDuffie was one of those obsessed with the menace of a patronage-laden executive, for if the King of England could resort to corruption in spite of his security of tenure, he reasoned, thus invoking the Old Country image of English liberty receding before executive usurpation, how much more would an American president be tempted? In fifty years, he predicted, 'the great aggregate of Executive patronage in this country will be, at least, greater than it was in England in the days of Sir Robert Walpole'.[11]

Extensive executive patronage, which would tempt men to fight ruthlessly for the presidency and to perpetuate themselves and their chosen successors indefinitely in office once they had won it; the corruptibility of congressmen and others in public life who might have influence to exchange for preferment: this was the combination which could spell the end of American liberties. So, at any rate, it was sometimes argued. John Quincy Adams himself privately recorded his belief in his diary in 1821 that 'About one-half' of members of Congress were 'seekers for office at the nomination of the President', and that of the rest 'at least one-half have some appointment or favor to ask for their relatives.' Some of the most lurid attacks on executive patronage and congressional vulnerability came after the celebrated 'corrupt bargain' of 1825, when the Speaker of the House, Henry Clay, helped to deliver the election to John Quincy Adams and was promptly appointed secretary of state, the traditional stepping-stone to the presidency. But this affair merely served to confirm long-standing prejudices. Dire warnings about the intoxicating effects of power, the subversive potential of executive patronage, and the frailties of congressmen and others, had been staples of political rhetoric since the eighteenth century. It was precisely these conditions, after all, which had led to the demise of liberty in England, or so the Americans who had rebelled against George III had largely believed, and it behoved the new generation of American republicans to ensure that their own rights and liberties did not succumb to the same unhappy fate. One way of averting this threat of an overweening executive was by amending Article II of the Constitution and several proposals were offered designed to curb presidential influence and congressional turpitude. Without some such reform, the proponents of these amendments insisted, the fateful conjunction of ambition, avarice and patronage, and the opportunity afforded by presidential elections, could make a mockery of the republic's proud boast of freedom.

Throughout the 1810s and 1820s congressmen, state legislators, editors and others continued to worry at the problems associated with presidential elections and presidential power, and occasionally indulged themselves with the hope that the defects of the American system of politics might somehow be eliminated for good. Perhaps some ingenious arrangement could be found which would ensure that presidential elections did not increase sectional pressures, that they did not encourage party formation, and that they did not tempt ambitious men to resort to bargains and intrigue. The district system amendment in particular found some favour with Congress, the Senate giving it a two-thirds approval in 1813, 1819 and 1822, but no amendment secured the constitutional majority of both houses in the same session necessary for it to be forwarded to the states. Because there were so many different remedies for the Constitution's supposed deficiencies, because the discussions were vitiated by partisan manoeuvrings, and because there were so many distinct interests to satisfy (the small states, for example, were opposed to any arrangement that might shift power towards the big states), the efforts to forestall the degeneration of America's political system by constitutional amendment came to naught. The trepidation aroused by the presidential contest thus was not stilled, and if anything was deepened by the revival of the two-party system in the late 1820s.

Yet the environment in which presidential elections had to be fought out was changing without the aid of a constitutional amendment. Some of these changes were welcomed by those who had found fault with the prevailing system. A greater degree of democracy, more uniformity between the states in the mode of choosing presidential electors, and a reduction of the role of Congress in presidential elections, had been among the objectives of many of the proposed amendments, and these goals at least were to achieve a measure of fulfilment.

In 1826 an article was reproduced in a number of leading newspapers proposing that the right to vote for president be vested in all free white males over the age of 21, the prize going to the candidate who secured most votes. This particular proposal may have had a mischievous intent (one effect would be to abolish the three-fifths weighting allowed the South for its slaves), but it reflected the fact that presidential elections were taking place in an increasingly democratic environment. It still remained with the states to determine whether presidential electors were to be chosen by popular vote, but the right of suffrage itself was becoming more extensive. By 1826, indeed, eight states had accepted the principle of universal suffrage (for white men), and several others gave the vote to taxpayers, which in most cases meant virtually all white men. Such property qualifications as now remained were usually fairly vestigial. 'Without the rights of suffrage, liberty cannot exist', conceded Governor De Witt Clinton of New York. 'It is a vital principle of representative government.' The change in principle was probably more important than the change in practice, since in most states the great majority of white men had long held the right to vote, but it was now widely recognized that any citizen, irrespective of wealth or social standing (if not of race or sex), should have a voice in the selection of public servants. The principle of majority rule was also furthered by spasmodic attempts to make election districts more equal in terms of population and to establish the secret ballot. If presidential elections were to become more popular in form, as the democratic imperative would seem to require, the candidates would find themselves displayed before a very extensive electorate.[12]

The state legislatures were, of course, bowing to the need to rest presidential elections more fully with the people. It did not need a constitutional amendment to underline the undemocratic nature of the system whereby the legislature appointed presidential electors. State parties which tried to cling to this privilege found themselves denounced at the polls by rivals who assumed a more democratic stance. Nine states (out of nineteen) used the legislative method in 1816, nine (out of twenty-four) in 1820, six in 1824, and only two in 1828. By the 1830s only South Carolina was obstreperously holding out against the trend. Elsewhere presidential electors were being chosen by popular vote. During the celebrated 'Revolution of 1800' the people had been able to go to the polls in the presidential election in less than a third of the states of the Union, the smallest proportion ever in American history. By contrast, Andrew Jackson in 1828 could not unreasonably claim to be the first president to be popularly chosen by his countrymen.[13]

Increasingly, then, presidential campaigns had to be directed to the people at large, rather than to Congress or to the state legislatures, although these bodies still had political roles to play. While the electoral system was becoming more democratic, the states themselves had surrendered none of their rights, and the sensibilities of a state's political leaders remained as delicate as ever. The politi-

cal influence of state chieftains may even have been enhanced by the
particular mode of choosing presidential electors which did ultimately prevail – the general ticket system. Used by only seven
states in 1816, it was used in nine in 1820, in twelve in 1824, in
eighteen in 1828, and by 1832 only Maryland and South Carolina
managed without it. Even Maryland, one of the doughtiest supporters of the district system, had succumbed by 1836. There have
been no detailed studies of the consequences of the triumph of the
general ticket system, but many contemporaries saw the general
ticket as an incitement to party organization, because statewide tickets had to be composed centrally. Since parties generally seem to
have preferred the general ticket to the district system, it may well
have served to encourage the growth of state political machines.
The 1830s did witness the emergence of what Richard P. McCormick calls 'the second American party system', in which state parties generally preceded a national organization.[14]

But whether or not the general ticket promoted state juntos,
what its triumph did achieve was to meet the demand for a method
of choosing electors which would be permanent and uniform
throughout the Union. In this sense the electoral environment became more predictable, and the plotting of a coherent presidential
campaign centrally was thus rendered more viable. An important
consequence of the victory of the general ticket, however, was the
confirmation of the state as the primary political unit in the federal
system. The principal objective of a presidential candidate came to
be not the winning of as many districts as possible, and not even
the winning of as many popular votes as possible, desirable though
that was, but the winning of as many states as possible. Each state
became a battleground of its own, and the winner in each would
carry off the state's electoral votes *en bloc*. Under such a system
attention naturally became focussed on the larger states, for they
were able to wield considerable electoral clout, particularly when
two or three of them acted together. In these years the two largest
states were the pivotal Middle Atlantic states of New York and
Pennsylvania, and during the life of the so-called second party system (1828–54) the party which carried those two states always won
the White House. Presidential campaigns had now to be taken to
the people, but to the people and their political leaders as loyal
citizens of their states.

The need for a presidential candidate to look to the people and to
the states for support was increased by the decline of the congressional caucus. Although in regular use by the Republicans since

1800, the party caucus had never been much acclaimed as a nominating device. Minority factions had frequently assailed it, such as the Peace Republicans who defected to DeWitt Clinton in 1812 and who described the caucus nomination of James Madison as 'hostile to the spirit of the federal constitution, dangerous to the rights of the people, and to the freedom of election'. In fact it is questionable whether the caucus could have imposed a president on the people. The early congressional caucuses were really called in order to agree on the vice-presidential nomination, the presidential candidate being a foregone conclusion, and for the Republican party there was never much doubt about which aspirant the party at large favoured. In the uncontested election of 1820 both the incumbent president and vice-president were willing to serve again, rendering the caucus superfluous. A meeting was in fact called, but less than a fifth of the eligible Republicans attended and it made no nominations. The caucus was a favourite target of abuse for those wanting to amend the format of presidential elections, and with the fragmentation of the Republican party in the 1820s its supporters dwindled. The caucus had long been moribund, and when little more than a quarter of Republican congressmen attended its meeting in 1824, its fate was sealed. Henceforth, more than ever, contenders for the presidency would have to mobilize support outside Congress.[15]

The general effect of the changes in the electoral environment in which presidential elections were conducted was to redistribute political authority downwards and outwards. If Congress lost some of its influence, so did state legislatures. From the 1820s presidents were in effect popularly elected, and by a very extensive electorate. The dispersal of power did not mean its dissipation, however, and much authority came to rest with state and local party chieftains. Any man whose ambition rested on the presidency would have a complex course to chart. A popular image with the people at large would further his interest, as would support from state political leaders across the Union, although sectional and other suspicions would make neither easy to achieve. If he found himself faced with a number of rivals, each the champion of some powerful faction, he would also be advised to cultivate support in Congress, for a multiplicity of candidates would increase the chances of an election being thrown into the House of Representatives. Many men in public life in the 1820s, indeed, believed that presidential elections in the future would normally take the form of contests between several different candidates. This belief did nothing to reduce apprehensions about the disruptive effects of battles for the White House.

The long-anticipated revival of the contest for the presidency, then, produced fear as well as hope. The growing role of the popular electorate made the outcome of elections less predictable. The increased size of the Union and the differing forms of economic and cultural development within its various sections tended to heighten sectional awareness and sectional tensions. Economic growth in itself brought riches to some and deprivation to others, while the Panic of 1819 reinforced the warnings of those who believed that wealth would bring corruption and of those who wanted the federal government to return to the strict constructionism of the early Republicans. In such a society, perhaps, one which seemed increasingly divided by economic, sectional and political discontents, and in which political authority had become so fragmented, it was easy to exaggerate the subversive potential of presidential elections and presidential power.

The varied attempts made during the misnamed Era of Good Feelings to reduce the dangers associated with the federal executive had met with little success. The rules of presidential politics had been changed, but not in ways which would clearly remedy the ills of party and faction, the strains of sectionalism, or the potential misuse of presidential power. Men were still frail creatures, and the institutions of the United States could still succumb to the ambition, greed and self-interest of those in public life. The renewal of the contest for the presidency could yet prove fatal to American freedom. With the divisions and temptations which now abounded, the republic more than ever perhaps needed the reassurance of virtue in the White House.

# CHAPTER THREE
# Towards the popular campaign: 1824

The 1820s were something of an anomaly in American political history. The semblance of order which is usually imposed on American politics by the operation of the two party system was momentarily absent. The Olympian battles between the Jeffersonian Republicans and the Federalists were now no more than distant rumbles from the past, while the party alignments which were to characterize the 1830s had not yet been clearly formed. For a brief, unsettling period American politicians had to play out their roles on the national stage without the aid of party. For the only time in American history, presidential elections were contests between candidates in their personal rather than party capacities.

If party competition has usually helped a later generation to make sense of the political history of the past, it has also probably served to simplify and clarify the American political world for its participants. A presidential candidate would normally have an identity and a role assigned to him by his party. A Lincoln or a McKinley or a Truman, it might reasonably be assumed, would more-or-less know what he was standing for and whose banner he was carrying. But for the presidential hopefuls of the 1820s this was not really the case. The disappearance of the old party divisions had been widely welcomed, but candidates for the Chief Magistracy were thereby denied a cause with which to identify and familiar cues to follow. Theirs had to be a highly personal quest for the presidency.

They were also seeking the hallowed prize in a highly uncertain political arena. If the party system had already crumbled the caucus system was fast following, leaving it unclear how a presidential aspirant might best be launched towards his goal. The trend towards the popular election of presidential electors – and towards universal suffrage – drew attention to the potential power of the sovereign people, but few were sure how to harness that power. The Panic of 1819 and the Missouri Crisis had also left their marks on the body politic, deepening both sectional and economic tensions, and these too could unpredictably affect the course of presidential campaigns. And no one could really know exactly how the American public would react when the presidential office could not be filled by a member of the Virginia dynasty or a hero of the Revolution. Never has the route to the White House been so stalked by hidden dangers as it was after the demise of Federalism as an effective national force.

The presidential election of 1824 was one of the most important in American history, more important in many respects than its celebrated successor four years later. It was in this election that a significant shift in political authority became apparent, as presidential candidatures were made and broken outside Washington. Although the election was ultimately thrown into the House of Representatives, the course of it was vitally affected by the interaction of grassroots sentiments. Established political leaders found that they could not always carry with them groups and areas they had counted as their own. Also, the campaign of 1824 has a good claim to be regarded as the first in which some kind of communication was effected between the candidates and the people. The communication was muffled, indirect and incomplete, but those who aspired to the presidency did find it possible to send signals of a sort to their electoral masters. Finally, the election of 1824 witnessed the introduction of new techniques to mobilize popular opinion behind a candidate, a new kind of campaign which anticipated the 'image politics' of later generations. In all these ways the distinction between presidential politics and popular politics was ceasing to have meaning. Presidential politics acquired a popular dimension which it was never to lose.

In the late 1810s and early 1820s the moribund nature of the Federalist party, together with the growing strains of sectionalism and the imperatives of the democratic ethos, served to hasten the dissolution of the Republican party. Deprived of a compelling reason to remain united, and subject to a complex mixture of economic, sectional, ideological and personal pressures, the Republicans were soon fragmented into a number of rival factions. The immediate occasion for this dissolution was the approach of the presidential election of 1824. With no Republican notable in a position to claim an indisputable right to the succession, a number of Republican leaders began to calculate their chances of winning the prize. Still very much subject to the convention that the presidency was an office which could neither be solicited nor declined, none of these men was brash enough to announce his intentions or to campaign too openly for the position. But their friends were less diffident. A multi-sided contest for the presidency in 1824 had been predicted even before the close of Monroe's first term, and so it proved. By the middle of his second term it was clear that a number of prominent Republicans were seeking to become his successor.

In the event, serious campaigns were launched on behalf of five candidates. One of the most formidable was Monroe's testy secretary of state, John Quincy Adams, who could perhaps claim the mantle as the most senior member of the administration (after Monroe) and as the favourite son of New England. The Virginia dynasty had ruled for long enough. A powerful rival, however, was the secretary of the treasury, William H. Crawford, a big, burly, affable Georgian who had come a close second to Monroe in the congressional caucus vote of 1816 and who might hope to benefit from such southern influence as remained. Also from the cabinet was the ambitious secretary of war, John C. Calhoun, who had won a patriotic reputation as a War Hawk before and during the War of 1812, and who, as a fervent nationalist, might hope to win some electoral support in the North as well as the South. Another former War Hawk was the popular Kentuckian Henry Clay, who had declined a seat in the cabinet and had created a powerful role for himself as Speaker of the House of Representatives, a position he had used to prey on the administration. By 1823 a less likely candidate had also emerged, the fierce hero of the Battle of New Orleans, General Andrew Jackson, but he had never served in a high civil office for any length of time and in the early part of the campaign he was not regarded as a serious contender.

Since all these men were accounted Republicans their candidacies were not defined by party. Jefferson in 1800 could allow his friends to run him for the presidency with good conscience, because he saw himself as representing a cause, a mission; he was the agent of the Republicans' determination to save the country from the errors of Federalism. Despite the diatribes against partisan activity, one of the virtues of party, as Albert Gallatin pointed out, was to keep in check 'the disordinate ambition of individuals' which many regarded as 'the greatest danger to our free institutions'. The absence of a clearly-defined party cause for the candidates of 1824 to champion presented them with the fearful problem of how best to conduct their campaigns. Tradition enjoined on them the example of the Mute Tribune. If they adhered to it scrupulously their campaigns would never take off; if they departed from it too conspicuously they would stand condemned of that self-serving ambition which was the bane of republics. Yet the candidacy of each of these men had in some way to be legitimized, and the electorate had to be given some reason to vote for him. In the event a number of ingenious strategies emerged and presidential politics underwent a remarkable transformation.[1]

One possible stance, of course, *was* to pretend to be the party candidate. This was the position assumed by William H. Crawford and his partisans in 1823–24. In the caucus of 1816 he had polled a respectable fifty-four votes to Monroe's sixty-five, and since that time as a major member of the cabinet he had become better known in the country. Further, as a native Virginian who had made his career in Georgia, he might hope to be seen as the heir of the Virginia dynasty, and he was indeed believed to be favoured by Jefferson and Madison if not by Monroe. Crawford's position as secretary of the treasury had also given him the opportunity to strengthen his credentials as the guardian of Old Republicanism. The Panic of 1819 had generated demands for a reduction in government expenditure, as the Missouri Crisis almost simultaneously had deepened southern sensitivity to states' rights, and Crawford's friends credited him with various 'retrenchment' measures. Certainly the national debt was substantially reduced during his stay at the treasury. If the people preferred 'the ancient principles of democratic republicanism, comprising economy in the public expenses, a strict accountability in the public officers, . . . a scrupulous regard for the constitution of the federal government, an equal respect for the powers and rights of the people and the states' and, indeed, 'security' for slavery, argued 'A Southron', 'then should Mr. Crawford obtain their suffrages'. So Crawford was presented as a Republican of the old school and his partisans determined to use the caucus to legitimize his candidacy. 'It was in this way that Mr. Jefferson was elected', said one Crawford editor, 'it was in this way that Mr. Madison was elected, and finally in this way it was that Mr. Monroe was elected.' The caucus, the Crawfordites defiantly maintained, was regular Republican party usage and the only means of concentrating opinion sufficiently to prevent a resurgence of Federalism. The caucus was 'the *only* mode of preserving the harmony, inviolability and predominance of the Great National Party whose interests and character have hitherto been promoted through it'.[2]

Crawford, then, was cast as the authentic choice of the Republican party, champion of states' rights and strict constructionism against the traditional enemy, Federalism. The caucus nomination of Albert Gallatin for vice-president, apart from being a bid for the vote of Pennsylvania, reinforced this identification, for Gallatin had been a leading critic of Hamilton's measures in Congress and had been closely identified with Jefferson as his secretary of the treasury. Crawford himself, while maintaining a close interest in the campaign and conferring and corresponding with his advisers, and allegedly building support through patronage appointments, kept a low public profile. He indulged in no overt campaigning. In fact he had little choice in that he was struck by a paralytic illness in September 1823 and suffered a relapse in the following May. Publicly he remained a dutiful secretary of the treasury, although he was unable to attend cabinet meetings for most of this time, leaving it to his friends to present him 'as the genuine Republican candidate'. But ultimately this party stance did not carry conviction, partly because the Federalist threat seemed a chimera and partly because only a minority of Republican members of Congress attended the caucus meeting that nominated Crawford.[3]

Quite a different strategy was adopted by John Quincy Adams, who at one stage seemed Crawford's most formidable rival. As imbued with conservative instincts as anyone, Adams not only repudiated the caucus but was also reluctant to think of himself as a party man of any kind. 'My career has attached no party to me precisely because it has been independent of all party.' It was the duty of a public officer, he believed, to advance the common good without reference to self or faction. He did unbend sufficiently to connive at a nomination by the Republican members of the Massachusetts state legislature, and even suggested that Federalists should be excluded from the meeting. (He had a Federalist past he wanted the public to forget.) He was prepared to discuss his views on such issues as the tariff with those who called on him, and when the large and pivotal state of New York came to choose its presidential electors in the legislature, Adams was moved to some quiet correspondence with his friends there. But beyond that he maintained what was dubbed 'the Macbeth policy', for Adam's stance recalled to a frustrated friend the Shakespeare line 'If chance will have me king, why, chance may crown me, Without my stir.' (The scholarly Adams replied by reminding his friend of the fate which had befallen Macbeth when he had stirred.) If he was to be a candidate, he insisted, it must be 'by the wishes, ardent and active, of others, and not by mine'. Virtuously turning aside all proffers of help, John Quincy Adams went conscientiously about his duties as secretary of state, which he interrupted only to spend September at the family home in Quincy.[4]

But Adam's stance was not without an element of calculation. In a day when partisan activity was regarded with distrust by many, when 'intrigue' was a dirty political word, and when potential candidates were expected to display a becoming reluctance, the 'Macbeth policy' might still prove a winning one. Given his long career in the public service, his distinguished position as secretary of state, the absence of other northern candidates and the recognition even by some southerners that the North had a claim to the White House, Adams could reasonably expect substantial support if the selection were made on the traditional grounds of public character and past services, and a more partisan and brash attitude might lose some of that support. So Adams seems to have convinced himself. There were those in his circle who believed that Crawford was injuring his own cause by his predilection for 'intrigue', and Adams was assured that his own 'very abstraction from all intrigues would be my principal recommendation'. On at least one occasion he prohibited his friends from making an arrangement with an editor he did not respect, on the grounds that support from such a dubious source would do him more harm than good. When so many were wringing their hands over 'corruption' in politics and bemoaning the loss of the public spirit of an earlier day, a display of old-fashioned virtue might be good policy.[5]

More than that, however, Adams's claims to the suffrages of his countrymen rested in part on his performance as secretary of state, which was certainly influenced by his desire to be president. 'Of the public history of Mr. Monroe's administration', he modestly informed his wife in 1822, 'all that will be worth telling to posterity hitherto has been transacted through the Department of State.' He could officiously go about his duties and trust that the public would give him due credit. And the positions that he took were in some measure conditioned by his perception of his political standing. In 1821 he was criticized for trying to boost his popularity after he had given a Fourth of July address in which he took a strongly nationalistic and anti-British line. He was always anxious to distance himself from the British, for whom conservative New Englanders were often suspected of harbouring an unpatriotic admiration. Ernest R. May has recently shown how John Quincy Adams's behaviour during the formulation of the Monroe Doctrine was influenced by his place in the presidential race. Needing to counteract the encumbrances of a Federalist father and a Federalist past, Adams was more insistent than his cabinet colleagues that the United States should reject the British offer of a joint stand on Latin America in favour of a unilateral declaration. More than his rivals, he had to show that he had no particular leaning towards Britain, and this in part explains the ultimate American decision to go it alone. His concern that his foreign policy be seen in its proper light was also revealed by his reaction to criticism, for on occasion he defended departmental honour by having the appropriate state documents published in the press and apparently he even wrote anonymous pieces himself for the *National Gazette.* In his eyes, of course, this did not constitute electioneering – 'to parry the daggers of assassins is not to canvass votes for the Presidency' – but it can scarcely be doubted that his thoughts were on the White House.[6]

Yet it was *services* rather than policies that Adams identified himself with. The differences between himself and his intermittent critic Henry Clay over such issues as the recognition of the Latin American republics were not likely to be clearly understood by the American public. And even his role in elaborating the Monroe Doctrine was obscured by the fact that the Doctrine was made public in the president's annual message. The American people, and the politicians who represented them, were probably more roused by domestic issues, if issues touched them at all, by the tariff and internal improvements and by the various questions of a sectional nature. 'Foreign relations being all quiet & pacific, and no high party feelings at present existing', reported Daniel Webster in November 1823, 'the necessary *excitement* of public sentiment seems only likely to be found in schemes of internal improvement.' Adams did respond to queries as to where he stood on such issues, but generally only in private conversation or correspondence, and to most people his views must have remained obscure. His partisans in the press did little to clarify them, and Adams may have been hurt by the southern suspicion that he was hostile to slavery. The signals that Adams sent out were aimed not so much at the people at large as at other political leaders and activists (though since the election was expected to be thrown into the House this was probably sound politics). But even with his peers Adams maintained a highly traditional pose. He was attached to no party, he publicly espoused no distinctive policies, and he took virtually no part in the campaign, resting his pretensions on his public reputation and his long and devoted career in the service of his country. In 1824 the Macbeth policy still possessed potency.[7]

Rather similar was the strategy employed by John C. Calhoun, although he spent infinitely more energy in promoting his own cause. He, too, conspicuously prosecuted his official duties, in his case as secretary of war. During Monroe's presidency he had reorganized the War Department, pushed back the military frontier, directed a fortifications programme, and advocated the improvement of military communication. The need to reorganize and improve the military in the years following the War of 1812, the campaign against the Seminole tribe, and the pressures for a reduction in the army establishment after 1819, ensured that the War Department got its share of public attention, and Calhoun made the most of his opportunities. But unlike Adams, Calhoun was not merely resting his claims on his services. Indeed, at the age of 42 in 1824 he was still a young man, and his years in the public employ did not equal those of Adams or Crawford. Further, he did not hold as great an office of state as his rivals. More than Adams, Calhoun allowed his views to become known on a number of issues. It was Calhoun who had introduced the bill to establish the second Bank of the United States, and in the same year he had spoken out for a protective tariff, arguing that the country would need its own supply of manufactures in the event of any future war. Calhoun also used military necessity to call for an expanded programme of internal improvements, and with a magnificent speech spurred his so-called 'bonus bill' through Congress in 1817, only to have it vetoed by a president with stronger constitutional scruples than his own. His movement to the War Department gave him less opportunity to speak out on such issues, but at least he was able to maintain his strongly nationalistic stance. Indeed, of all the members of Monroe's cabinet who aspired to the succession, Calhoun stood out as the strongest advocate of nationalist views. John Quincy Adams once said of him that 'He is above all sectional and factious prejudices more than any other statesman of this Union with whom I have ever acted.'[8]

The ambitious secretary of war further saw to it that his services and his views were given appropriate publicity. While he refrained from public speaking or public letter-writing, he worked assiduously to advance his own cause. He cultivated friends in several states and kept up a vigorous correspondence with them, soliciting information and advice and issuing guidance and instructions. He saw to it that he had his champions in the press, that they disseminated his views, and he probably wrote anonymous articles for them himself. Yet on the surface Calhoun's campaign remained relatively traditional. Ostensibly he was being presented to the public by his friends, who drew attention to his distinguished services and his nationalist views. More than most candidates, Calhoun could hope to transcend a sectional identification, for his nationalist economic and military policies should secure him some support in the North and the West, while his South Carolina base should bring him some southern support. As a scion of a Scotch-Irish family which had lived for a time in Pennsylvania and as a graduate of Yale, Calhoun also hoped for northern interest. One admirer, indeed, privately predicted that he would be taken up as 'the northern candidate'. His strategy rested on attracting significant support outside his own section, and while his friends drew attention to his nationalist principles and public services he went serenely about his business as secretary of war. In the event an unexpected surge of support for Jackson in Pennsylvania in the winter of 1823–24 deprived Calhoun of his anticipated northern stronghold and he was obliged to drop out of the presidential race. Opinion at the grassroots was to leave its unpredictable mark on the election of 1824.[9]

Outside the cabinet Henry Clay seemed at first to be the most formidable contender for the presidential succession. As a one-time War Hawk, peace commissioner at Ghent, and Speaker of the House, Clay had long played a prominent role on the public stage, and a somewhat distinctive one as the first westerner to gain real political stature. It was natural enough that he should eye the presidency, but his road towards it was less clearly marked out than those of his cabinet rivals. He had never held executive office, unlike most of those who had previously reached the presidency, and he lacked the option of displaying himself before the public in the sedulous performance of departmental duties. Also, he could not hope to be seen as the natural heir-apparent or as the regular party candidate. Clay more than anyone had to devise a new strategy to reach his goal.

Henry Clay was nothing if not bold. He in effect became the first presidential contender to run on issues, to identify himself with a number of clear policy positions. In the past, of course, candidates had sometimes been associated with a set of principles as party nominees, and in the current campaign both Crawford and Calhoun were identified with certain positions, but Clay went beyond them in enunciating detailed measures in the course of the campaign. His public character and past services played little part in his campaign strategy. Rather, he moved into a kind of 'opposition' position and tried to storm the White House with policies of his own.

It was the opinion of John Quincy Adams that Clay had first conceived a presidential campaign strategy in 1817, when, resentful at being passed over for the State Department he had refused other government offices and 'projected a new opposition, of which he should be the head, and which should in the course of two Presidential terms run down Monroe, so that he might come in as the opposition successor'. Whatever the truth about Clay's motives, he undoubtedly did use his position as Speaker to embarrass the Monroe administration. He made himself the principal American champion of Latin American independence, bitterly attacking the Monroe administration for what he considered to be its undue deference to Spain and its tardiness in recognizing the Latin American republics. He made eloquent speeches in favour of a protective tariff and of federal aid to internal improvements, on one occasion implying that Monroe's strict constructionist attitude towards the latter was tantamount to 'treachery'. By the opening of the 1824 campaign Clay had carved out for himself an independent position and could hope that others at odds with the administration might rally to his cause.[10]

The issue on which he decided to rest his hopes was the protective tariff, and at the end of March 1824 Clay stepped down from the Speaker's chair to present a classic defence of the protectionist case. The United States needed to build up her own industry, he insisted, both as a source of wealth and, especially, to provide a market for American farmers. The American economy had languished because of the inadequacy of foreign markets, but there was a remedy 'in adopting a genuine AMERICAN SYSTEM'. Clay called upon his countrymen to put aside their particularist apprehensions and support the measure as 'the cause of the country', which 'must and will prevail', and concluded with an appeal to God, 'in His infinite mercy, to avert from our country the evils which are impending over it, and, by enlightening our councils, to conduct us into that path which leads to riches, to greatness, to glory'.[11]

Formally Clay was addressing his fellows in the House; in fact he was reaching out to the electorate with an issue of his own. The speech was reprinted in the press and as a separate pamphlet and Clay caused copies to be sent to various friends and notables. The time and energy he had devoted to the tariff issue at the height of the campaign were considerable. He had, he said, 'almost prostrated myself on the Tariff'. He hoped in particular to win support in the Middle Atlantic states, which, when added to his own western stronghold and with some southern backing, should make him a formidable candidate. Yet a cause makes enemies as well as friends. By September Clay found it 'a little remarkable that my support of the Tariff has excited against me in the South, a degree of opposition, which is by no means counterbalanced by any espousal of my cause in Pennsa. and other quarters, where the Tariff was so much desired'. Clay had publicly proclaimed his platform and was in effect inviting the electorate to accept or reject him on it. He refrained from overt campaigning, except for an appearance at a public dinner given him by his constituents, at which he made a few bland remarks in favour of the tariff and internal improvements and was toasted as 'Henry Clay – May his nomination to the Presidency be the signal for rallying around the palladium of Internal Improvements and American Industry.' In order to distinguish himself from his rivals, then, and to give his cause some *raison d'être*, Clay used his position in Congress to dissociate himself from the administration and to embrace the policies which forever became attached to his name. But this brought him little support in 1824. This, after all, was not how presidential campaigns had been conducted in the past.[12]

The least likely presidential candidate of all in 1824 was Andrew Jackson. His fame rested above all on his military achievements, his dramatic victory over a larger British force at New Orleans in 1815 in particular making him the nation's greatest living military hero. But the traditional route to the presidency had been by loyal and distinguished service in high civil office, and in this respect Jackson had no real qualifications, apart from brief terms in the Senate and as Governor of Florida. When the idea that Jackson should run for president was first mooted few people took it seriously, including the general himself. 'I know what I am fit for', he is reported to have said in 1821, 'I can command a body of men in a rough way, but I am not fit to be President.' He seems to have remained relatively indifferent to the presidential question for some time. In the summer of 1822 the Tennessee legislature formally put him in nomination, though apparently not so much with the intention of running him as with using his name in certain local manoeuvrings. Jackson's response was in the highest tradition of the Mute Tribune. 'I shall leave the people free to adopt such course as they may think proper, and elect whom they choose, to fill the Presidential chair, without any influence of mine exerted by me', he told Andrew J. Donelson, insisting that his only desire was retirement. 'But as the Legislature of my state has thought proper to bring my name forward without consulting me, I mean to be silent.'[13]

Jackson held to this view with some tenacity. The most unconventional presidential candidate of all assumed the traditional self-effacing stance more convincingly than any of his rivals and justified it in terms of fundamental political principle. 'My undeviating rule of conduct through life, and which I have and shall ever deem as

47

congenial with the true Republican principles of government, has been neither to seek, or decline public invitations to office.' So he sternly informed one correspondent who asked whether he approved of his name being used as a presidential candidate. The presidency was 'interresting' to the American people 'alone' and 'as it should not be sought by any Individual of the Republic: so it cannot with propriety be declined when offered by those who have the power of selection'. Until late in the campaign Jackson scrupulously adhered to this position. He discussed the election with his friends, but he does not appear to have taken any active part in managing the campaign and he refrained from overt electioneering. In the fall of 1823, however, Jackson's associates in Tennessee decided to nominate him for the Senate, principally because he was the only man who could defeat the Crawfordite incumbent. Jackson appears to have had no part in initiating this move, being told of it only shortly beforehand and expressing himself 'astonished' at the event, which 'I regret more than any other of my life'. But he was duly elected and was obliged to take his seat in the Senate in Washington, knowing that his every action would be scrutinized for its bearing on the presidential race.[14]

In the Senate Jackson maintained a fairly low profile, adhering as best he could to the tradition of the Mute Tribune. He carried out his committee duties, voted for transportation schemes on the grounds of military necessity and for Clay's tariff bill, but he attempted no great speeches and did not seek to identify himself prominently with issues. What he did do, almost certainly with some calculation, was to repair relations with men with whom he had previously quarrelled and to present to this community – which was expected to make the final choice for president when the election was thrown into the House – a calm and stately bearing. His reputation for 'Passion and impulse', a friend had told him that summer, was being well exploited by his enemies: 'cannot something be done to counteract their Views'? Something could, and that winter in Washington Jackson buried his differences with Thomas Hart Benton, with whom he had once been involved in a tavern brawl, re-established friendship with Major-General Winfield Scott, whom he had once challenged to a duel, and improved relations with his old critic Henry Clay. 'This has destroyed the stronghold of my enemies who denounced me as a man of revengefull Temper and of great rashness', he told one friend. 'I am told the opinion of those whose minds were prepared to see me with a Tomahawk in one hand, and a scalping knife in the other has greatly changed and I am getting on very smoothly.'

James Buchanan later told Jackson that his popularity had increased in Pennsylvania, where fears about his temper had 'all been dissipated by the mild prudence and dignity of your conduct last winter, before and after the Presidential election'.[15]

During the 1824 campaign, then, Jackson did little beyond conduct himself with senatorial decorum. On occasion he furnished his friends with information and documents concerning his past or his views, chiefly material which could be used to refute the varied allegations made against him in the press, but he took no directing role and kept out of the immediate public eye. But he did make one significant innovation in campaign techniques, and that was his celebrated letter to Dr L. H. Coleman of Warrenton, North Carolina. Later it would become normal for presidential candidates to convey their views to the public in letters ostensibly written to their interlocutors, with the expectation that they would then be published, but it was Jackson who pioneered this means of reaching the larger electorate. The motives for this move are obscure. It may be that as someone whose name had been put to the people, as he explained to Coleman, he felt it 'incumbent on me, when asked, frankly to declare my opinion upon any political or national question pending before and about which the country feels an interest'. Jackson was the first presidential candidate to acknowledge that the people had a right to question him on his views, in effect to concede that there could be a dialogue between the electors and the candidate. It may be that Jackson felt a need to demonstrate that he was not merely a military hero, that he was capable of forming intelligent views on great public issues, and Clay had just made the tariff a campaign issue. Whether Coleman had been prompted to write Jackson his inquiring letter is not known. Jackson did say that he had received Coleman's letter only that day, in which case the skilful composition of his reply needs some explanation, for it does not have the appearance of a hasty production. Presumably it was intended for publication, for which Jackson subsequently gave permission. In the letter Jackson avowed his support for a 'judicious' tariff, which would enable the United States to preserve 'within ourselves the means of national defense and independence, particularly in a state of war', and used the occasion to pronounce the national debt a 'curse', to inveigh against 'a moneyed aristocracy' and to support the domestic market argument. While acknowledging the need for the right kind of industry, Jackson revealed his suspicions of the commercial nexus and his preference for the simpler republic of the past. The letter attracted notice, and the editor of the *New York Evening Post* was moved to observe 'how much more manly and honest' was Jackson's conduct than that of John Quincy Adams, 'who, when the whole people is in a state of agitation respecting a vital measure of national policy, and his opinion is looked up to, cautiously and cunningly keeps it to himself, and wears an impenetrable cloak of mystery?' The comment was not entirely fair, for it was Jackson who was breaking with tradition in seeking to reach out to the people.[16]

The candidates of 1824 thus evolved a variety of strategies designed to carry them towards the presidency. In the absence of a party cause, they had somehow to make clear their availability without departing too obviously from the stance of the Mute Tribune. A vigorous prosecution of official duties, a stance of conspicuous aloofness from party politics, a cultivation of a reputation for transcending sectional interests, a public adoption of a programme and defiance of the administration, an attempted resurrection of the old party cause, and a stately disinterested bearing combined with some attempt at public communication, were among the strategies evolved. Some of these attitudes were more likely to impress fellow members of the Washington community than the public at large, and this was an important consideration in an election which would probably have to be decided by the House. But the candidates also had their sights on the larger electorate and on local notables across the country.

All the candidates were well aware of the power of public opinion and all sought to take advantage of it. They themselves or their associates did what they could to cultivate support among state and local leaders, and their friends across the country tried to mobilize opinion by holding local meetings and creating electoral machinery. Compared with the hullabaloo of later years the rallies of 1824 were rather sedate affairs, but they were a mark of the growing popular involvement in presidential campaigns. One small sign of the future was the appearance for the first time of a kind of campaign button, brass medalets bearing the likeness of Andrew Jackson which could be pierced and worn on the person. But a much more important way of disseminating an image was via the printed word. The candidates in the cabinet established close connections with selected Washington newspapers, providing official patronage in return for support, notably Adams with the *National Journal*, Crawford with the *Washington City Gazette*, and Calhoun with the *Washington Republican*. These sent out signals to strings of local newspapers, and the support of friendly editors in such large and critical states as New York and

Pennsylvania in particular was sought. As influential as the press, perhaps, were the convention addresses, political pamphlets and campaign broadsides which were also showered on the electorate, and of which this campaign witnessed a marked increase. If the candidates themselves were reluctant to appear before the people, their friends could at least present them through the incalculable power of the printed word.[17]

In the place of the candidate, then, was the image. Since the personal part that a candidate could take in a campaign was limited, it may be that the image constructed around him was more important in advancing his cause than his own conduct. At any rate image-making, too, now became a major aspect of presidential campaigns. Publications appeared devoted primarily to the creation of an appealing representation of a candidate, the most important of which was the campaign biography. It was this above all which gave definition to a candidate's popular campaign.

The campaign biography appeared for the first time for the 1824 presidential election, and it was destined to became a regular feature of the campaign scene. If presidents were now in effect being chosen by the people, their character and careers had to be explained to the people. It was perhaps no accident that this distinctive electoral art form was invented for the 1824 campaign, when the candidates were obliged to appear before the people in their personal rather than party capacities. The first campaign biography was of the ambitious secretary of war. Still a relatively young man, Calhoun may have felt that his candidacy was likely to be overshadowed by his more senior cabinet colleagues and that he needed more exposure. At any rate, exploiting his close connections with the so-called 'Family party' of Pennsylvania, he had a memoir of himself serialized in their organ, the Philadelphia *Franklin Gazette*, in the spring and early summer of 1822. Its author is uncertain and may have been George M. Dallas, though Calhoun was himself not too modest to assume that role. Philadelphia was also the scene of the second campaign biography, when the *Columbian Observer* published a series of 'Letters' in 1823 promoting Andrew Jackson's cause, over the name 'Wyoming', a pseudonym for the general's friend, John H. Eaton (although Jackson himself did not learn of the authorship until the following year). Later the Letters were published as a 104-page book, and Eaton's earlier military biography of Jackson was updated and republished. Shorter sketches of the general also appeared. This flurry of activity on behalf of Calhoun and Jackson apparently had its effect on John Quincy Adams's advocates, who updated and republished an earlier sketch of their champion. Campaign literature on behalf of other candidates, of course, also appeared, although not in the form of promotional biographies.[18]

These early exercises in image-making reveal something about how the presidency was perceived in the early 1820s. The campaigns surrounding Calhoun and Adams retained many of the assumptions of an earlier generation. The publication on which the Adams image was based in fact had not originally been intended as a campaign biography, and the concessions that his partisans made to the popular audience were few. Their sketch reviewed Adams's academic career and described his youthful sojourn in Europe with his father, perhaps to the point of indiscretion. 'By remaining much longer in Europe', it was said of 18-year-old John Q., 'he saw the danger of an alienation from his own country, which would disqualify him for contentment with his condition in aftertimes, and he found himself contracting sentiments, manners, and opinions of European growth, . . . .' He hastened back to the United States, there to finish his education among his own people, though his identification with Europe was to provide his political enemies with ammunition. Because of his – and his father's – one-time Federalism, his promoters went to some trouble to emphasize John Quincy Adams's consistency of principle and to demonstrate that those principles 'have been, throughout the whole of his political life, essentially *republican*'. Yet ultimately it was his diplomatic career that was presented as his chief claim to his country's gratitude. Adams's mission to Russia in particular was accounted a remarkable success, his repeated triumphs over his adversaries raising his 'diplomatic character' to 'a point of pre-eminence, which posterity will long regard with admiration, and which his country cannot but feel proud to contemplate'. Adams, then, was projected as the polished, accomplished statesman, a man whose claims rested more on services performed than on views held or imputed. This was close to Adams's image of himself. There was no attempt to conceal the gentility of his education, indeed, attention was drawn to his cultivation of literature and the arts. This was the candidate as the cosmopolitan patrician, a man of good education, consistent republican principle and distinguished public service. He admirably fitted the traditional mould of political leadership.[19]

A variation on the candidate as statesman was produced on behalf of John C. Calhoun. In the columns of the *Franklin Gazette* he was an outstanding patriot, a leader possessed of an intellect and an integrity which raised him far above the ordinary. At school, it was reported, the budding statesman had suffered from a speech impediment, yet he became a brilliant orator, proof 'that all minor obstacles will vanish before the persevering energies of a great mind'. Grown to patriotic manhood, he took the initiative in Congress in having war declared on England, hence commanding the respect of the rest of the world for the power and integrity of the United States. 'The distinguishing feature of his mind', contended this eulogy, 'may be said to be the faculty of analysis.' Rising above sectional and party considerations, he used this magnificent instrument to peer ahead and formulate measures for the public good before others had realized their necessity. Moved by a desire to give durability to American republican institutions, Calhoun had no time for lesser considerations. 'To an ardent patriotism, he adds a stern and manly independence which disdains to calculate the personal consequences of discharging his duty . . .' the *Franklin Gazette* explained. 'He is not one of those timid and time-serving politicians who mark and follow "the shiftings of the popular breize".' Later writers would have hesitated before appearing to disparage the popular will. This portrait of Calhoun did nothing to suggest that its subject possessed the common touch. Like Adams he was presented as the lofty and far-sighted statesman of old, although unlike his more senior rival the emphasis was on his talents more than his services. 'If we are to believe one half they say in favor of their youthful candidate', sniffed one critic, 'his talents greatly transcend the limits we have heretofore ascribed to the human intellect.' Assuredly Calhoun had not been made an earthy man of the people; he remained the towering statesman, almost intimidating in his gifted yet lonely eminence.[20]

The most elaborate propaganda exercise of the campaign of 1824, however, was conducted on behalf of Andrew Jackson, both in the form of Eaton's Wyoming letters and in a separate array of biographical sketches which appeared to promote the Hero's cause. The publications centering on the controversial figure of Andrew Jackson far outweighed the attention given to his rivals. Jackson's partisans were early to grasp the need to make their champion the subject of a popular campaign, and they succeeded beyond their wildest dreams. Its impact was to reverberate through American political culture for a generation or more. Because it was of more than passing significance, the inventive image-making activity focussing on the figure of the Hero deserves extended analysis.

The nature of the campaign conducted on Jackson's behalf was governed very largely by the sheer implausibility of the Jackson candidature. It was widely assumed in the early 1820s that Jackson's nomination by his state legislature was not meant seriously, an assumption shared by some of the men who first proposed him for president. Henry Clay thought the Tennessee nomination a token honour and asserted 'very confidently that no other Western State will lend its support to him'. William H. Crawford was equally sure that 'There is no other state in the Union that will take him for President.' At the end of 1822 that hard-headed politico Martin Van Buren, in a private analysis of the prospects for the 1824 election, did not even mention Andrew Jackson. In a tour of New York in the summer of 1823 one politician found 'a general impression . . . that Gen. Jackson can not be Elected', while after a similar canvass of the Hero's own state Thomas Hart Benton reported that 'there is hardly any one who thinks he has any chance . . .'. Washington society feted Jackson when he arrived to take his Senate seat, but as late as December 1823, according to one congressman, 'all concur in the belief that he has no chance of success'. Not everyone took Jackson's prospects so lightly, of course, (John Quincy Adams was one canny exception), but probably few would have been prepared to stake money on him.[21]

Jackson, then, was widely held to be unelectable. Some reasons for his low rating are obvious enough. Most active politicians were committed to other candidates and had a motive for persuading themselves that Jackson was not a threat. It was widely expected that the election would be thrown into the House, where the other candidates had long been cultivating support. But it seems clear, too, that the professional politicians simply underestimated Jackson's potential appeal among the people. He did lack the conventional qualifications of a presidential candidate and he did lack serious experience in high civil office, and the traditional expectations of men in public life led them almost automatically to reject his pretensions. Yet beyond even that, the belief that Jackson could not be elected rested in part on a very genuine conviction that he *should* not be elected. Ultimately the objection to him was his military career and his high-handed reputation. One lesson that Americans had drawn from history was that a principal danger to republican government was the ambitious Military Chieftain, the Caesar or Bonaparte, and Jackson seemed uncomfortably close to this perilous model. 'The public esteem him *only* for his military Energy . . .', wrote one dismissive politician. 'There is more of the Dictator – than the Consul in his Character.' He was hardly the leader of a republic: 'This Nation is to be governed by moral, not physical Force.' The Jackson boom in Pennsylvania early in 1824 greatly upset William Plumer, Jr, who was moved to ask his father, 'Is it not a bad omen that mere military glory, for he has no character or reputation, as a Statesman, should thus captivate the popular feeling, and throw the nation headlong into the arms of a military despot?' That respected elder statesman Albert Gallatin held that precisely because Jackson had believed himself to be acting in the public interest on the occasions he had transcended the law during his military career, it was 'incomprehensible that he can be supported by Republicans and real friends of liberty'. The French had given 'a late sad example' of a people who had sacrificed 'their rights and liberties' to the shrine of 'military glory'. A similar concern was exercising the mind of Thomas Jefferson, who was visited in December 1824 by Daniel Webster, who promptly recorded the patriarch's conversation, not least his views on Jackson's possible election to the presidency: 'He is one of the most unfit men, I know of for such a place. He has had very little respect for Laws or Constitutions, – & is in fact merely an able military chief. His passions are terrible.'[22]

What was said in private was said even more brazenly in public. As early as 1819, when the House of Representatives debated Jackson's high-handed conduct during his pursuit of the Seminoles in Florida, Henry Clay had recalled the days when Greece and Rome had fallen to their own military heroes. 'Violence is in his blood', warned the *Washington Gazette* of Jackson, later adding that 'Military men have always occasioned the downfall of republics.' Jackson's career provided ample evidence of his penchant for violence and his disregard of the law and Constitution. He had killed and wounded men in duels and brawls; as a military commander he had had a number of militiamen shot for offences for which clemency might have been expected; during the Seminole campaign he had rather arbitrarily executed a pair of Englishmen he had captured; he had maintained martial law in New Orleans for two months after his victory there, and had arrested a legislator who had criticized him for this and then a judge who had issued a writ of habeas corpus on the legislator's behalf. These and other incidents revealed to Jackson's enemies an autocratic temperament, a willingness to resort to force, and little understanding of or sympathy with the principles of American republicanism. 'Rome had her Caesar, England her Cromwell, and France her Bonaparte, and the United States should profit by their example', it was said, and this unholy trinity was regularly invoked as a reminder of the fate of republics which entrusted themselves to military men. Jesse Benton, who had once put two bullets into Jackson, titillated the public with a lurid account of the general's blasphemous and bullying life-style, and concluded that it would be

well for the country 'should we not, by the appearance of another
Caesar in the history of republics, require yet another Brutus to
wind up the scene'. In short, not only did Jackson fail to conform to
the conventional yardsticks regarding presidential aspirants, but he
seemed to be exactly the kind of leader to which republican government was most allergic.[23]

It is hardly surprising that even Jackson's initial backers in Tennessee apparently had no great hopes that he would really be elected
president. As the *Richmond Enquirer* remarked in July 1822, Jackson
had occasionally been spoken of for president before that date, but
'we never supposed by any one, seriously'. Even when unanticipated
grassroots support developed for Jackson in such states as Alabama,
North Carolina and Pennsylvania, his partisans may have been
emboldened but they must still have felt that they faced a Herculean
task. They had, somehow, to transform this implausible contender
into a viable candidate. It is probably this which explains the promotional exercise on a scale thus far unsurpassed in the election of a
president.[24]

One way of allaying doubts about Jackson was to present him as a
human being of warmth and affection. The sketches of Calhoun and
Adams had portrayed their heroes as distinguished to the point of
aloofness, but Jackson's biographers sensed the appeal of a candidate
with a human touch. The sketches of Jackson were replete with
affecting anecdotes – Jackson the boy soldier in the Revolution
defiantly refusing to clean a British officer's boots; General Jackson's
yielding up of his horse to trudge on foot with his sick men; Jackson's adoption of an Indian infant found orphaned after a battle.
'Charity in him is a warm and active propensity of the heart', said
one biographer, 'urging him by an instantaneous impulse, to relieve
the wants of the distressed, without regarding, or even thinking of
the consequences.' The grateful shades of needy neighbours, hungry
and sick soldiers, and abandoned Indian children were summoned to
pay tribute to Jackson's good-hearted generosity. The message was
that a man of such impulsive benevolence could never turn into a
tyrant. Similarly, Jackson's biographers were anxious to counter the
charge that he possessed a violent temper. One tactic was to admit
that Jackson was a man of strong emotion, but to insist that the
emotion was patriotic ardour. Most of the incidents during the War
of 1812 which had been ascribed to high temper, in fact could be
'traced to strong provocation, operating . . . upon his patriotic zeal
and the very generosity and loftiness of his spirit'. Another response
was simply to deny that Jackson had a violent temper. It was not

Jackson himself who was 'desperate', argued some New Jersey admirers, but the enterprises on which he was sent; rather, he was 'cautious, prudent and deliberate' in forming his plans 'and cool and collected in the hour of danger'.[25]

The most ambitious attempt to demonstrate Jackson's fitness for the White House was made in Eaton's Wyoming letters. Throughout these, as throughout so much of early Jacksonian propaganda, lay an awareness that the accusation that had to be dispelled was that Jackson was a potentially dangerous Military Chieftain. There was, of course, the comforting precedent of George Washington, and Eaton opened with a reminder that a military man had taken charge at the very formation of the American government. Jackson, indeed, could even be compared with the revered Washington 'for abilities displayed, for firmness of purpose, for perils encountered, and devotion to the cause of liberty and his country'. In any case, Wyoming maintained, military service called forth those very qualities of mind needed by public men. 'Few highly distinguished military men have failed to make good statesmen'; he concluded, 'the peculiar cast of thought and judgment, necessary to constitute the one, eminently qualifies for the other.'[26].

But Wyoming's most ingenious argument, and one which he propounded through the entire book, was that the real menace to the republic was not Jackson but the civilian establishment. That the country was in peril he readily agreed, and like many of his generation Wyoming saw evidence of corruption and subversion all around him. But the culprits were the 'leading men' in Washington. 'Look to the city of Washington, and let the virtuous patriots of the country weep at the spectacle', he enjoined. 'There corruption is springing into existence, and fast flourishing.' In this adroit intellectual manoeuvre Wyoming reversed the tables on Jackson's critics. Where they had been exploiting ancient fears that republics were peculiarly vulnerable to executive ambition and military might, Wyoming was invoking an equally ancient fear – that republics were peculiarly vulnerable to internal corruption. 'Republics can only exist while the people, true to themselves, still adhere to principles and to virtue;' he intoned in language redolent of the eighteenth century, 'the instant these are abandoned, freedom must of necessity decline, and ultimately be laid prostrate.' The lesson of history was that an even greater danger to liberty than military ambition was the loss of public virtue.[27]

The Wyoming letters were studded with such words as 'intrigue', 'corruption', 'management', 'usurpation', and they invoked a republic which had once been happy, virtuous and free, but which had degenerated to such an extent that its very *raison d'être* was in jeopardy. Echoing the critiques of Walpolean corruption once propounded by *Cato's Letters* and by Lord Bolingbroke, the Wyoming letters located the source of the country's ills in ministerial patronage: the cabinet heads were distributing offices and favours to advance their own political fortunes and to buy support in Congress. That liberty was being lost was further confirmed by the caucus system, which took the choice of president out of the hands of the people and vested it in a set of men the Constitution had sought to exclude from the process. Together the patronage power of the Secretaries and the political power of the caucus constituted a system of corruption which menaced the rights of the people. The arrogant pretensions of the 'LEADING MEN OF THE COUNTRY' demonstrated that 'an ARISTOCRA-CY is rising in our land, and soon, very soon, the people of this country, with all their boasted privileges, will become the mere instruments of the men in power'. This vision of a once-proud people reduced to servility by the corrupt machinations of voracious office-holders is one which had been familiar in English and American political rhetoric for generations, and had once played its part in the American revolt against British rule. Whether consciously or not, Wyoming was reaching for something primordial in the American folk memory.[28]

American political leaders, then, had finally become those creatures of ambition and corruption which the Cassandras had for so long been warning against. Yet there was a solution. Andrew Jackson had saved the country once when it was in mortal peril and he could save it again. Only Jackson, after all, had stood aloof from the intrigues in Washington. He was not party to the electioneering which so beset the nation's capital, and not being in the cabinet he had no patronage to dispense. The very features which had seemed to disqualify Jackson for the presidency were thus at a stroke transformed into assets. As a political outsider he was untouched by the cancer that was gnawing at the republic's vitals; he was 'never in *Europe*' and 'never the HEAD OF A DEPARTMENT'. Jackson alone could restore the nation to its former principles, and that he was a true lover of republican government he had demonstrated by his repeated willingness to lay down his life for his country. He was now again but a 'private citizen, committed to no party, pledged to no system, allied to no intrigue, free of all prejudices, but coming directly from the people, and bearing with him an intimate acquaintance with their feelings, wishes, and wants, he can hardly fail to sustain himself with credit, and his country to advantage'. Here at last was Jackson's identification with the people, an identification made imperative *not* by his political philosophy but by the prior identification of the Washington politicos as the enemies of the republic. If the 'leading men' were conspiring to subvert the popular will, Jackson had to be cast as the people's champion, called out of retirement to save the body politic from the corruption at its heart. 'His resting ground is alone with the people, and the simple question to be decided is, *who shall govern this nation, the People or the Leading Men?*', concluded Wyoming. 'Yeomanry of the country look to this, and think of this!! For "that is the question". If you are freemen act fearlessly as such; or at once surrender and be slaves.'[29]

So Jackson was masterfully transformed from a potential Caesar to a potential saviour. The nation's experienced statesmen had been converted into dangerous subversives, and her republican destiny now rested with the virtuous Hero of New Orleans. For the last two generations and more a variety of pessimistic beliefs and assumptions had been sustained by American political discourse: that constitutions were subject to decay, that liberty was forever threatened by executive power and by the loss of public virtue, that republics were peculiarly vulnerable polities, that ministerial or executive patronage was a potent source of corruption and subversion. Weaving together disparate strands of English Country, revolutionary, and Old Republican thought, and exploiting the wistful nostalgia for the passing Jeffersonian arcadia, the Wyoming letters fashioned a devastating indictment of the political establishment in Washington and provided a compelling *raison d'être* for the candidacy of Andrew Jackson. The Hero's identification with 'democracy' was incidental to his rather old-fashioned purpose. Wyoming's object was to persuade the people to accept this unlikely presidential candidate by casting him as the champion, indeed as the saviour, of that republican freedom for which their fathers had fought.

This image of Andrew Jackson seems to have evoked a sympathetic response in some parts of the country. In such states as Pennsylvania, Maryland and North Carolina hardened politicians were surprised and sometimes alarmed at the apparently spontaneous enthusiasm generated among the people for the Jackson candidature, an enthusiasm which seems in part to have stemmed from a populistic resentment of the pretensions of established political leaders. In Pennsylvania the dominant 'Family party' leaders had hoped to deliver the state to Calhoun, but in February and March 1824 were forced to capitulate to the pressure for the Hero. At a state convention at Harrisburg, Jackson was nominated for president with but one dissenting vote. 'The truth is that the movement in Pennsylvania was made by the people altogether & not by the politicans,' grumbled one disturbed congressman. 'It seems that the people of North Carolina are taking up Jackson, as Pennsylvania did, against their politicians of their own mere will,' reported another surprised politician. 'So it is in New York.' 'What do you think of the people of Baltimore being all alive for Jackson?', asked Marylander John P. Kennedy, and a Baltimore editor agreed that 'The popular feeling in this city is decidedly, and without doubt, in his favor.' In North Carolina too, 'we are all in a buble for Jackson' except for 'the most considerate and firm men'; through most of the state Jackson 'is . . . unquestionably the people's President'. 'The truth is', echoed Daniel Webster, 'he is the people's candidate in a great part of the southern and western country.'[30]

The Jackson boom was no doubt a good deal less spontaneous than it seemed. Across the country ambitious local politicians and editors were not slow to volunteer for the Hero's cause. Yet not infrequently such men were themselves outside the governing circles in their states and felt an affinity with a candidate who could be used to mobilize opinion against a political establishment. Wyoming's sepulchral warnings (which had been reprinted in newspapers favourable to the Hero's cause) were often echoed in these local campaigns. 'The Great Augean Stable at Washington wants cleansing', said an early Jackson supporter in Pennsylvania, 'and we know of no other Hercules.' The *Columbian Observer* itself, the original outlet for Wyoming, played an influential role in the Jackson campaign in Pennsylvania. The Harrisburg convention adopted an Address which complained that the presidential succession was 'settled at Washington', inveighed against the 'intrigues . . . among the Official Gentry at Washington' and warned of the 'monstrous consequences' arising from this 'perversion'. The 'circean web' was said to be 'poisoning and strangling our Infant republic'. Another state in which an unexpectedly strong Jackson sentiment emerged was New Jersey. Isaac Watts Crane expressly acknowledged his debt to Wyoming in a speech denouncing 'the views of the trafficking politicians who draw their sustenance from the bee-hive of the Metropolis', and another group promised that Jackson would 'root out corruption and purify the polluted atmosphere of the city of Washington'. The New Jersey Jackson Convention itself urged that the people 'Take for your President a man from your own body, untainted by the corruption of a court and uninitiated in Cabinet secrets. So shall you restore the administration of our government to its primitive purity.' In Ohio, too, Jackson was presented as 'the CANDIDATE OF THE PEOPLE', corruptly opposed by 'an organised corps of *Leading men* and intriguing politicians, in almost every state of the Union... '. A Detroit supporter also warned of 'the cabals of the selfish and intriguing', while Kentucky Jacksonians disparaged the claims of the 'merely cabinet men', who, while Jackson had been fighting for his country, had remained safely 'in the circles of fashion and luxury, enjoying lucrative offices'.[31]

The ingenious propaganda campaign constructed around the towering figure of Andrew Jackson, then, seemed to strike a responsive chord in the electorate. In fact there is no way of measuring what impact, if any, this exercise in image-making had on the election. Much of the strength of the Jackson movement no doubt rested on the popularity the Hero had won at New Orleans, but John H. Eaton and his fellow propagandists exploited this popularity to the full. The candidacy which had at first been dismissed by several experienced politicians as a transitory diversion had by the spring of 1824 become a potent political force. Its true strength was revealed in the autumn, when Jackson carried eleven of the twenty-four states, scattered over every part of the Union save New England, and won 153, 544 popular votes, over forty per cent more than John Quincy Adams, who had finished in second popular place. Andrew Jackson did not win the election, which as anticipated was thrown into the House of Representatives, but he was never to be written off again as a presidential candidate. The Jackson insurgency had changed the nature of American presidential politics.

The presidential election of 1824 marked the end of one era and the beginning of another. In many ways there was much that was traditional in the relationship between the candidates and the electorate. No candidate moved very far from the stance of the Mute Tribune, accepting the convention that a candidate did not canvass for votes and that his claims rested largely on his known character and his public services. The anti-power attitudes of an earlier generation had not significantly abated, and candidates and their partisans continued to act on the assumption that republican liberty rested on the capacity of the people to resist corruption and the capacity of their leaders to resist ambition. Every candidate privately revealed a compulsive interest in his fate in the campaign (except Andrew Jackson who did not seem fully to succumb to the presidential bug until late in 1823), but in public each went conscientiously about his duties,

ostensibly adhering to the nostrum that the presidency should neither be sought nor declined.

Yet times were changing. The collapse of the old party system,
however much desired by the many men in public life who deplored
party forms, left the candidates without a cause. No candidate could
legitimately advance his own fortunes, and the passing of party deprived him of a patriotic *raison d'être*. Thrust into the electoral arena
in some measure in their personal capacities, the candidates gingerly
explored ways of distinguishing themselves from one another and
communicating discreetly with their peers and their constituents.
Strategies which were to become familiar features of presidential
campaigns in the *antebellum* era made their appearance, from the
conspicuous prosecution of official duties, through the revival of the
party cause and the vigorous espousal of distinctive policies, even to
the attempt to reach for electoral sympathy via the public letter.
Jackson's recognition that the voters had a right to his views marks a
growing awareness of the potent role of popular opinion, unpredictable though it was. To their surprise and dismay, candidates like
Clay and Calhoun found grassroots sentiments deserting them in
favour of Jackson, the least qualified candidate of all by traditional
yardsticks.

It was to the public at large rather than to the Washington community that Jackson's friends directed their main efforts. They perceived that in the political culture within which they were operating
the fashioning of a popular appeal through the printed word might
prove more effective in mobilizing opinion than the diffident conduct of the candidate. Even as the images fashioned around Adams
and Calhoun continued to portray them as high-minded statesmen to
whom it would be wise to defer, and as their partisans dismissed
Jackson as the very antithesis of a republican leader, John H. Eaton
in particular stumbled on a strategy which was to be imitated frequently in years to come. By converting the nation's leading men
into corrupt and voracious officeholders contemptuous of the liberties of the people, he simultaneously converted Jackson from a
potential Caesar to a potential Cincinnatus, ready to answer the call
of his country in its hour of peril. The Jackson campaign demonstrated both the need to take a campaign to the people and the value
of harnessing their highly conservative instincts. Ultimately Jackson's cause was the safety of the republic itself.

The resolution of the 1824 election, of course, seemed to confirm
all that Jackson's partisans had been saying about the wicked ways of
Washington politicians. The election was thrown into the House,

where Henry Clay swung his support to John Quincy Adams, the runner-up in both the popular and electoral vote, who was duly elected. Two days later Adams made Clay secretary of state and invited the remaining members of Monroe's cabinet to retain their posts. The uncouth Cincinnatus from Tennessee had after all been excluded from the suspect ranks of power. Wyoming's letters of 1823 had all but predicted the 'corrupt bargain' of 1825, which when it came could seem only like the fulfilment of a prophesy.

# CHAPTER FOUR
# *The conservative origins of the new party system: 1828*

Although the breakdown of the old party system had resulted in a variety of Republican contenders for the presidency in 1824, in the end John Quincy Adams and Andrew Jackson had emerged as the two most powerful combatants. Their campaigns had not been wholly dissimilar. Unlike Clay or Calhoun, neither had sought actively to manage his campaign and both of them sincerely believed that candidates should stand aloof while the people deliberated on their claims to office. Neither considered himself a candidate of a party and neither wished to take any initiative to advance his own cause. John Quincy Adams was presented as the embodiment of the conservative tradition of public service, patriotically giving of his best for his country without thought of reward, while Andrew Jackson was presented as the embodiment of the conservative tradition of Old Republicanism, an old-fashioned patriot ever at his country's call and yearning for the republican simplicity of an earlier and more virtuous day. They were not identified with parties, with policies, not even with principles, except the republican principles of public service. Yet there was a gulf between them. John Quincy Adams personified the presidential candidate of the early republic, a well-educated patrician who had spent long years in the country's service and who had distinguished himself in high government posts. Viewed from another perspective, he was a member of the officeholding class who counted on his fellow officeholders to sustain him in power. Andrew Jackson, on the other hand, seemed the most ill-equipped figure ever to have been presented for the presidency, an ill-educated frontier nabob with little government experience and, even worse, the capacity to become a military dictator. From another perspective, he could be viewed as a genuine republican champion who would rescue the people from the corrupt machinations of the power-hungry men in Washington.

Even in 1824 there was something of an ideological divide between Adams and Jackson. Although not clearly separated by policies or even party, they were separated by differing ideas about republican leadership. Over the next few years the gulf widened dramatically. In 1828 Adams and Jackson were the only presidential candidates, itself an unusual phenomenon, and their contest marked the advent of what has become known as the second American party system. This new polarization of American politics was the product of a variety of subtle pressures, but what helped to produce it were conflicting views about the nature of good leadership in a republic. In 1824 the rivalry between Adams and Jackson had not been a direct confrontation since they had not been the only candidates (the rivalry between Jackson and Crawford had been the more bitter). But now these different embodiments of republican virtue were brought into head-on conflict. In the eyes of one set of partisans, the electors were presented with a choice between a statesman and a military despot; to their rivals, the choice was between a corrupt spoilsman and a veritable Cincinnatus. Crude though these images were, they did reflect something of a deeper ideological divide. The second American party system, like the first, in some measure arose out of the differing conceptions of good republican government held by men in public life.

When Henry Clay accepted John Quincy Adams's invitation to head the State Department in January 1825 he inadvertently accelerated a process which was to have far-reaching consequences for American politics. By his act the so-called 'corrupt bargain' was completed and the Adams administration was irremediably branded with the sin against which the Jacksonians had long been inveighing. The framers of the Constitution had tried to eliminate the opportunities for bargain and intrigue in presidential elections, but their arrangements had never fully allayed fears that the electoral process might somehow be subverted, and Adams and Clay apparently proved the fears well-grounded. No act on the part of the administration could have been better calculated to give credence to the warnings which had long been issuing from Jacksonian presses. The charge of corrupt bargain reverberated across the stage of American politics and helped to bring about a new and dramatic alignment.

One consequence of the fateful events of early 1825 was the

commitment of Adams and Clay to one another in an irrevocable and binding fashion. Henry Clay, despite being temperamentally at odds with the president, now turned his prodigious political talents to the re-election of his new chief. Every president since John Quincy Adams's venerable father had been re-elected, and if vindication could be thus secured for the son, Clay's own turn might follow in due course. If executive influence could successfully be used to win presidential elections, the succession would thus be fixed until the impossibly distant date of 1840, a consideration which helped other ambitious politicians see the advantages of an alternative common front. Calhoun was now vice-president, but he was soon privately indicating his sympathy for an assault on the Adams–Clay coalition under the leadership of Andrew Jackson, whose own uncertain health might preclude a re-election. New York's adroit political manager, Martin Van Buren, was also 'morally certain that the present administration must go down & I firmly believe that such ought to be the case', and he persuaded many former Crawford partisans to tie their fortunes to Old Hickory's ascending star. Apart from some doubts about the aspirations of the New York governor De Witt Clinton (who ultimately dispelled them by dying), by the summer of 1826, as one correspondent of Andrew Jackson put it, 'Mr. Adams and yourself are the only persons spoken of' as candidates for the presidency.[1]

The candidates themselves could only act out the roles for which they had long been cast. John Quincy Adams was as determined as ever to avoid anything which might smack of electioneering. He did talk privately to his callers, confiding his views, sometimes furnishing evidence to disprove charges being made against him, and on occasion sending out political signals, such as one making it clear that William H. Crawford was not to be offered the vice-presidential spot on an Adams ticket. But beyond such quiet consultations with his friends he was reluctant to go, and he certainly did not direct his campaign. He avoided public functions and he refused to write letters for the press, declining a correspondence with an 'electioneering committee' in Kentucky on the grounds that such exchanges had 'not been customary with reference to the office of President of the United States, and I should not be willing to set the precedent'. He adamantly refused to contribute funds to the campaign, reminding one supplicant of William Lowndes's sentiment that 'the Presidency . . . was an office neither to be sought nor declined. To pay money for securing it, directly or indirectly, was, in my opinion, incorrect in principle.' He further vastly irritated

Henry Clay and others of his partisans by refusing to dismiss federal officials who were hostile to his administration or to make appointments for political purposes. 'Such a system would be repugnant to every feeling of my soul,' he told one remonstrating correspondent. He was periodically warned that such a course served to weaken him politically, for the appointment of an enemy to a coveted post in a given community could only frustrate and humiliate his friends there, but Adams seemed to take such complaints as evidence of his own virtue.[2]

Adams, then, was the presidential candidate as high-minded statesman, above party and above faction. Even as a party was forming around him he refused to recognize its existence and seemed almost to delight in turning aside the campaign proposals of his friends. As far as he was concerned, at any rate, Adams was decidedly not a party candidate. It may be that the corrupt bargain charge served to strengthen his determination to maintain a strict impartiality over such matters as appointments, for any other course would have lent credibility to the opposition's allegations. He wanted to be *seen* as a president who was working tirelessly and conscientiously for the benefit of all, a true patriot whose only thought was for the public good. The public pronouncements that he did make seemed to be a product of this attitude. While he remained discreetly circumspect on some of the issues of the day, such as tariff protection and public lands, there was one issue on which he made himself very clear, and that was internal improvements. No other issue carried such strong nationalist meaning.

Adams seized the opportunity of his first annual message to identify himself with this cause, advocating that the federal government actively pursue a system of internal improvements for the general welfare. So nationalistic in tone was this message that it gave pause even to Henry Clay and the cabinet. The president himself recognized the potential unpopularity of his proposal, but was reluctant to modify it. It seemed as if he were deliberately courting particularist opposition in order to demonstrate that he was president of the whole nation. 'It is not very material to me', he told his cabinet, 'whether I should present these views in the first or the last message that I send in to the Congress. But I feel it is my indispensable duty to suggest them.' In the event the message encountered the reception that Adams's advisers had feared. 'The friends of State rights object to it as utterly ultra,' observed Calhoun, 'and those, who in the main, advocate a liberal system of measures, think that the Message had recommended so many debateable subjects at once, as to endanger a reaction even to those measures heretofore adopted and apparently acquiesced in.' And so it proved. The Jacksonians had a field day in ridiculing the message's more fanciful schemes. Interestingly, the one quasi-electioneering jaunt that Adams did allow himself in 1828 was also apparently designed to identify him with this questionable cause. Although he had declined to attend the opening of the Pennsylvania Canal in 1827 because 'this mode of electioneering suited neither my taste nor my principles', he did agree to attend a Fourth of July ceremony in 1828 to break the ground for the Chesapeake and Ohio Canal and even to turn the first sod. He carefully wrote out his address beforehand because he knew that whatever he said would be 'severely criticized and misrepresented'. It was another rational plea for the enlightened use of the powers of the Union to further American progress. By this time it must have been obvious to Adams that his fervent commitment to a systematic policy of internal improvements was an electoral liability, but this simply proved to him that he put the nation first. The Adams campaign consisted of a zealous prosecution of his presidential duties and an almost contemptuous display of putting the Union above partisan and sectional considerations.[3]

Yet while the president was indulging himself in high-minded rectitude, some of his associates showed less scruple. Their fates, too, hung on the outcome of the election, and there was considerable activity below presidential level within the Adams administration to dispense patronage in a politically productive way and to find funds for party presses. Henry Clay in particular, although frequently annoyed with Adams's obduracy over appointments, in effect emerged as campaign manager and was vigorous in his efforts to stimulate the needed electoral machinery in the key states. But apart from tending to organizational problems, Clay also entered the campaign directly and became a kind of surrogate for the unenthusiastic president. He acceded to requests from Pennsylvania politicians to make a tour of that state in the summer of 1827, identifying the administration's cause with domestic manufacturers and internal improvements, and was congratulated on 'your late triumphant march through Pennsylvania' by a New York friend. He also found time to make some public appearances during the election year itself, in May attending a dinner in Baltimore, where he warned of the 'scourge' of 'military rule', and in August addressing an estimated 5,000 persons at Cincinnati, where he praised the American System, attacked the nullificationist symptoms which were appearing in the South, and stressed what the administration had done for the West. In this speech he also explained that his occasional addresses to the people, which had attracted some hostile criticism, normally occurred when he encountered receptions while travelling to his home in Kentucky, and that he had never 'resorted to such acts to promote my own election, or that of any other person'. During this election, of course, Clay was subject to much abuse for his alleged part in the corrupt bargain, and he was moved on occasion to defend his honour in speech or print, despite the president's opinion that it was better to remain silent. Other prominent men close to the administration also made speeches on its behalf, such as Daniel Webster in Boston in June 1828. Another, Tristram Burgess, was unwise enough to trust that God Himself would save the country from Jackson. 'Clay has given the cue to all his partisans throughout the country', complained the *New York Enquirer*. 'Eating, drinking & praying are all the go now-a-days.' John Quincy Adams himself had no direction over these surrogates, and showed little appreciation of their efforts.[4]

If the resolution of the 1824–25 election had made it even more necessary than ever for Adams to sustain the role of the patriotic and disinterested statesman, Andrew Jackson was equally inescapably thrust into the role of Cincinnatus. No one was more convinced than the Hero himself that he had been cheated out of the White House by the machinations of Adams and Clay and he was determined that right should triumph. He followed the ensuing campaign avidly and even took something of a directing role in it himself, regularly consulting with the committee which formed around him at Nashville and corresponding with his partisans in other parts of the Union. Yet it was a covert role. In his Wyoming letters of 1823 John H. Eaton had cast Jackson as the potential saviour of a republic whose very existence was threatened by the desperate intrigue and ambition of its leading men, and in the wake of the corrupt bargain this role assumed a new plausibility. It behoved Jackson to return to his farm to await the call of the people.

This meant giving up his seat in the Senate, which he promptly did when the Tennessee legislature obliged him with a new nomination for the presidency in the autumn of 1825. His excuse was that Congress was about to discuss proposals to amend that part of the Constitution relating to the election of the president, and now that he had been designated a candidate he could hardly take part in such a debate himself. He took the opportunity to make some pointed remarks about 'Intrigue and management' in Washington and to express the view that the executive could secure an influence over Congress through its power of patronage. 'It is through this channel that the people may expect to be attacked in their constitutional sovereignty, and where tyranny may well be apprehended to spring up in some favourable emergency.' With this invocation of Country and Old Republican sentiments, Old Hickory fired his first shots in the campaign for 1828.[5]

So he returned to the business of growing cotton and corn and raising hogs and horses. His friends urged him to stay quietly on his plantation and to avoid being drawn into the campaign. 'Weigh & bale your cotton & sell it;' said Eaton to the Cincinnatus he had helped to create, 'and if you see any thing about yourself just throw the paper into the fire . . . & go on to *weigh the cotton*.' 'Our people do not like to see publications from candidates,' added Martin Van Buren. 'It is a singular point that in almost every case in which they have (with us) been attempted on the eve of an election they have operated agt the cause they were intended to serve.' For the most part Old Hickory abided by this advice, though not without some cost to his blood pressure. He dutifully declined invitations to public functions, even missing the annual meeting of his local Bible Society in case 'I might be charged by my political enemies with having come forth hypocritically under the sacred garb of religion thus to electioneer'. Interrogatories that he suspected originated from a hostile source he ignored 'because my opinions were before the public'. On the controversial issue of the tariff Eaton advised him to confine himself to a 'laconic, very laconic' reference to his Senate votes, and even the Governor of Indiana was unable to secure more of Jackson's views on such issues than a reminder of his Coleman letter and an assurance that his constitutional principles had been 'imbibed in no small degree, in the times, and from the sages of the revolution'. Yet the prickly Jackson was sometimes drawn on matters that reflected on his honour. To charges concerning his execution of the militiamen, for example, or his alleged altercation with Captain Stephen Decatur in 1819 (when Decatur had supposedly stopped him caning a senator), Jackson issued statements denying any improper conduct which duly found their way into the press.[6]

Jackson's relative reticence was the more remarkable in view of the campaign conducted against him. As in 1824, of course, the principal charge was that he was a Military Chieftain with the potential to become a dictator, and in order to substantiate this his opponents had to point to every bloody, vengeful and lawless deed, real or imagined, of his career. John Quincy Adams may have been irked by the tiresome charges of corrupt bargain (which, in any case, were largely directed against Henry Clay, that 'Judas of the West'), but these did not touch his life, career and character in nearly as personal a way as the sustained and savage slanders against Andrew Jackson. No previous presidential candidate had ever encountered quite such hurtful abuse. John Binns's infamous 'coffin handbill', a widely-distributed broadside featuring a coffin for each of the men executed under Jackson's military command, was not untypical of the assaults upon him.

Jackson's advisers suspected that the real object of this vituperation was to provoke the irascible Hero into a violent response. 'They have taken pains to impress the public mind with the belief that your *temper* unfits you for civil government', Robert Y. Hayne cautioned him, '. . . and they *have put*, and will continue to put into operation, a hundred schemes to betray you into some act, or expression, which may be turned to their own advantage.' In March 1827 Charles Hammond of the *Liberty Hall & Cincinnati Gazette* published an article accusing Jackson's beloved wife Rachel of adultery, and soon after this, afraid perhaps that the enraged general might be moved to rashness, his friends and advisers in Nashville established a committee to detect and arrest 'falsehoods and calumny, by the publication of truth, and by furnishing either to the public or to individuals . . . full and correct information upon any matter or subject within their knowledge or power, properly connected with the fitness or qualification of Andrew Jackson to fill the office of President of the United States'. This group was kept busy refuting the extraordinary calumnies that were heaped on the Hero. The general supplied them with documents and information and made it clear when he expected them to act (they hastily published a defence against the charge that Jackson had been involved in the Burr conspiracy, for example, after Jackson threatened to issue a statement himself on the matter), but ostensibly the committee functioned independently of the general. Jackson apologized to a member on one occasion for not having visited him lately because 'I do not wish to be seen mingling with the members of the Committee *now*'. His enemies poured scorn on the 'White-washing Committee', as they dubbed it, but in view of the highly personal (and slanderous) nature of the endless allegations against Jackson it is difficult to see what other device he could have employed. Tradition (and his own campaign strategy) enjoined on Jackson a certain passivity, yet such charges as murder, treason, bigamy and adultery could hardly be allowed to pass totally unnoticed, and in several instances only Jackson himself knew where the evidence could be found to dispel them. Conducting a campaign in his personal capacity, Jackson ironically had been obliged to resort to a primitive form of party organization in his Nashville committee. If it was an innovation, as his critics claimed, it was one which had been forced upon him – and was intended in part to keep him personally out of the campaign.[7]

But Jackson could not remain at his plough throughout. He did make brief interventions into the campaign, though when he did so it was to reinforce his Cincinnatus image by reminding his fellow citizens of the corruption which was endangering their liberty. In June 1827 (soon after Rachel's name had been so unchivalrously dragged into the campaign at the behest, he believed, of Clay) Jackson wrote a letter which he must have known would be published in which he charged that in January 1825 Clay's friends had approached him with an offer of the presidency. The Hero, of course, had rejected 'such means of bargain and corruption'. To his subsequent embarrassment Jackson found that he could not altogether substantiate this allegation, but his personal intervention served greatly to magnify the corrupt bargain issue, which could only work to the political disadvantage of Adams and Clay. Some months later Jackson accepted an invitation to attend the anniversary celebrations of the Battle of New Orleans in New Orleans itself, and he and his wife and some of his principal advisers sailed down the Mississippi in the steamer *Pocahontas* in a well-publicized pilgrimage. He was met by large crowds along the route and was royally fêted at New Orleans, where he was obliged to deliver himself of short and graceful addresses. The occasion, of course, was ostensibly non-political, but Jackson managed a few backward glances at Washington in enunciating the principle that the government was 'constituted for the happiness of the people, and that its offices are the instruments of their will', and even referred to 'the great principle of rotation in office', the very 'channel of sovereignty' which protected liberty by removing the 'weak points in the system'. The general seemed to be promising to cleanse the Augean stables. His other public appearance that year was at a local Independence Day celebration, again formally a patriotic rather than a political occasion, when he invited the public judgment 'on those, who, for the sake of office, rather seek to kindle the angry passions, than to co-operate for the common good', and invoked those revoluntionary patriots from whom he had derived 'an hereditary hatred to whatever threatens the security of private rights, or poisons the sources of public virtue'. Where Adams was using his fleeting public appearances to suggest that he was the farsighted president of the whole nation, Jackson was using them to imply that there was something rotten in the state of Denmark. This was Cincinnatus signalling his willingness to be called from his farm to save his country in her hour of need.[8]

More important than the actions of the principals, however, in reaching the citizen masses, was the work of their partisans in the statehouses, county courtrooms, and printing shops across the country. Local and state conventions met to proclaim their commitment to their preferred candidate, as did legislative caucuses, and local committees of correspondence were formed to coordinate campaign activity and prepare addresses to the people. The prospect of federal jobs and patronage and the quiet funding of newspaper presses did much to invigorate the campaigns of the two parties, although both Adams and Jackson were largely oblivious of such activities. The popular excitement aroused by the contest was phenomenal. President Adams himself complained of the 'ward meetings or committee meetings of both parties every day of the week. It is so in every part of the Union. A stranger would think that the people of the United States have no other occupation than electioneering.' The partisans of Andrew Jackson seized the occasion of the anniversary of the Battle of New Orleans, 8 January, to hold rallies across the country. Both parties used Independence Day to stage political celebrations. Many of these occasions took the form of public dinners, at which addresses would be made and partisan toasts drunk. At Petersburg, Virginia, the diners were reminded that 'Caesar had his Brutus, Charles the 1st his Cromwell, and John the 2nd may expect the People.' These celebrations were sometimes given a more festive air by the firing of military salutes and by bands of music. As befitted a contest fought out before the people too, it was dramatized by the use of popular totems. Where the Jacksonians seized on the hickory tree as their emblem and paraded with poles of hickory, the supporters of Adams resorted to the oak to emphasize the sturdiness of their candidate. (It seems to have escaped comment that the hickory was native to North America while the oak had long featured in the imagery of England.) Campaign medalets appeared to honour both candidates, and a few brass clothing buttons with such inscriptions as 'JACKSON VICTORY' were produced. Another Jacksonian innovation in the art of popular electioneering took the form of jugs and plates bearing the Hero's picture. The active campaign workers across the country were becoming more ingenious than ever in their attempts to capture the public interest.[9]

More than the ecstatic campaign rallies and folksy iconography, however, it was the tidal wave of printed material which took the campaign to the people. In 1828 special campaign presses made their first appearance, that is, newspapers which were born and died with the election. One of the earliest was Charles Hammond's *Truth's Advocate and Monthly Anti-Jackson Expositor*, which appeared in Cincinnati in January and which soon made itself notorious by its attacks on Jackson's allegedly irregular marriage. *The Political Primer, or A Horn-book for the Jacksonites* appeared semi-weekly in Dover, Delaware, from April, another anti-Jackson paper costing $1 for the six months of the campaign. The Jacksonians themselves were not to be outdone in the publication of cheap campaign presses and they used the office of their Washington organ, the *United States Telegraph*, to produce the *Telegraph Extra*, a weekly 'devoted exclusively to the Presidential Election' published between March and October for the total of $1, and which in less than two months reached an extraordinary circulation of 20,000 copies. Even more extraordinary, if less influential, was *The Nose: Or Political Satirist*, published by William Piatt of Jersey Shore, Pennsylvania, which took its name from an incident in which the associate editor of the *Telegraph* had tweaked the nose of the president's son in the rotunda of the Capitol. Filled with nose-tweaking stories at the expense of the Adams party, this effusion at least managed to convey the impression that the pompous classes were aligned with the president while a healthy irreverence characterized the Jacksonians. In addition to the campaign press, of course, was the regular press, and both Adams and Jackson were served by scores of local newspapers scattered throughout the country.[10]

As influential as the press, perhaps, was an unprecedented torrent of published convention addresses, political pamphlets, campaign leaflets and broadsides, and even occasionally full-length books. Biographical sketches, particularly of Andrew Jackson, appeared in greater number than for 1824, and 'anti-biographies' too, in the form of publications designed especially to denigrate the opposition candidate. The printed campaign propaganda of 1828, for sheer bulk, dwarfed that which had enlivened the previous presidential election.

The battle for the allegiance of American souls, then, was largely fought out in the press and in the host of accompanying campaign publications. Neither Adams nor Jackson had much control over this propaganda war, but they were the subject of it. Both men tried to keep their distance from this aspect of the election, and neither liked to think of himself as the head of a 'party', but popular political parties had formed around each of them. Despite the self-effacement of the principals, these were highly personal parties. They were not associated very clearly with programmes or measures, but rather were defined by their candidates. This was reflected in the nomenclature of the campaign organizations. On the one hand there were the 'Administration Conventions', the 'Friends of the Re-election of John Quincy Adams' and the 'anti-Jackson committees', and on the other there were the 'Jackson Conventions', the 'Friends of Andrew Jackson' and the 'Hickory Clubs'. It was the respective merits of these highly personal parties which were broadcast in the rival exercises in propaganda, or rather the merits of the candidates, for it was their fitness for high office which was at issue. Yet it cannot be said that the election of 1828 was simply a personal contest between Adams and Jackson, for neither – consciously at least – was interested in office purely for its own sake.

Like the party battles of the 1790s, in the campaign of 1828 it seemed to be the republic itself which was at stake. Andrew Jackson and John Quincy Adams personified differing conceptions of republican leadership. If policies did not separate them, ideology of a kind did. On the one side there was the Adams persuasion, committed to upholding the principle of government by statesmen and to protecting the republic from the ruinous course that an ill-lettered and autocratic military commander would be all too likely to embark upon. To his critics Jackson's career fairly bristled with incidents which 'all proclaim him a dangerous depository of our liberties'. This seems to have been the sincere conviction of Adams himself, and it was the message of the massive press assault on Jackson. On the other side there were the Jacksonians, persuaded that the real danger to the republic was located in the halls and corridors of the nation's capital, where administrators and legislators were conspiring to fasten on the country a corrupt, self-perpetuating and power-hungry oligarchy. 'It will be for the people to decide whether they will put down this most violent effort to destroy our free constitution, or will, by sanctioning it by their suffrages, permit it to become a precedent, pregnant with mischief, and fatal to their liberties.' Only the election of the Farmer of Tennessee could redeem that freedom which Americans had once held dear, or so the Jacksonians told one another. The contest between Adams and Jackson in their personal capacities, it was said, was 'as dust in the balance' when compared with 'the great constitutional principles' which were at stake. In some measure, what was to become the second American party system originated in the differing political perceptions and ideological convictions of men in public life. What helped to sustain the Adams-Clay coalition and the Jacksonians in their assaults on one another was the belief that the republican system of government was in mortal danger. Neither Jackson nor Adams cared to be seen reaching for the presidency, but their candidatures were given a measure of legitimacy by the patriotic causes assigned to them by their partisans and by the press.[11]

Certainly the men around the candidates themselves seem to have been persuaded that they were engaged in a mighty battle for the soul of the republic. In a letter marked 'Private' and 'strictly confidential', an Albany correspondent of Clay foresaw in Jackson's election 'a fatal blow t[o] our republican Institutions. Your ideas of a Military President are justified by all history.' The fears which had been muttered in private in 1824 about the subversive potential of a Military Chieftain were muttered again. Henry Clay himself, in a confidential letter to Daniel Webster, found the rising Jackson sentiment 'sickening to the hearts of the real lovers of free Government'. Webster agreed that Jackson was 'wholly unfit for the place to which he aspires' and greeted his victory with the gloomy observation that 'My *fear*, is stronger than my hope.' John Quincy Adams also now believed that the Hero was 'incompetent both by his ignorance and by the fury of his passions'. The prospect of Andrew Jackson as president undoubtedly created deep forebodings among many men in public life. Jabez Hammond, who was to win distinction as an accomplished political historian of New York, later recalled that he had joined Adams in 1828 because the alternative was a 'military chieftain' who lacked 'literary, legal and statesman-like education'. To many Jackson was simply not a fit leader for a republic.[12]

But if the Adams men espied in Jackson the dread spectre of military rule, the men engaged in the Jackson campaign were convinced that the re-election of Adams would acknowledge that the presidency could be bought, that the electoral process was but a charade, and that republicanism in any meaningful sense was at an end. 'Adams & Clay must be put down, or they will speedily put down the Liberties of this nation,' William B. Lewis wrote to Martin Van Buren, warning that if executive power and patronage could re-elect Adams, then it could also deliver the presidency to Clay and thence to Webster and adding that he did 'religiously believe . . . that the very salvation of our Government depends on the elevation of Genl. Jackson.' 'The victory must be our's, or we are a ruined people forever', an Ohio politician wrote to Jackson. 'The same man who saved Orleans must save our republican institutions, or they are at an end.' In a 'Private' letter to Andrew Jackson, John C. Calhoun wrote as early as June 1826 that 'liberty never was in greater danger. . . . An issue has been fairly made . . . between *power* and *liberty*; and it must be determined in the next three years, whether the real governing principle in our political system be the power and patronage of the Executive, or the voice of the people.' Calhoun repeated the same points with such conviction to so many correspondents that it is difficult to doubt the sincerity of his views. 'The people will, they are determined to be free, the intrigues of monarchists and fedralists notwithstanding, pour souls,' wrote a friend of James K. Polk. Jackson's old friend, Hugh Lawson White, saw the contest as one between '*money, office*, the hope of office and every thing which can be included under the term patronage on the one side' and the 'intelligence and virtue of the people on the other'. The triumph of the former would mean 'nominally a Ruplican government: but practically a monarchy of the worst stamp'. (He was later to view the Jackson administration in much the same light.) It had been an ancient Republican (and Country) conviction that liberty could be imperilled by a corrupt and patronage-laden executive, and Jackson's own associates at least were convinced that only his election could now save the country from such a lamentable fate.[13]

What was said in private was said even more vehemently in public. A veritable Armageddon was fought out in the press and in party addresses to the people. If Andrew Jackson's chances had initially been widely discounted in the 1824 election, he was now a formidable candidate and his enemies excelled themselves in seeking to discredit his pretensions, desperately trying to demonstrate not merely that he was unqualified but that he was the very opposite of the good republican leader. 'We venture to assert that the *bloody and unforgiving temper* which is the *great characteristic trait* in Jackson's public and private life, has not a parallel in the history of the world', ventured one newspaper. Time and again his opponents picked at every incident in Jackson's life to show his lack of civil experience, his ignorance and contempt of the law and the Constitution, and his violent, arbitrary and authoritarian disposition, which together could make him a truly dangerous Chief Magistrate. 'Rome had her Caesar, England her Cromwell, France her Napoleon, Mexico her Iturbide', said a Louisiana address, extending the familiar litany. The anti-Jackson press teemed with such headlines as 'Julius Caesar and Andrew Jackson', 'Murder Will Out', 'Jackson & The Lord's Commandments' (he had broken them all except perhaps – as an orphan – the one about honouring parents), 'Six Militia Men', 'General Jackson's Violence', 'The Reign of Terror'. Ultimately the message was always the same: 'Let us be warned by the fate of the ancient republics, and learn to suppress in its infancy every tendency to military despotism . . . .'[14]

The strategy of the Jacksonian propagandists, of course, was that which had been so ingeniously devised for them in John H. Eaton's Wyoming letters in 1823. The republic was indeed in danger, but the danger lay in Washington, where an unscrupulous administration, which had originally secured office against the will of the people by corrupt means, was now desperately seeking to sustain itself in power through the use of executive patronage and influence. If it succeeded then liberty was no more. But the patriotic Andrew Jackson, uncontaminated by office, was poised to rescue his country once again as he had so valiantly rescued her at New Orleans. The wicked coalition threatened to 'domineer over this Republic', using its power to pass the succession 'from Adams to Clay, from Clay to Webster, until our Republic becomes a MONARCHY'. A Connecticut Address pointed to England as evidence that a government possessed of patronage was invariably tempted to use it to sustain itself, and observed that the Adams administration would be known as the first to introduce 'a general system of corruption; and Henry Clay will attain to the honor of being called the Walpole of America, who reduced to practice the maxim that "every man has his price"'. The *Albany Argus* ran a series of articles entitled 'The CONTRAST; or, Military Chieftains and Political Chieftains', which argued that the former had often risked their lives for the cause of liberty, which was more in danger from the 'inordinate ambition' of the latter, personified in this case by Henry Clay. Increasingly in the campaign Jackson was referred to not so much as the Hero of New Orleans but as 'the Farmer of Tennessee, the Cincinnatus of America'. In a variation on this theme he was toasted in Utica as

'*Andrew Jackson, the Moses of our country.* He will bring the people out of the wilderness of political intrigue.' In Jacksonian rhetoric the Hero was not a potential military tyrant but the saviour of his nation's liberties. He was the beneficiary of that old libertarian tradition which had defined a corrupt and corrupting government as a principal enemy of freedom.[15]

This is not to suggest that other issues were entirely absent from the campaign. At local level such matters as the tariff and internal improvements were sometimes discussed, and on the whole the Adams–Clay coalition was taken to be the more sympathetic to the American System kind of measures. But distinctions between the parties of this sort were never clear, partly because of Andrew Jackson's ambiguous utterances (and because of Adams's reticence on the tariff), and they did not dominate the campaign. Another hidden issue was slavery, the defenders of which hoped that Jackson would prove more respectful of states' rights than the Adams administration, with its suspected consolidationist tendencies. But these were not the banners to which the people were invited to rally. That such issues influenced voting behaviour is highly likely, but they do little by themselves to explain the two coalitions which grouped behind Adams and Jackson respectively. Those parties, like those of the early republic, found their coherence in divergent conceptions of good republican government. 'We are on the eve of a new election of President;' said Daniel Webster a little wonderingly in June 1828, 'and the manner in which the existing administration is attacked might lead a stranger to suppose that the chief magistrate had committed some flagrant offence against the country, had threatened to overturn its liberties, or establish a military usurpation.' That is precisely what many Jacksonians did believe, and those that did not at least affected to do so. Jackson as a candidate had neither significant governing experience nor a programme to offer; but he could stand as a champion of a mission the object of which was to sweep the enemies of the people from power and restore the republican virtue of old. This was a cause which could unite all the enemies of the administration, legitimize their furious opposition, and enable them to mobilize a popular assault on the White House.[16]

Andrew Jackson's victory in the election of 1828 demonstrated that presidential politics had changed in certain important ways but not in all. The Jacksonian movement, like many a successful movement, was an alluring blend of innovation and tradition. Jackson himself was an unlikely presidential candidate, a far remove from the statesmanlike public servant to which Americans had grown accustomed. In no small part because of his supposed ineligibility, the campaign on Jackson's behalf had been conducted largely outside Washington. Never before had a presidential candidate been presented to the people so vigorously, with an avalanche of propaganda which kept the printing presses in constant motion. His success showed that the presidency could be won through the mobilization of popular opinion and that a man could be returned to the White House against the wishes of many of the country's experienced statesmen. Unlike Jefferson, Madison and Monroe, Jackson had not been nominated by a congressional caucus. Unlike Jefferson and John Quincy Adams, he had not been elected by the House of Representatives. By 1828 there were many members of Congress working energetically on Jackson's behalf, but he seemed to owe little to the distracted Washington community, which had once rejected him and in which he had spent little time himself. American politicians with an eye on the presidency could conclude that even more important than the favour of congressional leaders or the backing of local notables was the creation of a compelling public image and the support of a popular party organization.

Yet while the Jackson campaign demolished traditional conceptions of the appropriate route to the presidency, it also exploited some highly conservative instincts. The stern figure of Andrew Jackson, simple, forthright and uncompromising, recalled the values of the Old Republic as it reproved the corrupt and unprincipled ways of the Washington politicos. The corrupt bargain charge in particular, in one reverberating accusation, invoked the lessons of history ancient and modern regarding the loss of public virtue and the fate of republics, nudged dim folk memories of the revolutionary cause and of the Republican crusade against Hamiltonian Federalism, and linked some of the Americans' oldest fears with the political events of the 1820s. Ultimately Jackson was the saviour of the republican liberty of old rather than the apostle of a new kind of democracy. The identification with democracy was there, but only because Jackson's libertarian role required him to be projected as the popular saviour who would cast out the proven enemies of the republic who were barricading themselves in behind Washington's closed doors. Only later was this association with the people to develop into the radical egalitarianism which distinguished Jackson's Democratic party in the 1830s. In 1828 Jackson's partisans were using novel techniques to conduct an essentially conservative crusade, and the formula was one which was to be imitated repeatedly by those anxious to win the White House.

The candidates themselves stoically acted out the roles in which they had long been cast in the election of 1828. Following the disintegration of the old two party system, presidential candidates in the 1820s had inescapedly been forced to seek the prize in their personal capacities; they were not the agents of party. Yet parties were necessary, and it was in a sense personal parties which took shape around Adams and Jackson. They formed in order to elect either Adams or Jackson and for no other ostensible reason; they had no programmes as such to offer. Yet each of these parties had a cause, and the cause was the republic itself. Each party saw in itself and in its candidate the only hope of preserving the liberties of American citizens. Even by the 1820s candidates could not run merely in their personal capacities; their candidatures still needed to be legitimized by a cause greater than themselves, by the cause of republican government.

Adams and Jackson personally made some minor concessions to the demands of the extensive electorate, but only minor concessions. For the most part they respected tradition by observing the nostrum that the presidency was an office which was neither to be sought nor declined. Adams went busily about his presidential duties, rebuffing those who wanted him to use money and appointments to further his own cause and underlining his almost perverse insistence that the public welfare was his only concern by a public commitment to an ambitious conception of internal improvements. His one brief campaign appearance signalled his idea that the government should assume some responsibility for the systematic development of the country's economic, social and political potential. Andrew Jackson resigned from the Senate and returned to his farm to don the cloak of Cincinnatus, although he occasionally broke into print and even into speech to defend his honour and to hint at the corruption in Washington. In their guarded departures from the stance of the Mute Tribune, both Adams and Jackson were fleshing out the roles they had earlier assumed, the former as the enlightened and public-spirited statesman, the latter as the untainted guardian of the virtues of the Old Republic.

The election of 1828, then, turned largely on the personal qualities of the candidates. It was their fitness for office which was weighed in the popular campaigns conducted on their behalf – whether Jackson's lack of civil experience and his military disposition disqualified him for the trust in question or whether Adams's supposed susceptibility to intrigue, cabal and corruption made him a dangerous repository of his country's liberties. Whatever personal or local motives led men into the Adams or Jackson camps, each party was united by a belief in good government and by the conviction that the election of the opposing candidate would imperil it. These personal parties were also ideological parties, given coherence by differing perceptions of the dangers which threatened the republic. In many ways the republic had not changed greatly since the days of the Founding Fathers. The presidency had always been regarded as a conspicuous and powerful office which an ambitious and corrupt incumbent could use to wreck the great experiment in liberty. This conviction had played a part in the shaping of the first American party system; it also played a part in the shaping of the second.

# CHAPTER FIVE
# The quest for the White House: Democratic style

The election of 1828 marked the origins of a new two-party system. In time the personal parties which had taken shape around Adams and Jackson became impersonal parties, that is, lasting political organizations which survived changes in leadership and which possessed programmes and characters of their own. The rival coalitions of 1828 did not remain wholly fast, and in the ensuing decade there was a good deal of reshuffling of party alignments. Yet it is possible to establish clear lines of continuity between the original Jackson coalition and the Democratic party of the 1830s on the one hand, and between the Adams-Clay coalition, the National Republicans of 1832 and the Whig party of the late 1830s on the other. Presidential candidates came and went, but the parties themselves survived, at least until the 1850s, and offered the nation a choice between contrasting political philosophies. This was the era of the so-called second American party system, when presidential elections essentially took the form of contests between the candidates of the two major parties.

The presidential candidate, then, now had to seek his goal through the medium of party. It was the convention system which gave shape and discipline to a party, and winning the blessing of a national nominating convention now became the first vital stage in a bid for the White House. The quest for such a nomination itself was an unpredictable process, being conditioned by the vagaries of district and state conventions (which sent delegates to the national body), by the subtle interactions between grassroots sentiments and the ambitions of local political leaders, by pressure from party chieftains and by the prospects of government patronage. The failure to secure a party nomination effectively removed a contender from the race (whereas the failure to win a caucus nomination had not necessarily been fatal), but for the nominee himself only the first hurdle had been surmounted. Whatever he thought of his party colleagues, his running-mate, or any platform that the convention may have adopted, he was now irretrievably connected with them. The history, composition and character of his party would play a part in determining his political fate, as would the fact that he was pitted against a single major opponent, who was also the chosen instrument of a party.

Yet while bearing the *imprimatur* of party, the candidate had also to seek the White House in a political environment which was highly democratic in structure, and, in this period, increasingly charged with sectional emotions. The popular vote had to be wooed, and by the 1840s in particular turnout at the polls was reaching heights not equalled in the twentieth century. Not only did virtually all white men have the vote, but the vast majority of them were now exercising it in presidential elections, creating an active mass electorate with no precedent in history. But this aroused citizenry were exercising their democratic rights within state boundaries, and local issues and state and sectional loyalties could powerfully influence their behaviour. These ultimately were the electoral masters to which the presidential candidate had to be presented. The pressures on the individual candidate were as complex as they were immense. He had to take cognizance of the traditions of the past, of the requirements of party, and of the primacy of a divided people.

Party alone, then, did not condition the nature of a presidential campaign, and the influence of party was not unchanging. The party system, like the wider political environment, altered in character with the passage of time. The transition from the 'personal' campaigns of the 1820s to the 'party' campaigns of the 1840s was not a sudden one and it was never complete, but the pressures on candidates subtly changed with the development of party forms. In the early days of the revived party system substantial political authority still rested with the national party chieftains. The first national conventions of the major parties, for example, were little more than devices for ratifying a choice already made or for choosing the *vice*-presidential nominee. But by the 1840s the national conventions, composed as they were of a host of ill-assorted and often assertive state delegations, really were making and breaking presidential candidatures. Taking shape initially in elections which were contests between persons – and forming around those persons – the major parties had at first been largely leader-oriented. But as the party system took deeper root across the country, and as the access of local politicians to the national decision-making body became institutionalized, parties became more responsive to the jumble of pressures from below. Their deliberations were not necessarily more 'democratic', but by the 1840s no single party leader could be confident of controlling a national convention. These changing circumstances, too, influenced the way in which a man might seek the White House.

Finally, a candidate's conduct was also conditioned by his precise location in the political universe. To be taken seriously he needed the endorsement of one of the two major parties, but the parties themselves differed markedly from one another, so that Democratic presidential candidates did not behave in the same way as their Whig rivals. There were third-party candidates too, though they usually played little part in campaigns they could not hope to win. (In 1832 an ephemeral party, the Antimasons, won the electoral vote of Vermont, and in 1836 the anti-Democratic vote was divided between a number of candidates, but thereafter, for the life of the second party system, the Democrats and the Whigs between them commanded every vote in the electoral college.) The Democrats regarded themselves as the majority party, and this was one consideration which bore upon the behaviour of their candidates. The Whigs, lacking the confidence which comes from repeated victories, seemed to feel they had to try harder, a feeling reflected in the campaign tactics of their nominees. Incumbency tended to suggest a different kind of campaign strategy from that resorted to by opposition candidates, and the advent of the popular or mass party system also introduced another variable – a pre-convention strategy might be different from a post-convention strategy. If the creation of the second American party system helped to make the political environment a little more predictable, it was becoming no less complicated.

One complication was that the new party system itself was not universally welcomed. Politicians had probably always been held in low esteem in the United States, victims of long-standing suspicions of power and ambition, and their more vigorous recourse to party forms did little to rehabilitate them. Presidential candidates now had to approach their goal through the medium of party, but some of them found party discipline as distasteful as did parts of the electorate. Yet adapt to party they did, some more successfully than others. The Democratic party in particular succeeded in identifying party organization with democratic principle, and its candidates were proud to see themselves as the servants of the people.

The Democratic party, which was originally formed around the redoubtable figure of Andrew Jackson, has traditionally been regarded as the party of innovation, the party which broke most completely with the genteel traditions of the past and adapted most successfully to the egalitarian ethos of the time. In some respects this judgment is a sound one. Certainly the Democrats exploited to the full the complex apparatus of party, and generally they were somewhat more successful than their rivals in mobilizing their vast army of supporters. In time their political and economic ideas were to take on a distinctly radical hue. But there *was* an important conservative aspect to the Democrats. Some scholars have noted the Democratic nostalgia for the Jeffersonian past, or the quixotic impulse to preserve the Old Republic from the encroachments of commercialism. There was also something old-fashioned in the way in which the Democrats approached presidential campaigns. The Jacksonian assault on the White House – in both 1824 and 1828 – had been launched in the name of republican virtue. Andrew Jackson himself during 1828, if not a perfect model of republican rectitude, at least retired to the Hermitage to sit out the campaign and largely avoided the public eye. For the most part, his successors as the Democratic flagbearers also generally retained a low profile. However novel the Democratic party machinery, and however efficiently it was managed, the party's presidential candidates themselves usually behaved with admirable circumspection, reviving for their own purposes the tradition of the Mute Tribune of old.

The presidential campaign of 1832 was fought out between parties which were still in some measure personal parties. The Antimasons, indeed, provided an exception to this, but their role served to show how far the other two parties were still commanded by their old leaders. Further, when it became clear that the Antimasons by themselves were a limited political force, the essentially old-fashioned and even Old World character of the campaign was more fully revealed. The principal protagonists were Old Hickory himself, running for re-election as the Democratic champion, and his great rival from the West, Henry Clay, the nominee of what was then known as the National Republican party. This was the only presidential election in the history of the second party system in which the head of the government was pitted against the leader of the congressional opposition. In that respect, the campaign of 1832 bore a distant resemblance to the kind of general election that was emerging in Britain.

From the moment when Andrew Jackson let it be known that he was prepared to serve a second term, there was never any doubt as to who the Democratic nominee would be in 1832. Since he had taken the oath of office, Jackson had established himself as the undoubted head of his own administration. His principal measures, such as the Indian Removal Bill and the Maysville Road Veto of 1830, whatever others may have contributed to them, reflected his own will and predilections. (He had made known his hostility to federal aid to internal improvements of a local character during the campaign of 1824.) His determination to be master of his own house, too, was demonstrated by his course during the celebrated Eaton Affair, which so embarrassed his cabinet officers and so titillated the country. (Jackson's friend and publicist, John H. Eaton, now secretary of war, had married a lady of doubtful repute; when other cabinet wives snubbed her, Jackson harangued their husbands and eventually removed them from office.) The political authority he held over his party was also demonstrated by his role in cultivating a successor. At the outset of his administration Martin Van Buren, his secretary of state, and John C. Calhoun, the vice-president, had both seemed potential heirs, but by the end of 1829 Jackson was making it clear to his intimates that Van Buren was his choice, while his toast at the Jefferson Day dinner in April 1830 made public his growing distance from Calhoun. Jackson had earlier expressed a desire to serve only one term, but party considerations now prompted him to reconsider. Van Buren, who had held a senior office of state for less than two years, still lacked the stature to claim the succession as of right, and an early retirement by Jackson would almost certainly precipitate a fratricidal battle between the New Yorker and Calhoun which could tear the party apart. The friends of the president and of Van Buren discreetly encouraged legislative caucuses in Pennsylvania and New York to call on Jackson to serve again, other Democratic meetings endorsed these overtures, and in January 1831 the new administration organ, the Washington *Globe*, announced that Jackson would not refuse a public summons. Jackson was clearly going to be his party's candidate, and he was formally so named by various legislative caucuses and state conventions. He was supported by Democrats across the country as their greatest electoral asset. His unrivalled hold perhaps derived from the nature of his party's birth, for it had originally formed around him and revolt against him was unthinkable – unless the rebel was prepared to leave the party. Jackson was not obliged to submit his credentials to a national convention; the party was his to lead.[1]

As it happened, the Democrats did eventually hold a national convention in May 1832, but only for the purpose of nominating a running-mate. Jackson's coolness towards Vice-President Calhoun had developed into an implacable hatred and it had become clear to those around the president that a new vice-presidential candidate had to be found. Calhoun in any case had by now effectively quit the party. Since Van Buren, who was forever being accused of being at the centre of every administration intrigue, was reluctant to give credibility to those charges by being the candidate himself, and since there was no other obvious choice, it was decided that party harmony would best be preserved by allowing a national convention to find a man. As it happened, before the convention met the United States Senate had caused a sensation by rejecting Jackson's nomination of Van Buren as Minister to England. This made Van Buren a Democratic martyr, and party meetings across the country demanded his vindication. The national convention then joyously named him as the Democratic vice-presidential candidate, and Van Buren accepted in the smug knowledge that his nomination seemed at the behest of the party rather than at the dictate of the president. In a sense, the Democrats' first national convention was held because the party was vulnerable to the charge of being controlled by its leaders.

Since Jackson had remained unequivocally at the head of his party, he had no special reason personally to court party members. As in 1828, the several state endorsements that he received were considered enough to make him a candidate, and they were little more than formalities once he had given the nod himself. The old soldier was thus able to maintain his earlier opinion that the presidency was not an office to be either solicited or declined. His own personal inclination, or so he persuaded himself, was for retirement, but his increasingly acrimonious feud with the Calhoun faction caused him to feel that his honour was at stake, so that, as he told Van Buren, 'I cannot retire now . . . . I will not be driven by my enemies.' Jackson was going to secure vindication from the people, but he was not going cap in hand for their votes.[2]

Jackson could not resort to the Hermitage for more than a brief retreat, but he could prosecute his presidential duties, and that he did with his customary vigour. Occupying the conspicuous station that he did, he could afford to comport himself in conformity with his distaste for electioneering. While he watched the campaign with committed interest, his active involvement in it was slight. The nominations that he received were in some cases prompted by his intimates, but there is no evidence that he had done anything to secure them, and he abstained from overt canvassing himself. He did privately encourage the nomination of Van Buren as his running-mate, but he embarked on no electioneering tours, delivered no speeches, and published no letters. He was content for the election to rest on his public character, the measures of his administration, and the perfidy of his enemies. By the spring of 1832 he was convinced that a coalition of desperate men in the Senate and in the Supreme Court had united to discredit him and to paralyse his administration. '*It all will not do*', he wrote determinedly to a friend. 'I have always relied on the good intelligence and virtue of the people. They will decide.'[3]

If Jackson did not formally electioneer, his actions nonetheless affected the course of the campaign. It had been his decision, for example, to veto the Maysville Road Bill in 1830, advertising his administration's hostility to the notion of federally-sponsored schemes of internal improvements, as it had also been his to issue ambiguous warnings to the Bank of the United States, the controversial national bank chartered for twenty years by Congress in 1816, and to prophesy the early elimination of the national debt. To many of his opponents it seemed as if Jackson was bent on the destruction of the American System. It was the principal champion of that system, Henry Clay, who became the National Republican candidate for president in the election, and after Clay had encouraged the Bank to seek a bill for its recharter during the campaign, it was Jackson's decision to veto that bill. It was Jackson, with Clay, who was defining the issues on which the election was to be fought. He was not submitting to a programme laid down by a party convention; rather, he was asking his party to support his own stances. The Democratic party was still substantially leader-oriented.

The election was of course a battle over measures as well as men. The decisions may have been Andrew Jackson's, but it was to a set of issues that he was committing his party (although they did reflect his long-held suspicions of government corruption and the commercial nexus). This was again perhaps a sign of the relative weakness of party. Jackson could not legitimately seek re-election in his personal capacity and had to find a cause larger than himself to espouse; party as yet did not seem quite enough. The party itself had to serve great principles. Issues were needed which would give legitimacy to Jackson's candidature, issues great enough to command his attention as president. By carrying out his public duties with belligerent devotion, Jackson could associate himself with causes without resorting to the kind of electioneering which had always been reprobated.

Jackson's official declarations nonetheless constituted electioneering of a kind. He knew perfectly well that his communications to Congress would be broadcast across the country, in a myriad of newspapers, pamphlets and broadsheets. He did not concern himself much with the detailed operations of the campaign, though he did meet frequently with Frank Blair, a close confidant and editor of the *Globe*. Andrew Jackson proved adept at this kind of indirect electioneering. His defiant veto messages may have been formally addressed to Congress, but their language was more suited to the hustings. His Bank Veto in particular, largely crafted by his fellow westerner and sometime editor Amos Kendall, was a brilliant exercise in populistic propaganda. His political opponents, indeed, were sure that his unpresidential utterances would prove his undoing and had copies of the Veto message distributed themselves. 'It has all the fury of a chained panther biting the bars of his cage', wrote a smug Nicholas Biddle, the Bank's president, and Daniel Webster piously denounced the message for inciting class warfare. But Jackson's judgment was the sounder. He had long seen himself as a kind of popular tribune, guarding the people's rights against the depredations of corrupt and special interests in Congress, and his message conveyed something of his empathy with the people. He himself never had any doubt that the people would vindicate his stand. 'The veto works well every where;' he told Major Lewis in August, 'it has put down the Bank instead of prostrating me.' Jackson had learned in the 1820s that it was better to have support outside Congress than inside, and he continued to depend on the people (and the party) at large to sustain him.[4]

Jackson, then, was adapting himself to the democratic environment. He was in his way seeking to reconcile the traditional conception of the presidential candidate, who was expected quietly to rest his claims on his public services, with the new political world which now existed. He was being cast as both the leader and the servant of the people. Yet there was still a personal element in presidential politics in 1832 which would diminish as parties became better established. Jackson did not see the election as simply another round in a regular party battle. He never really accepted the legitimacy of the opposition party. He needed an issue to legitimize his candidacy, and ultimately that issue was the republic itself. To Jackson the 'factious opposition in the senate' was propelled by base and selfish motives. Its ultimate object was to elect Clay or Calhoun to the presidency and 'a greater curse could not befall our country'. In Jackson's political universe, the public welfare was still paramount and the national interest indivisible and those who disagreed with his patriotic views were but a corrupt and selfish faction to be shunned by all good men. He spoke of party, but to him the Democratic party was indistinguishable from the body of the people, and political dissent could only be unrepublican and disloyal. '. . I can have no other view but to administer the government in such a way as will strengthen the democratic party, unite the whole and produce the greatest prosperity to our beloved country, and restore the administration to the rules pointed out by the express grants in the constitution', he told Van Buren. 'The opposition is broken and scattered, still tho scotched not dead, and it behoves us so to proceed as to unite and give energy to our democratic brethren, [and] prosperity to the whole union . . . .' The opposition would never be legitimate and would be better dead, but Jackson was persuaded that there would always be subversive elements which would demand the eternal vigilance of the Democratic party.[5]

No man ever again commanded the Democratic party as Jackson did. Where Jackson expected his party to defer to him, his successor, Martin Van Buren, scrupulously deferred to the party. If Van Buren had initially helped to create the party, he was also created by the party, and it was party, rather than personality or public services, which carried him to the White House. As Van Buren's enemies were quick to point out, prior to his elevation Van Buren was associated with no great public measures, had written no major treatises and prepared no major bills, and his career in federal office had been unspectacular. He had not even performed a great service for his country on the battlefield. Van Buren was raised to prominence by party services, and he ran for the presidency very much as a party servant rather than in a personal capacity. But as with Jackson, Van Buren at least came close to identifying the Democratic party with the bulk of the people, and a democratic philosophy seems to have underlain his conduct during presidential elections. He went even further than Clay in identifying himself with a comprehensive platform, and he was prepared to enter into a kind of dialogue with the electorate. It was Van Buren who popularized the use of public letters in presidential campaigns and he did so on the declared grounds that the people had a right to ask their public servants to avow their views. Van Buren could not run on a personal record, but he could run as the chosen agent of a democratic cause.

It was very much as a party candidate that Van Buren appeared on a presidential ticket. It was the rejection by the Senate of his nomination as Minister to England that had made Van Buren the inescapable vice-presidential candidate for the Democratic party in 1832, the Democratic party being determined to repudiate this blow to its pride. Van Buren had not sought the nomination and he took relatively little part in the campaign, not arriving back from England until July. But it was in this campaign that he established his letter-writing precedents. His nomination had not been warmly received in parts of the South, where there was unease over the support he had given to the tariff of 1828, and in some states there were movements to replace him with Philip P. Barbour of Virginia on the electoral ticket. Perhaps this explains Van Buren's decision to make a public statement. In any event, a public meeting at Shocco Springs, North Carolina, wrote to ask Van Buren and Barbour their views 'on the subjects of the protective system and its proper adjustment, internal improvement, the Bank of the United States, and nullification'. (A movement was under way in South Carolina to have the state annul – or 'nullify' – the federal tariff.) In his reply Van Buren acknowledged the public's 'right' to be informed of his opinions and made it clear that he stood foursquare with Jackson on internal improvements and the Bank and declared himself opposed to the principle of nullification. On the delicate question of the tariff Van Buren declared himself against measures which operated unequally on different parts of the country and looked forward to the anticipated extinction of the national debt to make further tariff reductions possible. Two weeks later, to some supporters in New York, he avowed that it was only through the 'doctrines of the old republican school' that 'civil authority . . . can be preserved from the insiduous [sic] approaches of wealth, ambition, and arbitrary power'. Yet he did not doubt the ultimate outcome of the struggle, for 'the people' had always virtuously triumphed over all 'attempts to overawe or to corrupt them'.[6]

This invocation of 'the people' was to become a familiar motif in Van Buren's campaigns. In 1836 he was, of course, the Democratic flagbearer himself, despite a distinct lack of enthusiasm for him in parts of the South and Southwest. He seems to have played little part in securing the nomination, which was largely a foregone conclusion. He was informed of this honour in a formal letter tendered by the officers of the convention, and in his reply Van Buren depicted himself as 'the honored instrument, selected by the friends of the present administration, to carry out its principles and policy' and promised if elected 'to tread generally in the footsteps of president Jackson'. After the nomination, in May 1835, he was prompted to take a more visible part in the campaign. He embarked on no tours and made no public speeches, but he did pen several letters for publication. Some of these were again designed to allay southern suspicions. Thus in a letter to a committee in North Carolina he promised to proceed to the presidency as 'the inflexible and uncompromising opponent of any attempt on the part of congress to abolish slavery in the District of Columbia, against the wishes of the slaveholding states; and also with the determination *equally decided*, to resist the slightest interference with the subject in the states where it exists'. Slavery would be safe under a Van Buren administration.[7]

But Van Buren's most ambitious production in the 1836 campaign was his celebrated letter to Sherrod Williams. Williams, a Kentucky Whig congressman, had written to the various presidential candidates insisting that it was 'the right of every citizen . . . to ask and demand and to be fully informed of the political principles and opinions' of any political candidate, whose 'imperious duty' it was 'to frankly and fully avow and disclose the opinions which he entertains'. In response, Van Buren welcomed 'the most liberal interchange of sentiments between the elector and the candidate' and acknowledged the 'duty of a candidate . . . to answer fully all enquiries made by an elector, undetermined as to his course, and seeking, in good faith, information as to the opinions of the candidate . . .'. As it happened, Van Buren felt that as presiding officer of the Senate he should defer giving his views on pending items until Congress had risen, a delay which earned him a sharp rebuke from Williams.[8]

The delay gave Van Buren time to consider his reply, which he evidently regarded as the most important public statement of his campaign. His own drafts of it reached 109 pages of manuscript, and when published as a pamphlet it stretched across eight-and-a-half pages of double columns. The president himself took an active interest in the letter and encouraged Van Buren to publish it early. Van Buren's reputation as a non-committal man may not have been deserved, but his prolix prose style served to blunt his points, for his readers needed concentration and endurance to discover what he was saying. There was nothing startling in the letter itself, which Van Buren used to align himself with the measures and doctrines of the Jackson administration: he opposed the annual distribution of federal revenue, agreed with the president's caution on internal improvements, held that Congress lacked the constitutional power to establish a national bank, defended hard money (the administration having lately taken moves against paper money), and welcomed Senator Benton's resolutions to expunge from the Senate record its 1834 censure of Jackson's presidential conduct. But the letter was significant in marking the first occasion on which a presidential candidate committed himself to a comprehensive platform and invited the electors to accept or reject him on it. The candidate, he was implying, was less important than the programme. The letter's most interesting feature was its repeated reference to the majority will. 'It is now for the majority of the people to decide' whether to make distribution temporary or permanent. 'The supremacy of the popular will is the foundation of our government', wrote Van Buren, and a powerful institution like the national bank could tend only to subvert that will. Given his own avowed hostility to the Bank, if a majority of people voted for him then clearly it was their will 'that there shall not be any Bank of the United States . . .'. Van Buren was saying that the people themselves should determine government measures – rather than men – through their choices at the polls. The candidate was but the servant of a party whose job it was to put into effect the popular will.[9]

This letter was well-received by the Democrats. Its hard-money stance appears to have done something to placate the Locofocos, the radical Democrats of New York City who were intensely suspicious of banks and paper currency. Several friends wrote to congratulate Van Buren on his success in repelling the allegation of non-committalism, 'You have boldly and publickly pledged yourself to the support of principles in consent with those always maintained by the republican party;' wrote Richard Riker, 'and essential in my judgment with a judicious and valuable exercise of power under our federal system of Government.' The *Richmond Enquirer* had 'never read a more masterly production' and defied anyone now to call 'Van Buren a *non-committal man!*' Charges of non-committalism, of course, did not cease with this production, which the Whig press for the most part discreetly chose to ignore. But the letter served to reassure factions within the Democratic party, pub-

licly committed Van Buren to Jacksonian policies and hence cor-
rected his reputation for evasiveness, and, perhaps most important,
established his candidacy on a democratic rationale. Van Buren, dis-
tancing himself from the Hero's style, cast himself as an agent
rather than as a leader of the people.[10]

Van Buren's election seemed a vindication for the party cause.
For the next four years he served his electoral masters from the
White House. Despite the Panic of 1837 and the depression which
seized the country during his term, there was never any question
that Van Buren would be his party's nominee in 1840. Van Buren
himself went serenely about his presidential duties, the nearest that
he came to electioneering in the pre-convention period being a
well-publicized visit to his home state in the summer of 1839. The
tour may have been designed in part to have some influence on the
congressional elections, as well as to provide evidence for popular
support for Van Buren. At any rate, the president proceeded at a
somewhat leisurely pace through Maryland, eastern Pennsylvania
and New Jersey to New York City. He later continued up the
Hudson, was fêted at several towns and villages along the route,
was given a warm welcome at Kinderhook, made his way to
Albany, took the waters at Saratoga Springs, and visited such cities
as Buffalo and Auburn before returning to Washington via New
York. He was, predictably, more enthusiastically greeted by his
own partisans than by his opponents and some Whig town councils
refused to allow him official receptions on the grounds that he was
engaged in a political tour. The first major reception, at New York
City, had been very much dominated by Democrats, and Van
Buren was accused of electioneering while 'receiving the honors of
the constituted authorities of the whole city'. This 'uncivil and insulting' act exposed him to the charge of being 'the very first President who thus avowedly started on an electioneering tour'. Van
Buren had indeed addressed his thanks to 'my Democratic fellow
citizens'. He was never really able to be anything but a party
candidate.[11]

The Democratic national convention in due course named Van
Buren for president without opposition. He had previously been
accorded several state nominations, and the national convention
again served as little more than a ratifying agency. (On this occasion
it could not even agree on a vice-presidential candidate, a sign that
it was becoming less easy to manage.) In the post-convention phase
it was again through the use of public letters that Van Buren sought
to communicate with the electorate, scrupulously avoiding the

stump-speaking to which his Whig rival was resorting. Throughout 1840 the newspapers were studded with Van Buren's replies to his correspondents: the Independent Treasury and hard money, the militia system, pre-emption and the price of public lands, wages, the general bankruptcy law, internal improvements, the public debt, and Congress's recent resort to the 'gag rule' to prevent the discussion of antislavery petitions, were among the topics on which he gave his strictly Democratic views. Never had a presidential candidate stated his positions on current issues so completely. A clear example of electioneering was a letter that he dated 4 July, in which he announced that he had 'this day signed the bill for the establishment of an Independent Treasury', which he described as 'the triumph of the popular intelligence...over the arts...and alarms of the interested few who desire to enrich themselves by the use of the public money'. But his most definitive production, characteristically wordy and carefully prepared, was addressed to John B. Cary and others of Elizabeth City County, Virginia, at the end of July. He reaffirmed his democratic conviction that the right of electors to call on candidates to disclose their public views was 'indispensable to the maintenance of republican government'. The letter itself consisted of an unremarkable collection of his views, often culled from earlier statements, affirming his soundness on slavery, his strict Jacksonian positions on the national bank and internal improvements, and dissociating himself from his secretary of war's militia reorganization, which was proving an electoral liability. In this and his other letters of 1840 Van Buren became the first president to issue public statements while seeking re-election. As always, they were deferential to the majority will, were grounded on the people's democratic right to be informed of candidates' views, were unequivocally Jacksonian and were loyal expressions of Democratic party policy. 'These productions are openly electioneering in their motive and character – plausible, astute and artful in their coloring, and fully support Mr. Van Buren's reputation of being "a very cunning man"', charged the *Richmond Whig*. Cunning he may have been, but Van Buren was at least making it clear where he stood, which was more than could be said for his Whig opponent.[12]

As the Whigs swung their colourful Log Cabin campaign into its final stages, the president conscientiously applied himself to his official duties and his public letters, eschewing the more novel forms of electioneering which were making their appearance. His vice-president, Richard M. Johnson, was less self-effacing, partly no doubt because the national convention had not endorsed him and he was compelled to conduct his own campaign for re-election, and he joyously took to the stump. Other dignitaries were also pulled into the canvass. Senator Silas Wright, Van Buren's loyal New York lieutenant, reported in August that he had taken up 'the – to me – new business of stumping'. The Postmaster-General, Amos Kendall, resigned from his cabinet post in order to edit the Democrats' principal campaign paper, the *Extra Globe*. Van Buren's close friend, Secretary of State John Forsyth, tried to counter continued southern unease about Van Buren by issuing an *Address to the People of Georgia*. Like some later incumbents, Van Buren was perhaps perceiving some advantage in the use of surrogates, though he was predictably accused of sending out his high functionaries to do battle for him as he quietly pulled the strings behind the scenes.[13]

In the end it was, ironically, a letter which undid Van Buren. His defeat in 1840 no doubt weakened his hold on the Democratic party, yet he was early regarded as its most likely flagbearer for 1844. There seemed to be a profound psychological reluctance to break with the old chief, at least among many northern Democrats. In November 1841 his friend Benjamin F. Butler was insisting that there was 'a general desire on the part of the friends of the late administration, that Mr. Van Buren should be a candidate for re-election' and in the following month the *Albany Argus* placed his name in the race. In fact Van Buren was likely to face competition, and in the early 1840s John C. Calhoun seemed his most dangerous rival in the party, for Calhoun had returned to the Democratic fold and had re-established himself as the champion of states' rights and a low tariff. It may have been with the thought of countering Calhoun's influence in the South that Van Buren embarked on his celebrated tour of 1842, the ostensible object of which was to visit Andrew Jackson. Certainly his southern and western friends urged him to make the most of it and promised him enthusiastic receptions. Thomas Hart Benton wanted him to press on to the territories of Iowa and Wisconsin and to the Falls of St Anthony on the Mississippi River, for 'it will be a sensation if you visit those remote parts'. He did not wander that far, but he did make the unlikely journey from the Hermitage to Ashland, where he and Henry Clay, who was sure to be the Whig candidate, may have reached accord on the vexed issue of Texas, which was currently seeking annexation to the Union. Fine receptions also welcomed Van Buren at St Louis, Cincinnati, Columbus and Indianapolis. The tour seemed to go some way to showing that he had regained public esteem, and the Van Burenites won some comfort from Democratic successes in the elections that autumn. Van Buren's pre-convention strategy continued to be largely preoccupied with averting the Calhoun threat. He and his friends considered the advantages of holding the national convention early, before the tariff, Texas or some other troublesome issue could be raised in the 1843–44 session of Congress, but in the end they decided they had little to fear by leaving it until May 1844. In the spring of 1843 Van Buren sought to deny Calhoun the free-trade issue by publishing a letter expressing anti-protectionist views. Late in 1843 the menace of Calhoun receded. He had suffered reverses in New York and Massachusetts, and in December, when the new Congress was organized, Van Buren's friends won the caucus nominations for their candidates for Speaker and other House officers. Concluding that the Democratic party was irremediably under the control of machine politicians, Calhoun then refused to let his name go before the convention.[14]

So Van Buren's nomination seemed assured, and so it would have been but for his celebrated letter against the early annexation of Texas. President Tyler had sought to restore his political fortunes by securing an annexation treaty with Texas, and his new secretary of state, John C. Calhoun, had embarrassed the northern Democrats further by publicly linking annexation with the protection of slavery. Many southern and western Democrats were enthusiastic for Texas, but in New York and other northern states antislavery Democrats were hostile to the measure. Van Buren was under pressure to take a stand, and in a letter published in the *Globe* at the end of April he made clear his opposition to the administration's treaty and to an early annexation. It may be that Van Buren was responding to the antislavery sentiments in his own state party; it may be that he was abiding by an agreement earlier reached with Clay, who had come out against annexation almost simultaneously; it may be that he was simply doing what he believed to be best for the Union. But whatever his motive, Van Buren's letter certainly did not advance him towards the presidency. The Virginia party finally broke its historic alliance with New York and other defections followed. Democratic leaders across the country found that they could not contain the excitement for Texas. The hitherto-flagging campaigns of other presidential aspirants suddenly revived, and such men as Lewis Cass, Richard M. Johnson, Levi Woodbury and James Buchanan let it be known that they favoured annexation. When the convention met the Van Burenites still had a majority, but a rule requiring a two-thirds majority for nomination had been something of a tradition with Democratic conventions, and the anti-Van Buren groups succeeded in having it adopted once more. Van Buren could not hope to roll up this total, but nor could his principal rival, Lewis Cass. In the event the deadlock was broken when the convention rallied to the dark horse, James K.Polk. The leader-oriented party of Andrew Jackson was now in the past. The convention had rejected the party's acknowledged leader ultimately because the party rank-and-file in much of the country lacked enthusiasm for him. As was his custom, Van Buren had made his views known and had invited his Democratic brethren to accept or reject him on them, and they had exercised their right not to endorse him. The anti-Van Buren sentiments stemmed from a variety of sources: southern scepticism about his soundness on slavery, widespread resentment over his politically-damaging stand on Texas, commercial distaste for his hard money policies, western jealousy of eastern leadership. Together these sentiments succeeded in blocking Van Buren, and the convention for once selected a candidate of its own choice – albeit one who was the first choice of none of its members. The convention had become an arena in which the host of state delegations, each reflecting local interests, attachments and ambitions, and each with its share of patriotic zeal, resolved their differences, on this occasion by compromise. The party had made its choice, by recourse to its now familiar party procedures.

James K. Polk's nomination did not come as an immense surprise to him. The Tennessean had really been angling for the vice-presidential spot on the Van Buren ticket, but the possibility of a deadlock and a consequent move in his direction had apparently occurred to Polk and his mentor, Andrew Jackson. But there was nothing much he could do to effect this beyond relying on the discretion of his friends at the convention, and he remained anxiously at home until he heard the extraordinary outcome. 'It has been well observed that the office of president of the United States should neither be sought nor declined', he wrote in his acceptance letter with a reasonably clear conscience. 'I have never sought it, nor shall I feel at liberty to decline it, if conferred on me by the voluntary suffrages of my fellow citizens.' If elected he promised 'a strict adherence to the old republican land marks'. At the same time he announced his intention of serving only one term, a course which had been very strongly urged upon him by his lieutenants at the convention, who had presumably come to an understanding with the friends of other candidates. Party harmony might be maintained by holding out the prospect of the succession to its more powerful and ambitious members. Like Van Buren, Polk, too, was a loyal servant of party – and hence ultimately dispensable.[15]

Polk the dark horse seems also to have concluded that his interests would best be served by maintaining his low profile throughout the campaign. He stayed quietly at home, eschewed the stump speaking for which he had a considerable reputation, and – with one noteworthy exception – refused to follow the Van Buren example of letter-writing. 'I am entreated on all sides to beg you to be cautious in your answers to the thousand communications which you will receive', wrote his friend Cave Johnson, 'fractions of our party in Penn & N.Y. & Ohio will be struggling to extract something from you to aid their fractions at home – ... I trust you will avoid answers wherever it can be done – your public life for 20 years is guaranty enough –'. There were evidently good party reasons to abide by the tradition of the Mute Tribune.[16]

Yet, as always, the political managers were looking to the decisive middle states, and Pennsylvania's large bloc of votes was not quite secure. H. A. Muhlenberg wrote to Polk that as a southern man he should lean a little to the North, as Van Buren had leaned discreetly to the South. There was 'but one' question which threatened his election, Robert J. Walker told the candidate, and that was the tariff. 'We must have the vote of Pennsylvania in order to succed [sic]. ... You then must not destroy us. The Texas question will carry the *South*, you must then go as far as your principles will permit for incidental protection.' Polk was thus induced to say something for the Pennsylvania Democrats, although not without misgivings. He sent his famed letter to John K. Kane with the request that it be left to the vice-presidential nominee, George M. Dallas, and to Polk's friend Henry Horn to decide whether it should be published. About two weeks later he tried to have the letter withdrawn, but the Pennsylvanians had already gleefully rushed it into print. Polk's statement that he was 'opposed to a tariff for protection *merely*' and was in favour of a revenue tariff which he would adjust in such a way as to retain 'such moderate discriminating duties, as would produce the amount of reserve needed, and at the same time afford reasonable incidental protection to our home industry' went further than had perhaps been anticipated in assuaging Pennsylvania's protectionist sensibilities. 'No candid man can compare his letter to Mr. Kane with his public course and votes', complained a Whig editor, 'without pronouncing that it was dictated by a spirit of *calculating interest*, and that its author was utterly unworthy of the first station in the world.'[17]

That there was calculation in the letter cannot be doubted, but thereafter Polk kept silent. He followed the campaign closely, of course, wrote careful private letters to trusted correspondents, enlisted Jackson's help in keeping some elements in the party in line, but he remained at home in Tennessee and took no conspicuous part in the canvass. Indeed, what seems to have preoccupied Polk most was a Whig allegation that his long-dead grandfather had been a Tory in the Revolution, and Polk expended considerable energy in having material gathered and published to refute this infamous slur on his family honour. In general, the Democrats were well pleased with Polk's caution, especially when his Whig opponent, Henry Clay, began to trip over his own public letters. 'The judgment you have exhibited in abstaining from writing letters for the Public', said a New York Democrat, 'is in singular and proud contrast with the course of your great competitor, I have heard more than one of our able men allude to it.' Polk's conduct even earned the commendation of that sometime foe of the Jacksonians, Richard Rush, who seemed to see in it a redemption of the republic:

All experience has shown that a primary danger to popular government , is in the shocks given to it by ambitious men struggling for an elective chief Magistracy; and of late years we have been witnessing the commencement of a downward career in our government – in the electioneering practised by our Presidential Candidates. To your name has fallen the fortunate lot of having given the first check to these alarming courses, unknown to the early day of our history.

Whether Rush changed his mind on the publication of the Kane letter is not known.[18]

Polk then left the conduct of his campaign almost entirely to his friends and to the party. The Whigs themselves drew attention to the lowness of Polk's profile with their scornful question 'Who is James K. Polk?' Yet there was a flicker of unease in the ranks of the Whigs as they lined up behind the towering figure of Henry Clay. 'Do you think it probable', asked one Whig of another, that James K. Polk 'whose qualifications & Claims are so small if not contemptible' – 'will defeat the election of such a man, such a Statesman & Patriot as Henry Clay?...I say *God forbid that he should.*' The power of party was demonstrated in the fall when a dutiful party servant was placed in the White House ahead of one of the nation's leading men.[19]

The restrained examples of Van Buren and Polk in general were followed by other Democratic contenders for the presidency. Seeing themselves as the servants of their party and of the people (two entities between which they could rarely clearly distinguish), they typically paid homage to Democratic principles and assumed a stance of dignified humility. The only action actually required of a candidate was a formal response to the ritual letter by which he was officially informed of his nomination. Lewis Cass 'carefully read' the resolutions of the national convention and 'I adhere to them as firmly, as I approve them cordially'. Franklin Pierce with 'surprise' accepted 'the nomination upon the platform adopted by the convention... because the principles it embraces command the approbation of my judgment', and tendered his acknowledgments 'to the convention... and to the people of our common country'. Apart from such solemn salutations to party, platform and people, the Democratic nominee was normally content to abstain from electioneering.[20]

In the early years of the revived party system, of course, the Democratic candidate usually had the advantage of incumbency, so was easily able to reconcile the need for visibility with the ancient proscription of personal canvassing. Later, when the Democratic nominee was less likely to be a foregone conclusion, it was in the pre-convention period that ambitious contenders were most tempted to resort to electioneering ploys. Hence Van Buren embarked on his celebrated tour of the South and the West in 1842, and wrote a carefully worded (and anti-protection) letter to the Indiana State Convention in 1843, in the hope of outflanking Calhoun, who was engaged in manoeuvres of his own. As the 1848 election approached, with Polk remaining true to his one-term pledge, reflective rivals for the succession again sidled into politic positions. The most vexed issue of the day was whether slavery should be tolerated in the land wrested from Mexico in the war of 1846–48, and in August 1847 Secretary of State Buchanan inched towards the South in a letter suggesting that the line of the Missouri Compromise be extended into the new territory. In the next month Vice-President Dallas at a meeting in Pittsburgh suggested that the decision whether to introduce slavery should be left to the territories themselves. Both were outflanked in December by Senator Lewis Cass, who in a letter to A.O.P. Nicholson of Tennessee articulated the popular sovereignty idea more clearly and forcibly, and also pointed out to his fellow northerners the evidence which suggested that slavery in practice was never likely to get established in the territories. Cass had been a powerful supporter of the Mexican War and of Polk's administration in the Senate, which had also helped his standing with his party. (His cabinet rivals were to some extent inhibited by a pledge they had made to the president that they would not seek the presidency while in cabinet office.) The dispiriting sectional confrontation was resolved for a time by the Compromise of 1850, and the various Democratic contenders of 1852 vied with one another publicly to express their support for the final solution, save for Franklin Pierce who was able to avoid a direct answer to the questions put to him on the pretext that he was not a candidate.[21]

After nomination, Democratic candidates characteristically retreated to their homes as their party went into action for them. Van Buren wrote his conscientious letters through 1840, acknowledging the public's right to question him, avowing his strict adherence to Democratic principles, and otherwise going about his presidential duties. James K. Polk confined his public utterances to his Kane letter, uneasily deciding not to follow the Van Buren example. Lewis Cass, his nomination secured by his performance in the Senate and by his popular sovereignty formula in the Nicholson letter, resigned from the Senate after nomination and made a long and leisurely journey home, making brief responses to the receptions he encountered on the way. Once in retreat he avoided writing public letters or making public appearances, though he did see to it that some of his Senate speeches were printed and distributed. Franklin Pierce, the wondering Democratic candidate of 1852, also accepted his friends' advice to remain quietly at home during the campaign. This was not without its disadvantages for a 'dark horse', which Pierce in some degree combated by sending out surrogates, New Hampshire friends who visited other states to talk to political leaders and make speeches on his behalf. Party chieftains like Lewis Cass and Stephen A. Douglas also loyally stumped for him. Pierce was occasionally forced to break his silence, as when denying allegations about his conduct during the Mexican War, and he infrequently graced local 'non-political' functions. His most public appearance was on the eve of the election, when he delivered a eulogy to New Hampshire's most famous son, Daniel Webster, in which he praised the Compromise of 1850. 'It is the finesse of a tricky politician, dicing with the bones of the mighty dead, and turning a funeral cavalcade into a party procession,' objected a sour *New York Tribune*. 'It ought to be rebuked and repented of.' But such formal ceremonies apart, Democratic candidates did not make speeches, and most of them did not issue public letters either if they could avoid it. The Democratic party, through its presidential candidates, kept alive the tradition of the Mute Tribune.[22]

The history of Democratic presidential candidates during the years of the second party system is, in a sense, a story of their ever-lower visibility. Jackson in large measure had been forced to seek the presidency in 1828 in his personal capacity, or at least as a patriot vaulting to the defence of his country in its hour of need. He himself publicly ignited the corrupt bargain charge and unashamedly defended his own honour in the press. By 1832, as a president with a fairly coherent party around him, he could afford to take little ostensible part in the campaign, but he certainly affected its course with his decisions on such matters as the Maysville Road, the Bank of the United States, and his choice of running-mate. It was in large part Jackson himself who dictated the issues for his party and its choice of successor. Van Buren was capable of no such effrontery, beyond acceding to the pressure of the party's radical wing for an Independent Treasury. He meticulously committed himself to what had become the standard Democratic measures, and tirelessly saluted the democratic electorate and party orthodoxy in his public letters. Only when a new issue forced its way into the electoral arena, one for which there was no clearly-agreed party position, did he find himself at odds with his fellows. And apart from their pre-convention manoeuvrings, his successors with rare exceptions did not even make use of public letters. They retreated to their homes and sat out the campaigns in seeming oblivion of the tempest around them. They launched no initiatives, proclaimed no highly personal causes, offered no leadership. Their private correspondence, of course, reveals a compulsive interest in their respective fates, and to varying degrees they advised their lieutenants, consulted party editors, and nudged intermediaries to seek understandings with restive factions. But publicly they were the disinterested agents of party. When formally apprised of their nomination they expressed humble gratification and pledged themselves loyally to the platform that the convention had already adopted. Hence their commitment to party principles was always clear. Once Andrew Jackson had passed from the scene, the person of the candidate was subordinated to the party.

The Democratic party, then, had ceased to be a personal party. Political issues were agitated in the press and in Congress, but ultimately it was the national convention which defined the platform, which it did in some detail, and chose the candidate. The party's presidential candidate had ceased to be the party leader; rather he was a dispensable instrument of the party's ambitions, as Van Buren discovered in 1844 and as Polk recognized with his one-term pledge. As such, the candidate in his personal capacity became almost redundant to the campaign. The party had come a long way from the days of Andrew Jackson when in 1852 it nominated for president a man whom few Democratic voters outside New Hampshire had ever heard of, and who did little himself in the course of the campaign to remedy that deficiency. The Democratic presidential candidate once more resumed the role of Mute Tribune, but only because his candidacy was integrated so completely with the machinery, the measures and the men of the Democratic party.[23]

The Democrats, however, had made the Mute Tribune a highly democratic figure. Andrew Jackson had been elected as a defender of the people's liberty, as a resolute Old Republican, but in time the Democrats came to equate their cause with 'the people' almost more than with 'liberty', although to them democracy and liberty were indistinguishable. Jackson's successors pursued this identification to its egalitarian conclusion. The party, 'the Democracy', was held to be virtually synonymous with 'the people', a popular fellowship committed to protecting the people's republic against the subversive designs of its aristocratic enemies. The conduct of its presidential candidates was grounded on avowedly democratic principles. They on occasion acknowledged the right of the people to ask candidates to disclose their views. More important, in committing themselves to the party platform, and in recognizing that the candidate was less important than the programme, the nominees were implying not only that the people should rule, but that the people *could* rule in a practical sense – by going to the polls to vote for the measures they wanted. The self-effacing conduct of the Democratic presidential candidates in these years was part of an attempt to put into effect the will of the majority.

# CHAPTER SIX
## The quest for the White House: Whig style

It was the Whig party which was primarily responsible for the hullabaloo which was introduced into presidential campaigns in these years. However conservative the Whigs may have been in other ways, as campaigners they were innovators, and they bequeathed a theatrical tradition to American presidential politics. In the 1820s the partisans of Andrew Jackson had made some use of popular devices, as they brandished their hickory sticks and sang the Hero's praises at campaign rallies, but in the succeeding decades the Whigs carried popular campaigning to truly sublime heights. Long and extravagant processions, bibulous banquets, and mass meetings stretching over a number of days became regular features of presidential campaigns, as did memorabilia of all kinds, from medallions, satin ribbons and bandanas to hand-mirrors, shaving-soap and knives, bearing the likenesses or names of the candidates for president. The celebrated Log Cabin campaign of 1840, when the Whigs sought to establish the earthy origins of their candidate by depicting him as living in a log cabin and drinking hard cider like any other hardy pioneer, had been anticipated by some colourful Whig canvassing in 1836 and was to be repeated with appropriate variations in succeeding presidential elections. The Whigs were never bashful when it came to wooing the people.

The Democrats, of course, also participated in the creation of hullabaloo, but it was the Whigs who contributed the lion's share. The famous mass meetings of the 1840s, for example, which not infrequently attracted some 20,000 or 30,000 citizens, on occasion even an estimated 50,000 or 100,000, were pioneered by the Whigs and the newspapers of the day reported more such Whig meetings than Democratic. Popular insignia were more often associated with the Whigs than with their rivals. For the election of 1840, for example, some seventy-five distinct medalets and clothing buttons depicting the Whig candidate, William H. Harrison, have been identified, compared with only ten for the Democratic candidate. In 1844 there were over sixty such emblems for the Whig nominee and nine for the Democrat. Other extravagances, such as the introduction of giant balls or live animals into campaign rallies, were usually Whig. The Democrats for the most part avoided such excesses and in 1844 inserted a plank into their party platform condemning 'factitious symbols' and 'displays and appeals insulting to the judgment and subversive of the intellect of the people'. It was the Whigs who believed in the virtues of bread and circuses.[1]

In the midst of the Whig carnival was the presidential candidate, who departed ebulliently from the tradition of the Mute Tribune. While Democratic candidates for the presidency busied themselves with their official duties, penned occasional cautious letters, and meekly took refuge in their country homes, Whig candidates travelled the country, delivered themselves of a host of impetuous letters, and even took energetically to the stump. While there were constraints upon them, it was the Whig candidates who did most to change popular expectations about the proper behaviour of presidential candidates and who prepared the way for the whistle-stop campaigns of the future.

The high visibility of Whig candidates in these years owed something to strategic considerations. No Whig candidate, for example, ever entered an election as an incumbent (once Millard Fillmore had been passed over for the nomination in 1852), and so the dignity of the presidential or vice-presidential office could not be exploited. By the same token, the Whig candidate was also normally the opposition candidate, expected not merely to retain votes but also to win over voting support for his party, and this may have encouraged an aggressive approach. But there was something in the Whig party character, too, which served to invigorate the candidate. Like the Democratic party, the party which had its origins in the Adams-Clay coalition of the 1820s also in time became less leader-oriented and acquired a separate existence of its own. It, too, abandoned its old chieftains when they ceased to be electoral assets and sought candidates who would further the party's interests by winning elections. But the Whig conversion to the creed of party was never complete. The Whigs were more sensitive than the Democrats to the popular prejudices against politicians and parties, prejudices which they shared. There seemed to exist in the Whig mind a nostalgia for the patrician leadership of old. Many Whigs did feel that the president should be a disinterested patriot, acclaimed for his virtue and his public services rather than for his party zeal. This was the fatal flaw in Whiggery, which found itself resorting to party forms to resist the idea of party, a contradiction which contributed to its early demise. The Whig candidates themselves frequently did not care to be seen as mere party men, and this consideration tended to push them into the thick of the fray, since they had to present themselves in their personal rather than their party capacities. The colourful innovations of the Whig campaigns, both the hullabaloo of the party enthusiasts and the energetic electioneering of the presidential candidates, ironically served a highly conservative purpose, that of restoring an earlier political world.

The precursor to the Whig party, the National Republican party, was still very much Henry Clay's to command in the election of 1832. It had long been assumed that Clay would succeed John Quincy Adams as the party's presidential candidate, and so it proved. Yet Clay left little to chance. He had retired to his home, Ashland, on Jackson's victory in 1828, though even before he had relinquished the secretaryship of state he was sounding out his friends on the timing of his own candidacy. 'Precipitancy and tardiness should be equally avoided', he counselled in January 1829. ' . . . To present formally candidates for the succession, before the President-elect enters on the duties of his office, would be premature and offensive to the quiet, that is, the larger portion of the community.' (The silent majority, it seemed, might ultimately be aroused to expel the barbarians from the White House.) Besides, it was impossible to predict at that point who else might be in the race. While in bucolic retirement Clay was able to indulge in the luxury of attending public dinners, travelling around the country, and making occasional speeches on behalf of the American System. By the summer of 1830 his conspicuous non-candidacy was having the desired effect, and he was toasted at Fourth of July banquets through the North and began to win nominations from local conventions. Finally, on 9 December 1830, Clay was nominated for president by a large convention in Kentucky. From this time he considered himself to be formally before the people as a presidential candidate. He now abstained from any activity which could be construed as electioneering, citing 'the existing relation to the community in which I have been placed'. Since his name had been presented for the presidency, he explained in the autumn of 1831, 'I have not accepted, nor, whilst it remains thus before the public, shall I accept, any public entertainment tendered on my own account'.[2]

This abrupt reversion to the pose of the Mute Tribune in the post-nomination period, however, was not without its drawbacks. For one thing, the Antimasonic party, the product of an intense and widespread hostility towards freemasonry, was in the field and it was not impossible that it would attract more votes than the National Republicans. A number of National Republican editors and politicians, impressed by the Antimasonic example in calling a national convention and anxious to maintain harmony themselves, began to press for a national convention of their own. Clay himself seems to have been unenthusiastic about the idea, but once it had been widely bruited in the press it seemed expedient to bow to it, and such a convention would at least provide an opportunity for improving the party machinery. The fact that an Antimasonic candidate would also be seeking opposition votes put some pressure on Clay to assume a more prominent stance, and when it became known that that candidate was the respected William Wirt, who might conceivably find some favour with the National Republican convention, the pressure on Clay to assert his leadership increased. A poor performance by the National Republicans in the congressional elections in Kentucky in the summer of 1831 also raised the dread thought that Clay might not be able to carry even his own state (he had been embarrassed by its loss to Jackson in 1828), and his friends began to urge him to secure election to the Senate to counteract such an impression. Behind their promptings was a very real fear that the Jackson administration was doing irreparable harm to the republic. The president had already thrown down the gauntlet with his Maysville Road Veto, he had been issuing ambiguous warnings to the Bank of the United States, he was prophesying the early elimination of the national debt, and, most disturbing of all, the nullification crisis was brewing. On a personal level, Clay as the most prominent champion of the American System, could hardly fail to see Jackson's messages and measures as constituting a direct challenge to him. On another level, they seemed a challenge to the republic itself.[3]

This was the message of Clay's friends, who now beseeched him to leave his Ashland retreat and take a place in the Senate. 'An army is preparing much more formidable than has ever yet assaulted . . . the leading and important public interests', Daniel

Webster told him. 'Not only the tariff, but the Constitution itself, in its elementary and fundamental provisions, will be assailed with talent, vigor, and union. Every thing is to be debated, as if nothing had ever been settled.' John Sloane wrote from Ohio to point out the approaching extinction of the national debt and the need for Clay to make public his views on subsequent policy. Another friend wrote from Rhode Island warning him that the next Congress would need his presence because there was to be an attempt to overthrow his system of national policy. 'The times are portentous', wrote General Dearborn of Massachusetts, 'and there is no man in the land who can do so much to restore confidence in the stability of the Republic.' Finally persuaded that the fate of his country was at stake, Clay consented to abandon the traditional role of Mute Tribune and to return to Washington as Senator for Kentucky.[4]

By going to the Senate Clay was able to assert his leadership over the National Republican party without resorting to open electioneering. The national convention met in December 1831 and duly nominated Clay as anticipated. The Antimasons had failed to make any real inroads into National Republican strength, and Clay's was the only name formally presented to the convention. Every delegate voted for him, except for one who expressed no preference. Less predictable was the vice-presidential nomination, which in the end went to John Sergeant of Pennsylvania, in the hope that he would be able to detach the Keystone state from the Jackson cause. As with the Democratic convention that year, the choice of the party's presidential candidate had not really been at issue. Clay was already the acknowledged chieftain, and the convention did little more than ratify his nomination.

By the end of 1831, then, the Kentuckian was both a senator and the formal presidential nominee of the major opposition party. This unusual dual role did not go unnoticed by the Democrats, particularly as Jackson himself had so virtuously retired from the Senate in 1825 when he had been named a candidate. Since it was the constitutional function of the Senate to advise the president, it could be – and was – argued that Clay would not be in a position to offer disinterested advice. 'This attitude', observed a Cincinnati paper, 'no politician in these United States has ever before Mr. Clay had the audacity to assume.'[5]

But Clay was now committed to his course. The Senate was the arena in which he proposed to fight the election of 1832. There he could resist the president's destructive measures with propriety (at least in his own eyes) while keeping himself in public view. He could also raise issues of his own. In early February he delivered a long speech in favour of protection and the American System, which dutifully found its way into the National Republican press and into pamphlet form, and Clay sent copies to prominent men around the Union. There followed his report on public lands, which favoured distributing the revenue from land sales to the states for internal improvements, and this was similarly distributed. A more blatant political ploy was Clay's resolution calling on the president to proclaim a day of prayer and fasting to avert the threatened cholera epidemic. He had never previously displayed the evangelical sentiments that touched some of his party, and the *Albany Argus* dismissed his resolution as 'pharisaical cant', reminding its readers of Clay's reputation as a gambler and duellist. But Clay's principal electioneering device was of course the Bank bill. Although he had originally favoured leaving an application for a recharter closer to 1836, he now seems to have perceived some political advantage in raising the issue before the 1832 election. If Jackson accepted the recharter Clay could claim the credit, and if he rejected it the Democratic party would be divided and Pennsylvania at least would desert Jackson in the election. So Clay apparently reasoned, and he and Webster persuaded Nicholas Biddle, the Bank's president, to submit a recharter bill. Henry Clay steered it through the Congress, and when Jackson did veto it Clay delivered himself of a ferocious assault on the president. As the election campaign heated up with the summer of 1832 so did the Bank War.[6]

So the respective candidates for president closed in combat with one another during the spring and summer of 1832. In a sense, this battle of the giants was a fitting resolution to their rival campaigns. Both Jackson and Clay had taken command of their respective parties as if by prescriptive right. Neither had been obliged actively to seek nomination, and the two major national conventions had functioned as little more than legitimating devices, acclaiming choices already made. Taking their ground in their official stations, in the presidency and in the Senate, Jackson and Clay had then chosen the issues on which they were to fight. It had been Clay's decisions to defend the American System, propose a land bill and press Nicholas Biddle to submit the recharter bill. It had been Jackson's decisions to veto the Maysville Road and to launch an offensive against the Bank of the United States. The renewed party system had not yet reached maturity. Jackson and Clay were operating in a system of politics which was still substantially leader-oriented. They had taken command of their parties, defined the issues, and expected their supporters to follow them into battle.[7]

Henry Clay adapted less successfully than Jackson to the need to reach the people at large. Clay's speeches were addressed to his Senate colleagues, and when published as pamphlets were distributed to notables. They were long, complex, and replete with sophisticated economic and historical arguments. In short, they were addressed to the politically-informed community, to the local and state leaders and editors with whom Clay was used to conferring and corresponding. Clay had the capacity to bewitch his congressional colleagues and to inspire the loyalty of leading politicos across the country, but he never quite reached a *rapport* with the people. Yet if he lacked Jackson's populistic instinct, he shared with him the conviction that the election was not simply another round in a regular party battle. Each needed an issue to legitimize his candidacy, and ultimately that issue was the republic itself. Clay had been induced to go to the Senate on the grounds that the country was being imperilled by Democratic madness. There he spoke eloquently for the Union, the laws and the Constitution, and in his one speech outside the Senate he identified his cause with the fate of the republic. In May 1832 Clay addressed a convention of National Republican Young Men which had assembled in the city of Washington. 'Our greatest interest in this world, is our Liberty,' he told them. 'The eyes of all civilized nations are intensely gazing upon us, and it may be truly asserted that the fate of Liberty throughout the World, mainly depends upon the maintenance of American Liberty.' But Clay was never entirely convincing in his role as the saviour of the people's – and the world's – freedom.[8]

Henry Clay's energetic performance in 1832 was a hint of things to come. Few Whig presidential candidates were to prove reluctant to parade themselves in the public eye. This was evident in the election of 1836, when the Whigs first properly displayed their talent for political innovation and extravaganza. Setting aside the gentlemanly manoeuvrings of Daniel Webster, who eventually won little support outside Massachusetts, the two principal Whig (or at least anti-Van Buren) contenders that year were William Henry Harrison of Ohio, who was later to be dubbed 'Old Tippecanoe', and Hugh Lawson White of Tennessee, a sometime friend of Jackson who had broken with the administration. Both men imparted something of a western spirit to the campaign.

The Jacksonian Democrats had once received powerful support

in the South and Southwest (other than in Calhoun's South Carolina and Clay's Kentucky), but in the course of Jackson's second term this began to crumble. Jackson's alleged insensitivity to states' rights, as reflected in his forceful resistance to South Carolina's attempt to nullify the tariff, his high-handed treatment of his cabinet, his stand against commerce and enterprise as reflected in the Bank War, and his designation of Van Buren as his successor – all these hurt Jackson in different ways in the South. Men who had voted for Jackson in 1832 now began to look around for another champion for their interests, some of them still ostensibly 'pro-Jackson' but apprehensive that Jackson himself had succumbed to the influence of sinister northerners. Jackson's home state, Tennessee, witnessed some significant defections, and in December 1834 a caucus of rebel congressmen from that state nominated Hugh L. White for president. This was something of an 'anti-party' movement by men who claimed that they themselves had remained consistent to principle, but that they could not stomach the party discipline being imposed on them by the administration – the party voting in Congress, the attempt by Jackson to dictate his successor, the Van Burenite style of politics. White himself played up to this strategy admirably. Like Van Buren he was prepared to answer public letters, and in these he affirmed his soundness on slavery in the District of Columbia, and took a strict constructionist (that is, hostile) stance on both the Bank and internal improvements. His opinions, he said, 'conform to the true Jeffersonian creed'. The implication was that Jackson was the apostate. This theme was carried further in a speech White delivered in August 1836. The citizens of Knox County, Tennessee, had held a formal dinner for him, and White delivered himself of a lengthy address in response to the toasts. Dinners of this sort were not uncommon, although this occasion could claim to be the first in American history when a presidential candidate delivered what was in effect a stump speech. (Candidates had .occasionally made brief remarks at ceremonies.) Announcing himself again to be 'a republican of Mr. Jefferson's school', White castigated his former colleagues for abandoning their principles and cast himself as one assaulted by the administration and thus with a right of reply. He had reluctantly succumbed to overtures to be nominated for president when he had become convinced that the Democrats were putting into effect a '*system*' which would '*destroy* the *freedom* of *election*, which was *intended to transfer all federal power into certain hands, who by like process would transfer it into the hands of others at their pleasure* . . . .' Jackson's attempt to force on the nation his own successor, insisted White, was a threat to republican institutions. The people's tribune, presumably, should not remain mute when the republic itself was in danger.[9]

But it was William Henry Harrison who really threw himself enthusiastically into the occupations of speech-making and letter-writing for 1836, and his campaign, too, sought to exploit popular misgivings over the phenomenon of party. Harrison was hitting the campaign trail even before he was formally put into nomination. His name had started to surface in presidential talk in the winter of 1834–35, and in the summer of 1835 he had toured Indiana, Illinois and Kentucky making speeches. This was novel behaviour for a presidential aspirant, for not even Clay had undertaken quite so blatant a political tour on his own behalf. In August, for example, Harrison was given a sumptuous dinner at Louisville, after which he delivered himself of some complimentary remarks and a toast to Kentucky's patriotism and valour. In September various local meetings and conventions proposed Harrison for president, and in December the Pennsylvania and other state conventions more formally put him in nomination. Harrison, of course, had won some repute in the War of 1812, but since that time had not been much in the public eye. His pre-nomination travels were perhaps prompted by a desire to test the political water and to make clear his availability.[10]

By the beginning of 1836 Harrison could be regarded as a candidate rather than a contender. 'Let him say not one single word about his principles or his creed, let him say nothing, promise nothing...', counselled Nicholas Biddle. 'Let the use of pen and ink be wholly forbidden as if he were a mad poet in Bedlam.' This advice, if it ever reached him, Harrison ebulliently ignored, embarking on a wholly unprecedented campaign of travelling, letter-writing and speaking. For the first time a presidential candidate made a determined effort to reach out directly to the electorate. His lack of high public office, perhaps, was a reason for making himself more visible, as were his relatively advanced age and his suspect health, public reservations about which he had to dispel. His military record eased the adoption of such electioneering tactics, for several of the occasions that he graced were ostensibly to celebrate old victories. And, as with White, the conviction that the republic was in peril made it a positive act of patriotism on his part to sound the alarm.[11]

Harrison's letter-writing was not greatly inspired, save for his attacks on party discipline and presidential usurpation. He parried various Democratic stabs at him, denying for example that he had once voted in the Ohio legislature to sell imprisoned debtors (that is, white men!) into slavery. His answer to Sherrod Williams was both shorter and more equivocal than the vice-president's, favouring the distribution of the surplus revenue and 'strictly national' internal improvements financed therefrom, supporting Clay's land bill while emphasizing that land should be disposed of in such a way as to create 'the greatest number of freeholders', and suggesting that the federal government should fairly try the experiment of doing without a national bank, which, however, might be rechartered if its absence clearly harmed the public interest and if there were 'unequivocal manifestations of public opinion in its favor'. Finally, although Sherrod Williams had made no mention of it, Harrison adverted to the executive veto and usurpation at some length, promising that 'it would be my aim to interfere with the legislation of congress as little as possible'. Like White, Harrison made opposition to presidential and party usurpation the grounds for his candidacy, as he made clear in his letters accepting the presidential nomination. He assured the Maryland convention that if he became president 'the influence and patronage of that office shall never be used to control or impair' the people's right to choose their officers. He followed this thrust at 'the office-holders' with a promise to the New York convention that he would carry into the presidency 'a mind uninfluenced by the passions and the prejudices, which the heat, and violence of the late contests have unfortunately produced'.[12]

Harrison was determined to be seen as well as heard. In August he embarked on another summer excursion, this time eastward. He repaired first to drink the waters at Delaware Springs, Ohio, and then to the more celebrated Hot Springs in Virginia. In September he made a leisurely return from Washington via Baltimore, Philadelphia, Trenton, Princeton, New York and Pittsburgh. He was generally greeted by large and friendly crowds and resplendent receptions. In Philadelphia, for example, so crowded was it that the horses were unhitched from his open barouche, which was pulled by the citizenry from the Chestnut Street wharf to Independence Hall, while bands played such tunes as 'Yankee doodle' and 'See the Conquering Hero Comes'. The Conquering Hero responded to this and other receptions by making brief speeches, though they appear to have been expressions of thanks rather than philippics against the administration. One friendly editor remarked that Harrison had given the lie to Democratic slanders that he was a broken-down old man, commented on his 'plain farmer-like appearance' and 'quick and intelligent eye', and concluded that if Van Buren and Harrison had undertaken such a tour together and the election had turned on 'the impression respectively produced by the manners, appearance and speeches of each', then 'General Harrison would beat the favorite son – clean out of sight'. The Democrats were predictably less impressed by the old general's performance, contrasting his antics with the dignified reserve of Van Buren, and castigated Harrison (and his running-mate Francis Granger) not merely for travelling about in his own state, as the Democratic vice-presidential nominee Dick Johnson was accused of doing, but 'actually traversing the union from *State* to *State* . . . .!' 'For the first time in the history of this country', complained the *Frankfort Argus*, 'we find a candidate for the Presidency traversing the land as an openmouthed electioneerer for that high and dignified station.' The Virginia Democrat William C. Rives was doubtful whether the exercise did Harrison much good, writing caustically to the president that 'The grand electioneering tour seems to have been as abortive & unhappy in its results as some of the military campaigns of the same distinguished personage.'[13]

The various anti-administration candidates of 1836 had been nominated by legislative caucuses and state conventions, for the Whig party was not yet sufficiently formed as to make possible a national convention. Harrison (like White) thus could not present himself unequivocally as *the* candidate of the Whig party; nor was he tied to any formal Whig platform or address. Harrison was inevitably in some measure a candidate in his personal capacity, and he later stated that he had run 'pretty much on his own hook'. He was not short of experienced advisers, but without the endorsement of a national body it was his own qualifications that he had to present to the electorate. But he also needed a cause to legitimate his personal canvassing, and that cause was the dire threat to the republic posed by a power-hungry and corrupt administration. This cause served the Whigs at large well enough, for their attacks on party and on presidential management could make their own organizational failings seem positively virtuous. The primitive state of their party structure served to put a premium on personal leadership and tempted White and Harrison into their innovatory forays at the hustings.

In spite of, or because of his personal canvass Harrison in fact scored fairly well in the autumn election, carrying seven states. Perhaps even more impressive was the geographical spread of his support, for in addition to his western base Harrison picked up electoral votes in New England, the Middle Atlantic and the border states. This inter-sectional appeal at once made him a serious contender for the next presidential election, and almost as soon as Van Buren had been inaugurated politicians in such states as Ohio and Pennsylvania began to raise Harrison's name once more. The ageing general conducted himself much as he had in the last election, though perhaps a little more circumspectly. This time there was a real chance of success and experienced politicians moved in with advice. In the pre-nomination period Harrison employed his now familiar mixture of travelling, speaking and writing. This time, he knew, there was likely to be a national convention and Clay and Webster would probably be rival candidates for the Whig nomination. He wrote letters favouring pre-emption (that is, recognizing squatters' rights on public land) and denouncing duelling, the latter at least (to a citizen of New Jersey) probably being designed to show him to advantage in the middle states against Henry Clay, who had been involved in a number of duels. In November 1838 an Antimasonic 'national' convention met in Philadelphia, predominantly Pennsylvanian in composition, and nominated Harrison for president, an honour which he duly acknowledged in a letter which carefully kept open the possibility of his being selected 'as the candidate of those opposed to the principles of the present administration'. In another letter of 1838 which evidently looked forward to the Whig nomination he committed himself to one term, assuring James H. Birch, editor of the *Missourian*, that if 'elected President under no circumstances would he again be a candidate'. Harrison would be 67 in 1840 while Clay would be 63 and perhaps the younger man could be induced to wait for four more years. In 1838 also Harrison again took off for a summer tour, this time of Indiana and Ohio, which again provided an opportunity for public dinners and a little speech-making. Not that he wanted to be president, he stressed, casting himself as a reluctant Cincinnatus: 'There was not a man in the nation who could in truth say, that any suggestion which had the least tendency towards the expression of a wish to become a candidate for the presidency ever came from his lips or his pen.'[14]

During 1839, as Whig conventions met to elect delegates to the national convention in December, Harrison retreated to North Bend, contenting himself with his correspondence. His principal rival, Henry Clay, made clear his availability by a well-publicized tour through the North that summer. In the event, of course, the Whig nomination was secured for Harrison. As the formal Whig

candidate he wrote further letters, delivered longer and more partisan speeches, but travelled around less, remaining within the borders of Ohio.

Harrison now behaved with greater caution, seeking advice on
campaign matters both from other Whig leaders like Clay and William C. Rives (a recent defector from the Democratic party) and
from a group of men who had gathered around him at Cincinnati.
One correspondent who wrote to the general for his views received
a reply from a 'confidential committee' saying that Harrison could
not respond personally to all the many letters he now received and
that the policy was that 'the General make no further declaration of
his principles, for the public eye, whilst occupying his present position'. It was explained that Harrison's views had already been put
fully to the public (and would in any case be reproduced in a pamphlet), and that the Whig national convention itself had made no
new declaration, thus, it seemed, obliging its candidate to remain
similarly reticent. The Democratic press jeered joyfully at the candidate who was thus kept in 'apron strings' by men who had made a
'monstrous avowal of non-committalism', and Harrison was
obliged to return to issuing letters over his own name. These were
now reluctant and few, mainly devoted to rebutting charges of
federalism, abolitionism, and nativism, often by citing his earlier
letters, such as that to Sherrod Williams. In a letter to some New
York Whigs he pointed out that his opinions on important subjects
had been fully expressed during the course of a long public life.
'Further than this I cannot suppose intelligent persons could desire
me to go', he insisted. 'The people of this country do not rely on
professions, promises and pledges.' Apart from being a slighting reference to Van Buren's virtuously democratic letter-writing, this
was an invocation of the traditional image of the presidential candidate, whose claims were founded on his public career. This stance
suited the Whig charge of executive usurpation. 'Congress should
be left as much as possible untrammeled by Executive influence in
the discharge of its legislative functions;' said Harrison, linking the
tradition of the Mute Tribune to the Whig promise of presidential
restraint, for 'a better guarantee for the correct conduct of a Chief
Magistrate may be found in his character, the course of his former
life, than in pledges or opinions given during the pendency of a
doubtful contest'. He pointed out that it would be more relevant to
seek the opinions and pledges of candidates for the legislature.[15]

In his written statements, then, Harrison was wriggling away
even from his 1836 precedent of epistolary equivocation. He was

now reluctant to write letters himself, and when he did so he tried to avoid making new statements. But on the stump he was less reticent. His travels in 1840 did not go outside Ohio, and he protected himself further against the charge of electioneering by making visits to old forts and battlegrounds the ostensible reason for most of his forays. In June he attended a great celebration at the site of old Fort Meigs, where he was fêted by a mass meeting of perhaps 25,000, which he addressed for nearly an hour. Further speeches followed that summer at Columbus, Sydney, Urbana, Carthage, Dayton and Fort Greenville. Some of them were quite lengthy but they contained little of substance. He denied being a Federalist and asserted his belief in republican institutions; he damned abolitionist agitation as against the spirit of the Constitution; he repeated his old straddle on the national bank; he assured the foreign-born that he was not anti-immigrant; and he reiterated his refusal to be drawn into promises or pledges. A candidate, he told the Fort Meigs assembly, should not solicit votes for the presidency; that office should be bestowed by the people 'spontaneously, and with their own free will'. The people should choose their president through 'a review of his past actions and life', he repeated at Dayton, not by exacting pledges from him, for the effect of the 'pledging plan' would be 'to offer the presidential chair to the man who will make the *most* promises'. The history of all republics showed, it seemed, that their decline was marked by the making of promises to secure office. Washington, Adams and Jefferson had been asked for no pledges, for their past careers had been guarantees of their presidential conduct, and a return to such propriety would advance the nation 'safely, rapidly and surely in the path of prosperity'. A candidate chosen for his known character, Harrison was suggesting, could be trusted not to abuse the powers of his office. As it was, the seeds 'of monarchy that Patrick Henry had espied in the Constitution had grown fearsomely. '*This government is now a practical monarchy!*' The one defect in the Constitution was the absence of a limit on presidential tenure, and the one pledge that Harrison was prepared to give, '*before heaven and earth*', was, if elected president, '*to lay down at the end of the term faithfully that high trust at the feet of the people!*' At this point the reporter of the speech was lost for words: 'Here the multitude was so excited as to defy description.'[16]

Old Tippecanoe, unlike his opponent, was not committing himself to issues during the campaign of 1840, despite his wordy effusions. He was mindful, perhaps, that his party was less than fully united on such issues as the Bank, and that in any case the Whigs were disposed to reduce the role of the president in passing legislation. He referred his interrogators to letters he had written years before, tried to have it both ways on subjects he could not avoid, equated the expression of views with 'pledges' or 'promises' and these in turn with corruption, and coyly offered himself as a latter-day Cincinnatus who would save the republic from Democratic despotism. This, of course, was much the same strategy that Jackson's friends had adopted in the 1820s. In his own speeches Harrison had the audacity to hold up the model of the Mute Tribune as one that should be returned to. His image of the Chief Magistrate was one above self and party, above demeaning promises and self-serving ambition. He was invoking the traditional conception of the presidency as a means of establishing the illegitimacy of the Democratic incumbent. Harrison thus resorted to new modes of electioneering in order to broadcast a very old-fashioned message. The 67-year-old general also resorted to them to demonstrate his physical fitness for office. 'As he stood, uncovered, before the multitude assembled', it was said of his Fort Meigs appearance, 'all were struck with the elastic vigor which he yet possessed, and particularly with his keen, piercing eye, which yet retains all the fire of youth'. His speech evidently confirmed his virility: 'His full, clear voice gave another demonstration of the falsehood of the charge of imbecility and decrepitude, which the Locofocos have seen fit to heap upon the worthy Soldier.'[17]

Another 67-year-old Whig candidate was Henry Clay, who in 1844 also conducted a very vigorous campaign of speaking and letter-writing, though with rather more content and less success than his predecessor. Declining cabinet office in Harrison's administration, Clay had assumed leadership of the Whig party in Congress. When Harrison's death had made John Tyler president, and when Tyler had proved most un-Whiggish on the Bank question, Clay once more led his troops into opposition. From his seat in the Senate Clay imperiously established his authority, and, having identified himself as 'the embodiment of Whig principles', he retired to Ashland again to await his reward. 'So far as I can learn', wrote his friend John J. Crittenden in May 1842, 'Clay's retirement has had the happiest effect upon the public feeling and opinion in respect to him, and all the indications seem to be that, without the aid of any convention, he will be the candidate of the universal Whig party.' Clay himself favoured a national convention 'not to nominate a

Candidate for the Presidency, but to *concert measures to give effect to the popular nomination, and to nominate a Candidate for the V.P.'*. A year later, when other contenders seemed to be manoeuvring for the nomination, Clay was having misgivings about a convention, but in the event one was called by the Whig congressmen, who were anxious to unite all the fragments of the party behind Clay.[18]

As the day for the convention drew near, when his nomination seemed assured, the restless Clay embarked on a tour of the South, where he was received with the enthusiasm now customarily visited upon travelling contenders for high office. (In the autumn of 1842 he had also signalled his availability by a tour of Ohio and Indiana.) Although he insisted that he had set out on his travels 'with the intention to keep his lips sealed', he was nonetheless 'compelled to speak' – a compulsion which on some occasions drove him wordily on for hours. For the most part he addressed himself to traditional Whig principles – a reasonable and discriminating tariff to provide revenue and encourage home industry; the distribution of the proceeds of the public lands to all states; a sound currency maintained by a national bank; a curb on the power of the executive and support for the one-term principle. The one topic on which he carefully refrained from commenting was Texas (although the administration did not announce its Texas treaty until 12 April, towards the end of his tour). His major effort was at Raleigh, where Clay delivered a carefully-prepared speech which was largely devoted to showing how the Democratic party's failure to respect the law and the Constitution was endangering republican institutions. Unlike the patriotic Whigs, it seemed, the Democrats put party before the public good.[19]

Clay was able to make these speeches because 'he had never yet consented or declared to any one that he was a candidate for the presidency', indeed, he claimed, 'at present he was a plain farmer, earning his labor by the sweat of his brow...'. Confident of the nomination that had not yet been bestowed, Clay contrived to use his southern tour to place himself on record again as the champion of Whig policies while not yet formally the candidate. Once the national convention had met, Clay conspicuously put electioneering aside. His formal letter of acceptance was brief, making no mention of the Whig platform and accepting the nomination in the belief that it was the will of 'a majority of the people of the United States'. In a public letter to the *National Intelligencer* two days after his nomination Clay explained that he would be unable to accept

121

further invitations to public functions. The election of the president was exclusively the concern of the people and the very preservation of free institutions rested on their choice. 'In making it they should be free, impartial, and wholly unbiased by the conduct of a candidate himself', sermonized Clay. 'Not only, in my opinion, is it his duty to abstain from all solicitation, direct or indirect, of their suffrages, but he should avoid being voluntarily placed in situations to seek, or in which he might be supposed to seek, to influence their judgment.' Just how the people were to make their judgment was not very clear – presumably by reference to the candidate's past services and published positions. This abrupt reversion to the stance of the Mute Tribune seemed close to the Harrison position that a candidate should not give pledges, that he should somehow remain above the party fray, though more virtuously than Old Tippecanoe Clay would not go near it at all. Indeed, apart from acknowledging his nomination, Clay made no mention of the Whig party, depicting the election as something exclusively between the electorate and the candidate.[20]

Yet Clay did not remain exactly mute. Although he ceased to attend public functions, he did write letters for publication. Through the summer of 1844 he tirelessly and tiresomely refuted the varied allegations against him and restated his familiar views on such matters as protection, internal improvements, the bankruptcy law, and duelling (his reputation was still suffering from the suspicion that in 1838 he had encouraged a duel which had resulted in the death of a congressman called Cilley). His most critical letters, however, were those concerning Texas. Towards the end of his southern tour, while at Raleigh, Clay addressed a letter formally to 'the editors of the *National Intelligencer*', itself a change from the usual practice of writing ostensibly to a third party (a private citizen or local committee). This seemed to imply that the public had a right to his views, and he explicitly stated that now the administration was making annexation a public issue he felt it 'my duty' to present his opinions 'to the public consideration'. Written at a time when it was expected that the Democrats would nominate Van Buren (whose views on Texas Clay claimed privately to know), the letter may have been intended to remove the issue from the campaign. It warned firmly that annexation meant war and that it would in any case serve to divide the Union. This stance perhaps encouraged many antislavery Whigs in the North to stay with Clay rather than defect to the Liberty party. But the Democratic revolt against Van Buren very much made Texas an issue, and the Democrats swept into the campaign urging annexation 'at the earliest practicable period'. As annexationist zeal mounted in the South, Clay softened his position in his so-called 'Alabama letters' – written to an Alabaman paper – explaining that 'far from having any personal objection to the annexation of Texas, I should be glad to see it, without dishonor – without war, with the common consent of the Union, and upon just and fair terms'. He added, somewhat unrealistically, that 'I do not think that the subject of slavery ought to affect the question, one way or the other.' These letters were not well-received by the antislavery elements in the Whig party and Clay appears to have lost some critical support in New York. 'Ugly letter, that to Alabama', complained Thurlow Weed to a friend, 'Can't stand many such.'[21]

These letters, of course, and others like them, exposed Clay to Democratic charges of trimming, of being '*pro* and *con* on all subjects'. Weary of continued misrepresentations, Clay finally decided to write no more. In yet another public letter to the editors of the *National Intelligencer* on 23 September he said that he had originally intended to decline answering public questions put to him, since a candidate who committed himself prior to taking office might subsequently find himself deprived of the advice of cabinet, Congress and public opinion, but that he had succumbed lest he seem to be 'unwilling frankly and fearlessly to submit my opinions to the public judgment'. Now he would answer no further queries. But Clay's vow of silence came too late. The Democrats mercilessly exploited the apparent anomalies in his statements and northern antislavery Whigs felt betrayed by his Alabama letters. 'I am more and more convinced of the *Expediency* as well as the perfect propriety of a Presidential Candidate when once nominated to abstain entirely from answering all Enquiries regarded public measures – ', wrote a harassed New York Whig to Crittenden. The expediency of such a course was obvious, while its propriety was demanded both by the candidate's own dignity and by his recognition that when the people nominated him they 'knew what they were about'.[22]

There remained a wistful regard for the values of the past both in Clay's own attitude towards the presidency and in that of some of his fellow Whigs. Clay as a formal candidate had virtuously declined invitations to public functions and retired to Ashland, lest he inadvertently influence the will of the people. He even claimed to doubt the propriety of writing public letters, lest they commit him in advance – like Harrison he would go into office unpledged. At the same time he had persuaded himself that the public had a 'right' to his views on the major issues of the day, and so had released his ill-conceived statements. Temperamentally Clay found it difficult to remain in seclusion as the electoral storm raged around him. But there was also a strange ambivalence in him, as if he were caught uncertainly between the patrician political world of old and the new egalitarian world of Jacksonian America. Before his nomination he hit the stump with enthusiasm, but after it he seemed to hope that the people would turn to him without further prompting, as if recognizing his transcendent qualities of leadership. As before the 1832 election, he even doubted the need for a national convention. Ideally, it seemed, the people themselves would somehow spontaneously designate the candidate, without the intervention of party devices and without being influenced by the candidate. All that might be expected of a candidate was that his views be a matter of public record. In Clay's case the record was a long one, though in the past he had principally chosen to expound his views in Congress, where he had skilfully deliberated with his peers on the affairs of state. But now Clay had to address the voters at large rather than the Senate, and his attempts to placate differing interests in different parts of the Union proved his undoing.

Another Whig candidate with a penchant for writing letters was Zachary Taylor. 'Old Rough and Ready', of course, was the military hero *par excellence*, a professional soldier who had never previously dabbled in politics and indeed had never even voted. His candidacy well illustrated the Whig ambivalence over party, for Taylor liked to regard himself as a candidate of the people rather than a party, although party support was clearly necessary to his cause. The stream of letters that flowed from his pen was largely a product of this dilemma, as he sought to present himself as both a party and a non-party man.

The Taylor movement dated from 1846, in the spring of which he secured some early victories over the Mexicans at Palo Alto and Resaca de la Palma, and Whig politicians began to wonder whether his military fame could be turned to party advantage. Taylor himself brushed aside the first suggestions that he be a candidate, but by the end of the year had agreed not to rule himself out. Then in March 1847 came his great victory at Buena Vista, and the Taylor boom was away. It was not exclusively a Whig phenomenon, for some Democrats and independents saw possibilities in a Taylor candidacy, and the editor of the *Cincinnati Signal* wrote to Taylor asking his views on public issues, condemning any attempt by either Whigs or Democrats to appropriate him for themselves and suggesting that the time had come for an independent 'president of the people'. These sentiments seem to have touched a responsive chord in Taylor, who in June replied that his military position precluded him from discussing public policy, although he indicated approval of the *Signal's* editorials and concluded that 'In no case can I permit myself to be a candidate of any party, or yield myself to any party schemes.' This and subsequent letters of similar import caused an uproar among northern Whigs. Some forcefully rejected the Taylor candidacy, some discreetly backed away from it, and some gamely argued that such high-minded independence was a fundamental Whig principle. The general then sought to recover himself with further letters which continued to cast him as a candidate of the people but conceded that he was 'a whig – not indeed an ultra partisan whig – but a whig in principle'. This and his assurance that had he voted in the last election it would have been for Clay helped to mollify the committed Whigs, though did him little good with the groups of Democrats who had been attracted by his banner. 'Taylor has lost ground greatly, and will probably be ruled off', remarked Calhoun in the autumn of 1847. 'He has written too many letters, and some of them very illy advised.'[23]

The chief beneficiary of the waning Taylor enthusiasm was Henry Clay, once again making a bid for the Whig nomination, whose partisans fiercely attacked Taylor for refusing unreservedly to embrace the Whig cause. Taylor's busy pen continued to supply them with ammunition. He declined to make any 'pledges' to the Whigs and he accepted nominations from the 'Independents' of Pennsylvania and even from nativists, which exasperated those Whigs who attributed their defeat in 1844 to the foreign-born vote. The general's managers finally closed in around him and the result was the carefully-constructed 'Allison letter' of April 1848. The Whigs' attacks on executive usurpation in the past had led them to emphasize the primacy of Congress, and Taylor's advisers now used this belief to strengthen his cause. In the letter Taylor reiterated that he was 'a Whig, but not an ultra Whig' and if elected would not be 'the mere President of a party'. But he moved close to the Whig position on the veto, which he thought should never be used 'except in cases of clear violation of the Constitution, or manifest haste and want of consideration by Congress'. On such vexed subjects as the tariff and the currency he argued that the executive should carry out the will of the people as expressed in Congress – a stance which allowed him to avoid expressing his own views on such subjects.[24]

In the end Taylor avowed himself enough of a Whig to secure the nomination, though not without a further flurry when he said that he would not withdraw his name if Clay became the Whig nominee. (His embarrassed managers, recognizing that they could hardly present to the convention a candidate who would not abide by its decision, explained rather feebly that all Taylor had meant was that since he had not proposed his name himself he could not withdraw it himself.) His brief and formal letter of acceptance made no mention of Whig principles. After his nomination Taylor remained at his military post, from which he continued to transmit his vexatious letters. Democratic allegations that he would not veto the Wilmot Proviso (designed to prohibit slavery in any territory acquired from Mexico) led him indignantly to remind a southern correspondent that he was a slaveholder. He also returned to his familiar refrain. 'I am not a party candidate', he told one correspondent in July, 'and if elected cannot be President of a party, but the President of the whole people.' He repeated the same sentiment to the erratic Democrats of South Carolina, who had made an independent nomination of him, adding that he would even have accepted a nomination from the Democratic national convention. 'Taylor ought to write no more letters', groaned the Whig Senator for Delaware, John M. Clayton, and his friends advised him 'to make no replies whatsoever' to correspondents. But the South Carolina letter produced another rebellion in the ranks, and Whig meetings were called in New York State to nominate Clay. To contain this Taylor and his managers determined upon another careful letter to Captain Allison, in which he explained that as head of the army he had originally avoided making political pronouncements which might have divided his men (who were of both parties), that he had always 'declared myself to be a Whig on all proper occasions', that an acceptance of a Democratic nomination would not have caused him to change his opinions 'one jot or tittle', and that the Whig convention had 'adopted me as it found me – a Whig – decided but not ultra in my opinions; ...'. He was not a party candidate 'in that straightened and sectarian sense which would prevent my being the President of the whole people', but he understood this was 'good Whig doctrine – I would not be a *partisan* President' who would 'lay violent hands' on public officers who differed from him or who would seek to coerce Congress.[25]

In the event Taylor won the election handsomely, though probably more because of the split in the Democratic party ranks than because of his own inspired idiocy. Taylor, like Jackson in 1828, had wanted to see himself as the candidate of the whole people, untainted by the machinations of party that he ill-understood, and he instinctively sought to exploit the popular prejudices against party and against politicians. But the institution of party itself was now too firmly entrenched in the American polity to be bypassed, and the general was obliged to make his tortuous accommodation to it. Yet, like other Whig candidates, he retained something of an 'above party' style. He avoided speeches and public appearances, remaining dutifully at his army post or at home on his plantation. He did write letters, but he did not give 'pledges' and for the most part he contrived to avoid discussing issues, addressing himself mainly to the relationship in which he stood with the people and the party. To a degree he embodied that nostalgia, which many Whigs felt, for a president who was somehow above party and faction, a president who would come into office uncommitted to any programme and who would serve the whole people. Ironically, such a president was now acceptable to many Whigs only if he left the problems of government to Congress.

Towards the end of the Whig party's life, as it was lacerated by sectional tensions and weakened by the poison of nativism, it was perhaps only with a military hero as its flagbearer that it could hope to maintain a precarious unity. Military heroes, unlike politicians of the order of Henry Clay and Daniel Webster, were not given to discoursing on the affairs of state. At any rate, General Winfield Scott evidently hoped to be allowed this soldier's licence in 1852. Scott had in fact long been close to the New York Whigs, with their suspect antislavery sympathies, and he hoped to make northern support the basis for his own bid for the nomination. Prior to the Whig national convention he kept a fairly low profile and resolutely forebore from publicly committing himself to the Compromise of 1850. This did help his cause with the northern Whigs, though it also exposed him to severe pressure from southern Whigs to demonstrate his soundness on slavery. Outwardly he remained unmoved, but as delegates made their way to Washington and Baltimore the harassed general began discreetly to give way, privately giving spoken and written assurances that he would support a party platform which endorsed the Compromise. In the event these blandishments did not prove enough for the southern delegates, who caucussed and demanded – successfully – that the convention adopt

127

a Compromise platform prior to receiving the nominations. The Whigs were finally recognizing that the logic of party meant putting measures before men. Scott's candidacy went ahead and eventually on the fifty-third ballot he won just enough tired and suspicious delegates over to secure the nomination.[26]

Scott was evidently walking a tightrope. President Millard Fillmore had failed to win the nomination because northern Whigs considered his administration leaned a little too far in a southerly direction, while Daniel Webster's attempts to accommodate himself to southern convictions had failed to win over the South as they lost him admirers in the North. At a fortunate remove from the wasting fray of day-to-day politics, and keeping discreetly mum, General Scott proved the most available candidate. Once nominated he maintained his stance of high visibility and low commitment. Remembering perhaps the troubles of Clay and Taylor, he kept his letter-writing to a minimum. But he did undertake an ambitious electioneering tour. Ostensibly he was carrying out his official duties, for Congress had asked the army to find a location in the West for an asylum for disabled officers, a mission of such commanding importance, apparently, that it needed the personal attention of the army chief himself. In the autumn of 1852 Scott set out on this quest chaperoned by a Democratic colleague, General Wool. His travels took him out through Pennsylvania and Ohio to Kentucky and Indiana, and his return route brought him back through Ohio, New York, New Jersey and the border states. His journey, it was said, was 'a complete triumphal march', as he was greeted by large crowds and fêted handsomely at each stop. 'It is a pleasant sight to the friends of Gen. Scott', mused one editor, 'to see him thus vindicating his own noble manhood, his fine mental powers and attainments, and their good judgment, by meeting and speaking with the people face to face.' His brief speeches did give him an opportunity to try to mend a few fences, as when he tried to shake off his reputation for nativism by complimenting a questioner on his Irish brogue and also by refuting a story that as the commanding general in Mexico he had had fifteen Germans tied to a tree and flogged. But on the whole Scott's speeches were vacuous affairs, containing flattering references to the town he was currently visiting, evoking old military engagements, and summoning patriotic sentiments. The good people of Pittsburgh were no doubt reassured to be told that he was for 'the Union, the whole Union, this great and glorious nation, which ought and ever would remain one and indivisible'.[27]

It may be that Scott was drawn into speech-making more than he intended, and his antics certainly aroused considerable criticism in both the Democratic and the independent press. 'For the vote of "the foreigner", to whom but a few years since he would have denied the rights and franchises of freemen', snorted *The Union*, 'he now supplicates by imitating the low arts and fawning hypocrisy of the pot-house politician.' James Gordon Bennett believed that Scott was 'perpetrating a positive suicide' and complained that he talked nothing but 'campaigns, and battles, and old soldiers, with the exception of some observations about the weather, and his blarney of "the rich Irish brogue" . . .'. Much was made of the fact that Scott was travelling at the expense of the public, the 'first instance on record' in the United States in which a public salary had been devoted to 'electioneering purposes'. 'With the exception of General Harrison', worried the Philadelphia *Public Ledger*, 'he is the only candidate for the Presidency who has made *electioneering* speeches, and we hope that he will be the last.' Electioneering of this kind had still not been generally accepted as legitimate. Itinerant speech-making by a candidate was thought, at least by some, to bring dishonour to the high office of the presidency.[28]

Yet Scott was conducting himself more-or-less in accord with Whig tradition. If Taylor had not made speeches, Harrison had, and so had Clay before he was formally designated the candidate. And in keeping with most of his Whig predecessors, too, he was not discussing policy or making pledges. Apart from his affirmation of 'the Union' (with its ambiguous evocation of the Compromise of 1850). Scott was not identifying himself with any platform or programme. (He contrived even to avoid mentioning the Compromise in his bland letter accepting the nomination.) In that sense, he did not present himself as a highly partisan candidate, as committed to carrying out his party's measures. He was still in some degree running on his reputation as a public man, whose evident merits he was trusting to the people to acknowledge.

Whig presidential candidates, like their party, were simultaneously pulled in two directions. Receptive to innovation in their quest for votes, their political values were nevertheless distinctly old-fashioned. As the Whig party at large bemused the electorate with its riotous displays, the candidates themselves did their active part, palpably travelling the country, presenting speeches, issuing letters. Yet if in this important respect they departed from the tradition of the Mute Tribune, they also paid a kind of obeisance to it by saying little of substance in their public performances. (A partial exception was Henry Clay, but even he ceased to give speeches once nominated and he eventually thought better of his letter-writing.) The Whig tribune may not have been mute exactly, but he at least had the grace to be either vacuous or equivocal. In making himself so conspicuous yet so vapid, he was inviting the electorate to take him for what he was, not for what he said.

The Whigs may have cherished the patrician tradition of personal leadership, but like the Democrats they became less dependent on their leaders with the development of party organization. In 1832 Henry Clay had been very much in command of the National Republican party and with Andrew Jackson had defined the issues of the campaign. Yet in 1839–40 and in 1848 Clay found that he, too, was dispensable, as did President Fillmore when the party passed him over for renomination in 1852. Zachary Taylor vexatiously discovered that he was obliged to declare himself some sort of party man, however qualified, in order to be accorded the nomination, while the last Whig national convention asserted its sovereignty by adopting a platform before adopting a candidate, for which it needed three days and fifty-three ballots. The Whig party was no one's to command.

Yet the Whig capitulation to party was grudging and incomplete, for the very *raison d'être* of the Whigs was hostility to party forms. They had taken shape to resist the Democratic party, the very manifestation of the kind of politics which they believed was destroying the republic. This at least was the message which their candidates often sought to convey. They divulged a desire to be chosen 'spontaneously' by the people, without recourse to personal electioneering or even, ideally, to party-nominating conventions. The latter, they sometimes managed to imply, were little more than convenient devices for ratifying the already clear choice of the people. Whig presidential candidates made a show of avoiding what they called 'pledges' or 'promises', which they intimated were a species of corruption to which only those interested in the spoils of office would stoop, they usually ignored or passed lightly over the measures with which their party was normally associated, and in their prolific public statements they invoked their military exploits or delivered themselves of fearless sentiments about 'the people', 'the republic' or 'the Union'. The one topic on which they allowed themselves to be drawn was the unrepublican nature of executive usurpation and the partisan use of public patronage, in brief, the way in which the Democratic party was changing the constitution of American politics. They promised to turn out the spoilers, to confine themselves to one term, to defer to the will of Congress and to be the president of 'the whole people'. Making opposition to the Democratic conception of party their primary cause, the Whig candidates had somehow to minimize their own dependence on party organization and to emphasize their fitness as persons. They seemed to expect that they would be judged for their past services and their known opinions and characters, rather than for their adherence to a party or a set of policies. Somewhere in their minds there survived a pre-party image of the president as a reluctant statesman rather than as a party functionary. Ironically, this lofty conception of the presidency required them to take their campaigns to the people, for they could not project their personal candidatures by repeating a party litany. So they took to the stump and to the press to try to resurrect that bygone if mythical day when public-spirited statesmen serenely conducted the affairs of state without recourse to the corruptions of party. If the characteristic pose of the Democratic presidential candidate was one of low visibility and high party commitment, the characteristic pose of the Whig candidate was of high visibility and low commitment.[29]

But the stance was an unsatisfactory one. The Whigs could not convincingly be a party which was anti-party. They, too, had acquired a loyal army of partisans and a set of economic and other policies, even if they did not care to avow them too boldly at election time. Whig candidates were evoking something genuine in Whiggery when they virtuously refused to make pledges and invited the people spontaneously to choose a president, but, as Zachary Taylor found, their party colleagues did not allow them to carry such ecumenicalism to the point of accepting nominations from non-Whig groups. The Whig party was fatally divided between that impulse which turned to Henry Clay as 'the embodiment of Whig principles' and that impulse which produced the promises of Harrison and Taylor to end the rule of party. There was a contradiction, too, between the Whigs' emphasis on the personal qualifications of presidential candidates and their belief that the role of the president should nonetheless be restricted. These divergent strands in the Whig persuasion put impossible demands on the party's presidential candidates. These unfortunate men found themselves obliged to avow that they were Whigs while promising to rise above party considerations as president, and also obliged to promise an end to corruption even as they offered to abandon an independent role for the executive. These contradictions in Whiggery were in large part produced by the movement's deep-seated hostility to the Democratic party and all its works, to that deplorable party's use of party discipline, to its tendency to regard the president as a popular tribune, to its willingness to take issues to the electorate, and to those issues themselves, with their essentially anti-commercial thrust. What ultimately gave coherence to Whiggery was its political conservatism, but this was no more an electoral asset than its internal contradictions. The Whig hullabaloo and the energetic electioneering of Whig presidential candidates, however novel and however demotic, still managed to carry a hint of an age when loyal constituents might be royally fêted at election times as long as the serious affairs of government were left in the hands of the better sort.

# CHAPTER SEVEN
# *Military heroes, dark horses and single terms*

Viewed from the perspective of the candidate, the presidential race is first a contest for a party nomination and then a contest for the White House. Viewed from the perspective of the party, the presidential race is first a quest for a candidate (or rather a pair of candidates) and then a contest for control of the executive branch of government. Candidates might adopt particular strategies to win both nomination and election. Parties, as rather amorphous bodies, cannot plot strategy quite so readily, but the nature of their composition, the rules and procedures they adopt, and the calculations of their members, do affect their choice of candidate and the party's performance in the campaign. In short, the party reveals something of its character in the candidates it adopts, while the degree of success of a particular candidacy may reveal something about the larger political system. Whether or not a country gets the politicians or the government it deserves, different political environments do breed different kinds of politicians, and an examination of the characteristics of successful presidential candidates in a given period exposes something of the forces which raised them up.

Foreign visitors to the United States were among those who pondered the question of what kind of men became president. They wondered at the apparent reluctance of Americans to send their 'great men' to the White House, their Daniel Websters and their John C. Calhouns, for often it seemed that names which were known in the Old World were passed over in favour of those that were not. Many visitors were troubled by the political excitement generated by military fame and doubted the wisdom of placing the destinies of the republic in a soldier's hands. And they were bemused by the frequency of elections in the United States, by the way in which Americans always seemed to be replacing their harassed agents in government. The more astute visiting Europeans realized that they were watching the operation of the principle of 'availability', the way in which American politics seemed to put a greater premium on popularity than on ability in candidates for high office. More even than in most periods, availability was a leading characteristic of presidential politics in the second quarter of the nineteenth century.[1]

What gave a measure of political order to this period was the second American party system, which lasted from about 1828 until 1854, and in those years every successful presidential candidate, with one exception, could be described either as a military hero or as a dark horse. (The exception, Martin Van Buren, is often defined as a northern man with southern principles, another potent political formula of the time.) With one outstanding exception, too, incumbent presidents were not re-elected. The availability of military heroes and dark horses, and the unavailability of the men in the White House, were not entirely the products of chance. The respective characters of the major parties, the closeness of the competition between them, the uncomfortable presence of third parties, the continued political weakness of the executive, the deepening sectional and other antagonisms in the political system, and the ineffable will of the American people, all played a part in determining who should and who should not become president.

There can be little doubt that the military hero made a redoubtable presidential candidate in mid-nineteenth-century America. The phenomenon, of course, was not altogether a new one: George Washington had been the towering example of the warrior as statesman. The benign example of Washington, indeed, probably did much to still the quivers of apprehension produced by the idea of a military man in politics. With magnificent circumspection he had demonstrated that an American soldier could safely be entrusted with the civil power, and subsequent soldier-politicians sought to fold themselves in his comforting mantle.

But the role of the military hero in politics cannot be explained simply by reference to the illustrious Washington. For over thirty years after Washington's retirement the presidency had been filled by statesmanlike public servants, and only in the Jacksonian era did the military hero become a political force to be reckoned with. In every presidential election from 1824 to 1856, with the exception of 1844, a military hero was a major candidate and on four occasions was returned to the White House. (It would be five if Franklin Pierce's dubious claims to military fame were admitted.) The military hero was highly available as a presidential candidate in those years, because by his very nature he lacked serious political enemies or implacable opposition, because he tended to personify certain values esteemed by the Whig party, and because of the resonance he achieved with popular political culture.

It was Andrew Jackson who first convincingly demonstrated the availability of the military hero. As we have seen, when the old general first began to be mentioned for the presidency he was widely held to be unavailable. Apart from his other disqualifications, his very success on the field of battle was seen as a liability, for educated Americans had long learned the lesson that republics were highly vulnerable to the vaulting ambition of the man on horseback. It has earlier been suggested that much of the propaganda surrounding Jackson's presidential bids in the 1820s was designed to allay those deeply-held fears of the Military Chieftain, and to convert Jackson into a highly available candidate by demonstrating that the real threat to the republic stemmed not from the Old Hero but from the intrigue and corruption in the nation's capital. To guarantee that republican institutions would be safe – and could only be safe – in his hands, Jackson was transformed from a Caesar into a Cincinnatus. He was not a party or a sectional champion, but the people's champion, rescuing them from the wicked wiles of power-hungry office-holders.

The unease over Military Chieftains never quite disappeared, but political managers now knew how to combat it. The strategy devised for Andrew Jackson in the 1820s was employed for William H. Harrison in 1836 and again in 1840, for Zachary Taylor in 1848, and even, in some measure, for Winfield Scott in 1852. General Harrison, it was said in 1836, was a candidate for the presidency 'not by his own choice – not by the dictation of a self-constituted convention – not by the prompting of a midnight caucus – but at the call of the democracy of the land'. He had sprung from the people, 'chosen by themselves from their own ranks', and unlike others he had 'carried no spoils into private life'. The swelling of support for him in 1840 was attributed to 'the prevalence of the consciousness that the country needed, not to be governed, but TO BE SAVED'. Old Tippecanoe was the people's candidate who would rescue the government 'from the hands of the spoilers'. Old Zach, too, was 'the people's candidate', summoned by them because the 'Republic is in danger' from the 'spoilsmen and corruptionists, who have so long preyed on its vitals', and his election was imperative if 'all that is valuable in a free Government' was not to be forever lost. It was more difficult to cast

Scott as the people's candidate pitted against a corrupt and despotic administration since there was a Whig in the White House at the time, but his virtue could be emphasized by comparing him with his Democratic rival, who would be the 'chief of a mere party, executing the petty schemes of such as are bound together by "the cohesive attraction of the public plunder", and dwarfing the government into the exercise of such functions only as will serve to satiate the voracity of those who throng the doors of the Treasury'. If there were perils in Military Chieftains, there were at least as great perils in corrupt officeholders and an over-powerful executive, as history had also shown, and on occasion a Cincinnatus had to be called from his plough to save his country from the machinations of those in government. This rationale did not altogether satisfy those who felt that entrusting a military hero with high civil office was a bad precedent. In 1847, when his own party was weighing the availability of both Zachary Taylor and Winfield Scott, Horace Greeley in a private letter still found it 'strange and mysterious to nominate a General fresh from a war of invasion for President. The consequence will soon be wars and conquests for the sake of the Presidency.'[2]

As the Jackson-Harrison-Taylor campaigns against 'the office-holders' demonstrated, the availability of successful generals rested on more than a momentary public acclaim. The *éclat* of New Orleans and Buena Vista undoubtedly helped launch Jackson and Taylor to political stardom, but Harrison's military renown had remained undiscovered for about a generation, while perhaps the most able military commander of the period, Winfield Scott, could not ignite great popular enthusiasm. Military heroes seemed to function best as opposition candidates, when they could exploit not only their own military fame but also popular distrust of the politicians in government. Americans had been taught to fear power and to distrust ambition, an equation which perhaps made it necessary for them from time to time to find a champion to turn the officeholders out before their sinister designs had become irreversible. As 'the people's' candidates military heroes seemed to rise above both party and section and even above government itself. Fighting for their country on the battlefield, they avoided being assigned sectional, factional and ideological identities more successfully than professional politicians, and their trade seemed an infinitely nobler one.

In an era of implacable sectional jealousies, the military hero could be a potent political force. The incomparable advantage of Jackson's candidacy in the 1820s was its capacity to attract support across sections. He was evidently popular in Pennsylvania and New Jersey, and could win votes in New York, as well as through the South and West. In 'contra-distinction to all the other candidates', insisted one admirer, 'he is unconnected with party politics, local feelings or sectional jealousies, and of course the only one among them who can go into the Presidential chair, unpledged to any thing but the interests of his country'. His ability to carry several states outside his own section made him the most formidable presidential candidate of his day. William Henry Harrison won the nomination of the Whig national convention in 1839 because, in addition to support in the West and in New England, he was acceptable to the delegates of the Middle Atlantic states while Clay was not. In the election itself he carried states in all sections. In 1848 Zachary Taylor enjoyed some of the same advantages as Jackson in the 1820s. As a slaveholder he was warmly favoured by southern Whigs, but as a career soldier rather than a politician he lacked a strong sectional identification and won substantial support in the North, especially in the critical Middle Atlantic. 'The peculiar state of our national affairs', professed a mass meeting in New York, requires that the presidency be filled by a man free from 'all sectional prejudices and partizan obligations' and designated Taylor as that man. Military heroes combined the advantages of high visibility with a relatively low sectional identification and hence could hope to keep the disparate geographical elements of a party coalition together.[3]

Perhaps as potent as the supra-sectional appeal of the military candidate was his supra-party identification. The traditional suspicion of the corruptibility of officeholders, which had made possible the fashioning of the Cincinnatus image, was also related to a long-standing unease about the legitimacy of political parties and a popular distaste for politicians. To many Americans, to return a party leader to the White House seemed a fatal betrayal of the ideals of the Founding Fathers. The military hero, however, who was at once an active patriot and a political outsider, could be represented as above party, indeed as a candidate of 'the people'. Old Hickory, Old Tippecanoe and Old Rough and Ready were each in turn presented as 'the people's choice', as authentic tribunes spontaneously called forth by the people without the devices of party. Horace Greeley had little doubt that military heroes benefited from the low regard in which Americans held their politicians, who so often seemed to enter politics for private gain. 'This is the reason why military candidates are preferred by the masses, who honor distinguished public services of every kind, but feel safe above all with a man who with great abilities and a memorable career has not exposed his integrity to any of the stains which are so often acquired in the more tortuous and difficult sphere of politics.'[4]

The military hero was honoured because he had evidently fought for his country rather than for his section or his party, and this was a politically potent image. In an age when politicians were not slow to espy unrepublican implications in one another's actions and words, the military hero held the incomparable claim of an attested patriotism. When Henry Clay sought to draw attention to the dangers of military men in politics he was soon shouted down: 'Because they loved liberty, and fought for it and won it to them we would deny it. ... Because they have *proved* their patriotism and their worth, they must be made the victims of unrelenting jealousy, of cold, unfeeling, indignant suspicion!' The transcendent republicanism of the military hero, who had risked his very life for the cause of freedom, could not be safely questioned, even as the fidelity of others to republican values was questioned on all sides. 'The position of an army officer is peculiarly national', reflected Josiah Quincy Jr on the death of Zachary Taylor, 'He feels that he belongs to the public, and the nation feels he belongs to them.'[5]

Yet there was a partisan dimension to the military hero. He was essentially a Whig figure. Andrew Jackson, who in any case first entered the White House when the Democratic party was in but a formative stage, was the first and last Democratic military hero in the *antebellum* era, not counting Franklin Pierce, who returned from a brief foray in the Mexican War with the rank of brigadier-general and a reputation for falling off his horse. The Whigs, by contrast, ran a military hero in every presidential election except 1844. Indeed, with the passage of time the Democrats turned from being defenders to being critics of the entry of military men into politics. Because of the success of Washington and Jackson, snorted the New York Democrat Churchill C. Cambreleng in 1840, the Whigs 'think they can elect any old drum stick to superintend the affairs of a great nation'. The Democrats ridiculed the political pretensions of Harrison and Taylor, arguing that Jackson at least had had some prior civil and government experience of significance. The Whigs' claim that Harrison was entitled to consideration for his '*past services*' was dismissed by one Democrat who insisted that more relevant were 'his talents and capacity *now to serve the people* in the office for which they propose him'. By the time of Scott's candidacy in 1852 Democratic stump-speakers like Stephen A. Douglas and James Buchanan were ringing the changes on all the old charges against military men in politics.[6]

The Whig preference for soldier-presidents was the product of both party character and electoral calculation. As a number of scholars have pointed out, and as we have seen from the behaviour of their presidential candidates, the Whigs still nourished a strong strain of antipartyism. Old-fashioned conservatives like the New York patrician Philip Hone, dreaming of the gentlemanly days which never quite were, found the machinations of party politics deeply distasteful and equated the rise of the party professional with the degeneration of American public life. Evangelical Whigs, strong in those Yankee-settled areas touched by religious revivalism, who seemed to have replaced the old ideal of republican harmony with a kind of fervid moral absolutism, uneasily viewed parties as the profane vehicles of selfish interests. These patrician and evangelical elements in Whiggery yearned for a more wholesome political order in which party was subordinated to the common weal, and for them the patriotic hero held a seductive allure, the 'people's candidate' who would reunite the country after the infamously partisan government of the Democratic spoilsmen. Indeed, Zachary Taylor's repeated protestations of being above party were turned by ingenious Whig editors into evidence of his fundamental Whig faith. Nonpartisanship, said the Baltimore *Republican*, was 'of the essence of Whig principles'. His promise not to be 'the President of a party' but to devote himself 'to the public good', added the New York *Courier*, was 'the spirit and the temper' of true Whiggery.[7]

This conservative temper in the Whig persuasion, the nostalgic desire for a champion who would rise above mere party and restore the republican virtue of old, also served to incline the Whigs towards men of stature, which military heroes undoubtedly were. The Whigs, as the behaviour of their presidential candidates betrayed and as a later chapter more fully shows, tended to esteem *leadership* rather than *service* and retained a measure of deference towards great men. 'What we seek in a candidate is, first, a great character', divulged the *Whig Review*. The choice before a Whig national convention was commonly limited to a few notables, as with Harrison, Clay and Scott in 1840, or with Webster, Fillmore and Scott in 1852. (In Democratic national conventions, in contrast, the great often found themselves joined in the arena by a profusion of unremarkable and sometimes downright obscure contenders.) In their search for a candidate, the Whigs seemed to hanker for a great man who was not closely identified with party, and before the advent of the modern entertainment industry such a candidate could normally only be found in the army. The Whig fondness for the military hero was a reflection of the essential conservatism of the party, which recent studies of the liberal Whigs of New York have tended to obscure. But ironically, in the years of party warfare the Whigs had come to play down the role of the president in the American constitutional structure and to emphasize the role of Congress in governing the country. It was essentially the responsibility of Congress to deliberate the issues of the day and to determine laws and policies, they suggested, while it was but the modest duty of the executive to carry out the congressional will. If this view did not sit very well with their hierarchical disposition to reserve the White House for great men, it was compatible with their preference for military heroes. They could argue, as they sometimes did, that it was 'not a matter of so great importance' for a president to 'have been bred a statesman', or to know much about public affairs, for his function was simply to be 'a firm executive officer', administering the laws passed by Congress. For this task, a successful general, with his expertise in marshalling men and *matériel*, it was suggested, might be better-suited than an opinionated legislator. The rather ambivalent attitude of the Whigs towards political leadership, which combined a patrician taste for men of distinction with a limited conception of presidential power, fairly logically tended to direct their attention towards the military hero.[8]

But if the character and composition of their party encouraged Whigs to look towards military candidates, so did considerations of electoral advantage. The Whigs, albeit marginally, were a minority party, particularly at state level. In the period 1834–53 Whig presidential electors secured 46.1 per cent of the vote (to the Democrats' 53.9 per cent), while Whig governors secured only 39.7 per cent. In the same period the Whigs took 42.6 per cent of the seats in the House of Representatives, while the Democrats took 54.9 per cent. Whig presidential candidates, it seems, tended to run ahead of their party, necessarily so if they were to have any hope of winning, for the regular Whig vote at sub-presidential level was rarely enough to deny the Democrats control of Congress. To win a presidential election, the Whigs needed not merely to hold onto their regular supporters, but also to entice into the polling stations independents, unhappy Democrats and third-party voters, and men who did not ordinarily vote. They needed candidates who would *attract* voters, especially in the crucial states of Pennsylvania and New York, and it was difficult to see how they could do this with flagbearers who were obscure or were encumbered with highly partisan or sectional images. Clay was a hero to the party faithful but only to the party faithful, while Webster never commanded much enthusiasm outside New England, not even after his fateful Seventh of March speech, when he sacrificed much of his own constituency without attracting compensating support elsewhere. The military hero seemed the ideal solution to many of the problems besetting the Whig party. 'Tremendous meetings are being held by all kinds of people in favor of *Harrison*', rejoiced a Whig editor in 1840. 'Not only the *Whigs*, but the Democrats, Jackson men, working men, radicals, and all sorts of people are flocking to the *Harrison* standard.' The attraction of military heroes for the Whigs perhaps increased in the 1840s when the Democrats adopted an aggressive and nationalistic foreign policy, to the disapproval of the Whigs who nonetheless had to show that they, too, were patriots. It was urged in favour of Taylor's nomination in 1848 that he would be bound to carry the states won by Clay in 1844, and that in addition he would also carry those others won by Harrison in 1840, and hence a Whig victory would be assured. More than that, the 'prestige of his name' and his popularity 'with all classes of the people, except the few who adhere to "the obsolete idea" that defeat under one banner is preferable to success under another', would secure Whig majorities in both houses of Congress. Being in some measure above section and faction, a military hero might keep the quarrelsome Whig coalition together, and as a celebrated patriot relatively untainted by party politics he might bring over to the Whig banner just those extra votes needed for victory.[9]

If the military hero did bring added strength to the Whig cause, it may have been in part because he did touch instincts deep in the American political psyche. It was possible for him to embody the American destiny in a way which was beyond mere politicians. Transcending section and party, the military hero came closer than others to defining the national purpose. The nation had, after all, been born in war, and had reaffirmed its proud independence in the War of 1812. Americans had also been told, in countless Fourth of July orations, popular songs and poems, and school textbooks, that God had assigned them a unique mission in the world, and that that mission was the protection and nourishment of human liberty. Military valour and the cause of liberty were indissolubly bound together in the annals of popular American mythology. The eagle, that 'carnivorous, ravenous, plundering, destroying, fighting' creature, had been chosen as the national emblem; American history textbooks in the *antebellum* era devoted three times as much space to military events as their modern counterparts. As the Revolution itself receded into the past Americans looked to other events to affirm that they were remaining true to their sacred trust to advance the cause of liberty, and not least to the ever-moving frontier. Westward expansion became associated with the American mission, for with each extension of American territory the area of the globe devoted to freedom and civilization grew larger. The military conquests associated with the process inevitably became battles for American liberty. If there is 'anything in this world particularly worth living for, it is freedom;' vaunted an American folk hero, albeit apocryphally, as he rode towards his death at the Alamo, 'anything that would render death to a brave man particularly pleasant, it is freedom'. Military men were the heroes of the popular culture of the young republic, for they had offered their lives for the cause of American destiny, and, more, by their very victories had strengthened and perhaps enlarged the great experiment in republican freedom.[10]

In an era when Americans were still very anxious about the fate of republican institutions, and were burdened with the knowledge of their unique yet vulnerable destiny, the military hero offered hope. The extraordinary celebrations prompted by military candidacies for the presidency were reminiscent of the excitement surrounding the visit of Lafayette to the United States in 1824–25, when Americans seized the opportunity to be told by this illustrious comrade of Washington that they were indeed remaining true to the trust bequeathed by the Founding Fathers. If the individual voter felt his loyalties to be circumscribed by section, community, party, sect, or ethnicity, he could assure himself of his true patriotism by identifying with the cause of the military hero. If Americans were uneasy that the republic was going awry, if they were fearful lest virtue was being lost and the great experiment sacrificed to personal ambition, they could reaffirm their commitment to the selfless ideals of republicanism by honouring those who had stridden fearlessly in the vanguard of America's mission. In this perspective, the victorious general was not a threat to the republic but its very embodiment. It was said of Harrison, as it was similarly said of Jackson, Taylor and Scott, that he 'appears to have been reserved by Providence for the use of his country, and destined to be again the instrument of its safety'. It was not only the horny-handed Farmer of Tennessee who invoked restorationist sentiments. The military hero, too, became the focus of a widespread yearning to return to the days of republican virtue.[11]

At the opposite end of the political spectrum to the military hero was the dark horse. If it was his visibility and his patriotic renown which contributed to the availability of the military hero, it was the reverse which made the dark horse a formidable political figure. The dark horse, of course, was the man who emerged unexpectedly from obscurity to win his party's nomination. On occasion a national convention would choose for its presidential candidate someone whose name had not even been entered in nomination in the first place, someone who hitherto had not equalled in stature the party chieftains who so coveted the prize. In the period of the second party system two such candidates, James K. Polk and Franklin Pierce, were triumphantly returned to the White House.

If the military hero was predominantly a Whig candidate, the dark horse was exclusively a Democratic creation. He was the product of the Democratic party structure, of the rules governing the party's national conventions, and, in a sense, even of the ethos of the party itself. The delegates to a Democratic convention, of course, did not assemble with the intention of nominating a dark horse for president, but this was an expedient to which they could have recourse in a way unthinkable to the Whigs. The dark horse was a democratic phenomenon in part because in certain circumstances the relatively humble and obscure were acceptable contenders for that party's nomination.

'What has James K. Polk ever *done* to recommend him to the people for the high office to which he aspires?', asked an incredulous Whig. While the Whigs may have exaggerated Polk's obscurity with their celebrated question, 'Who is James K. Polk?', their ridicule was not without foundation. Every serious contender for the presidency hitherto had been a man of some political weight, but on the eve of his nomination Polk's political career had seemed all but over. He had achieved a modest success in the House of Representatives in the 1830s as a defender of Jackson's administration, and he had served briefly as Speaker. But after returning to Tennessee and winning the governorship in 1839, he had been defeated for re-election in 1841 and had lost the gubernatorial race yet again in 1843. His career thus blocked in a state which was becoming predominantly Whig, Polk had turned his sights somewhat desperately once more to the national scene, hoping against hope that his party colleagues would rescue him from oblivion by naming him the vice-presidential candidate in 1844. The well-known story of how the Democratic convention, locked in an implacable stalemate between the partisans of Martin Van Buren and Lewis Cass, had eventually resolved its crisis by going for Polk, need not detain us here. Suffice it to say that while Polk, as a regular party member, may have been known to several of the delegates, he was not well-known to the public at large. There was nothing more predictable than the Whig merriment at the ' idea of Jem Polk being President of the U.S.!!!'[12]

Eight years later the Democrats surpassed themselves by nominating for president the even darker horse Franklin Pierce. The son of a distinguished New Hampshire politician, Pierce had moved readily into politics as a young man and had eventually reached the United States Senate. But his congressional career had not been spectacular, and concern for his wife's health (together apparently with his own fondness for drink) had led him to retire from politics in 1842. It is doubtful whether many of the Democratic delegates had ever heard of Pierce as they converged on Baltimore for their convention ten years later. But again the chieftains of the party, Lewis Cass, James Buchanan, Stephen A. Douglas and William L. Marcy, divided the vote between them, and on the forty-ninth ballot the weary delegates finally abandoned the fight by bestowing the crown on the Granite State's obscure son. At least one Democratic editor confused Handsome Frank with a congressional namesake and proudly announced the party's champion to be 'General John A. Pierce.... A better nomination it is not possible to have made.'[13]

'We have fallen on great times for little men', complained the *New York Tribune* after Pierce's nomination, 'and this wretched machinery of National Conventions is one potent cause of it.' The Democratic party, like its major rival, was composed of a host of sectional, factional and ideological groups, and with the ending of the Jackson – Van Buren hegemony its national convention became a battleground for several rival contenders. It was not easy for any single candidate to secure even a majority of delegate support, but what made it peculiarly difficult for the Democrats to reach a swift decision was the operation of the two-thirds rule. At the first Democratic national convention, largely in order to demonstrate solid support for Van Buren, it had been agreed that a two-thirds majority was necessary for nomination. The same rule had been used in 1836 though dispensed with as unnecessary in 1840 (Van Buren had no longer to be shielded from the charge that Jackson had chosen his own successor), but in the 1844 convention the anti-Van Buren forces rammed the two-thirds rule through again in order to prevent the anti-annexationist New Yorker from winning the nomination. But while the friends of Lewis Cass, James Buchanan and Dick Johnson might make common cause to keep Van Buren out, they could not themselves roll up the required total for any of their champions. With the Van Buren forces adamantly opposed to yielding to '*the damned rotten corrupt venal* Cass cliques', and with most other delegates unwilling to capitulate to the ex-president because of his stand on Texas, Polk's friends seized the opportunity to present him on the seventh ballot as a candidate who could be stomached by most factions. Polk had been a fairly loyal supporter of Van Buren, was sound on money and banking, and yet favoured the annexation of Texas. Had an overall majority been required Van Buren could have won on the first ballot, but the two-thirds rule deflected the lightning in an unexpected direction. With so much emotion vested in it, the two-thirds rule remained to rack the nerves of later Democratic national conventions. In 1852 none of the four major contenders could win even a simple majority of the convention's votes, let alone come within striking distance of the magic total, and in the end the delegates surrendered their favourites to announce their support 'For General Franklin Pierce, (God bless him!)'.[14]

The two-thirds rule in a sense gave a power of veto to minority factions, at least in certain circumstances. The Van Burenites could not deliver the nomination to their chieftain in 1844 but they could deny it to the Lewis Cass they so despised. The Cass forces could not win the prize for their ageing leader in 1852, but they could help to frustrate the bids of Cass's principal rival, James Buchanan, and of that abrasive upstart from Illinois, Stephen A. Douglas. Anti-voting manifested itself at national conventions as much as at the polls, and the two-thirds rule helped to turn Democratic conventions in particular into cauldrons of sectional, factional and ideological hatreds. 'In a multiplicity of candidates, with friends and adherents intensely devoted to each,' observed the *Springfield Republican*, 'and with the consequent impossibility of uniting a force of two thirds upon any one candidate pitted in such a direct antagonism – the only alternative is, to take a candidate, to whom all being equally indifferent, will be equally attached.'[15]

The Democrats themselves seem to have had few qualms about choosing dark horses. The nominations of Polk and Pierce were greeted with widespread relief that the party had found a way of holding together. But there seems also to have been something in the Democratic persuasion which made relatively minor figures acceptable candidates. The Democrats looked not so much for distinction in their flagbearers as party regularity, and the common feature of all their presidential nominees after Jackson was their history of loyal service to the party. Polk and Pierce were nothing if not party regulars who had both defended Jackson's administration in Congress years before. Democratic conventions were customarily confronted

with more contenders than Whig conventions, among them a significant number of optimistic near nonentities. At the 1844 convention
Van Buren and Cass shared the limelight with James Buchanan,
Dick Johnson, Levi Woodbury, John C. Calhoun, and Charles Ste-
wart. Four years later it took Lewis Cass four ballots to reach the
two-thirds total, having faced competition from James Buchanan,
Levi Woodbury, George M. Dallas, William J. Worth, John C.
Calhoun and William O. Butler. In 1852 those two old rivals, Cass
and Buchanan, were joined in the lists by Stephen A. Douglas, William L. Marcy, William O. Butler, Sam Houston, Joseph Lane, Linn
Boyd, Henry Dodge, R. J. Ingersoll, William R. King, and Daniel S.
Dickinson. The Whigs, by contrast, characteristically confined their
attentions to a few prominent dignitaries. The humble as well as the
great could have their names placed in nomination at the Democratic
convention, as long as they were loyal party servants. 'Fifty years of
masterly inactivity in the service of Democracy have qualified the
New-Hampshire Senator', sneered the *American Whig Review* in
1852, noting that the Democratic party's negative government philosophy seemed to call for such a nonentity. '... The absence, not
the excess of talent, is needed for a representative of Negation.'[16]

The Whigs indeed charged with some justice that the Democrats
favoured loyal functionaries. A national convention, said Horace
Greeley, 'is under very strong temptation to *make* a candidate for
President, instead of merely *presenting* one whom the People have
already fixed upon; since in the former case the candidate's obligation to the delegates is far greater, and his gratitude will probably be
proportionate'. The Van Burenites eventually turned to Polk in 1844
at least in part because they hoped that he would accord them a
measure of influence and patronage which they knew they would
not receive from Cass, while a similar thought probably flitted
through the minds of the Buchanan men who eventually went over
to Pierce in 1852. But there was also a suspicion in the Whig ranks
that the Democratic party did not really like chieftains. Buchanan,
Cass and Douglas were spurned by the Democrats in 1852, said one
Whig editor, 'for the very reason that they were eminent and influential. .... The Machiavels of Democracy do not wish to be controlled, but only to control; they desire not to have a master, but an
assiduous servant.' Since the time of Jackson the Democrats had insisted that they were the obedient servants of the people, and as such
a loyal party regular was perhaps even better qualified for the presidency than a candidate with a will of his own. The Democrats, after
all, had enhanced the powers of the president on the grounds that he

was the authentic popular tribune, but he could only use those powers safely if he deferred to the wishes of the majority, which were best translated through the Democratic party. Years of loyal party service were an essential qualification for the Democratic nominee.[17]

If the Democratic party composition and the rules of the national convention sometimes interacted in such a way as to exclude the party's leading men from the nomination, the Democratic ethic of party discipline served to legitimize the dark-horse contenders. But probably this state of affairs was tolerated, too, because of its electoral advantages. The Democratic dark horses, after all, won their races. The Democrats were the majority party nationally, and Democratic leaders seemed to believe this even more confidently than the figures warranted. 'No man, military or civil, can be elected President of the United States by a *majority of the votes of the American people* unless he is supported by the democratic party', remarked Churchill C. Cambreleng privately in a typical Democratic aside. Unlike the Whigs, therefore, the Democrats did not need a presidential candidate who would *win over* votes. Their need was for a candidate who would not *repel* votes, a candidate who would retain the loyalties of regular Democratic voters. From this perspective, it was safer to run a loyal party functionary than a controversial man of stature. A dark horse might not attract many votes, but the obscurity of his views should ensure that he would not repel them, while the efficient Democratic party machinery would get the voters to the polls. Democratic managers did not set out looking for dark horses, but they felt comfortable with them when circumstances produced them. In contrast to the Whigs, the Democrats were helped by candidates of low visibility but of strong party identification.[18]

There was after all some reason for thinking that prominence in political life could be an electoral disadvantage. A national convention, Horace Greeley complained, 'is almost certain to set aside all candidates who have any positive character, any notable history, and definite ideas, and propose instead some negative, half-and-half, small-minded personage, who has never been of sufficient consequence to offend or excite jealousy, and who never had an idea beyond the pale of his party catechism'. Alexander Mackay, a Scottish visitor, concluded that great men were too identified with one section or another, and that only an obscure candidate could prevent internal divisions within a party. The best nominee was 'the one least objectionable to all', for 'if admirers were few, so were enemies'. Philip Hone came to a similar conclusion after the 1844 election, comforting Henry Clay with the observation that a 'statesman' such as himself, 'prominent as you have been for so long a time, must have been identified with all the leading measures affecting the interests of the people, and those interests are frequently different in the several parts of our widely extended country. . . . . Give me, therefore, a candidate of an inferior grade, one whose talents, patriotism and public services have never been so conspicuous as to force him into the first ranks.' What the Whigs generally did, of course, was to select a candidate who had not been prominent in *political* life. The dark horse was the Democratic answer to the military hero. Both were highly 'available' in their different ways; in an electoral system subject to 'anti-voting' there was a premium on the politically enigmatic.[19]

The prominence of the military hero and the dark horse among successful presidential contenders in these years was a mark of the highly fractious nature of American politics. The United States was a vast and unwieldy enterprise, filled with peoples all too conscious of the differences between them. Slaveholders feared the expansionist ambitions of free men of the North; Pennsylvanians were jealous of the commercial and political pre-eminence of New York; the growing numbers of wage-earners were becoming aware of their distinctive interests as a class; devoted Protestants feared for the safety of the republic as the Catholic church expanded rapidly; immigrants from many countries brought old animosities with them and sensed the antipathy of many native Americans; rural and small-town Americans viewed with unease the mushrooming populations of the big cities. The political parties of the period became the receptacles of all these fears and animosities and more, and political managers wrestled with the problem of forging electoral majorities from the discordant elements which comprised the body of the people. In presidential politics availability was the key, the ability perhaps to attract and especially not to repel votes, and this characteristic was most often possessed by those who had not been much involved in political battle, by those who were in some measure above party, like the military hero, or those who were not too closely identified with a particular factional interest, like the dark horse. Another kind of available candidate was the man from one section who espoused the views of another. Thus the Democrats sometimes nominated 'a northern man with southern principles', notably Van Buren in 1836 and 1840, Cass in 1848, and, after the ending of the second party system, Buchanan in 1856. All these men had gone to some trouble to emphasize their soundness on matters relating to slavery. Conversely, slaveholding candidates usually sought to conciliate northern interests, as Polk did with his Kane letter in 1844 and Henry Clay hoped to do on various occasions with his American System. The Whigs even indulged the wishful hope that Winfield Scott could reconcile the various sections: 'being a Southern man by birth, a Northern man by residence, and a Union man by sentiment, his great moral influence will still forever the bitter waters of sectional controversy'.[20]

But availability was a fragile quality and all too easily lost. If political outsiders were held to be available, the very act of bringing them into the political game endangered their status. In a sense, complementary to the military hero and the dark horse was the single term – presidents did not normally survive for more than four years in the White House. The single term, too, was largely a product of the fractious nature of political parties and the deep divisions within the American Union.

During the history of the first party system (say approximately 1790 to 1820) every president except one had served two terms. In the period of the second party system Andrew Jackson alone was re-elected; not until Abraham Lincoln thirty years later was that feat to be repeated. Since the two-term administration was later again to become the norm, the *antebellum* era stands out as something of an exception in American presidential history. The American political process at that time (together with occasional nudges from Providence) militated against long tenure in the White House. The precarious nature of the party coalitions, the growth of democratic ideology, and the long-standing suspicion of executive power, all in some measure heightened by the destructive forces of sectionalism, together helped to create the one-term presidency.

The insecurity of presidential tenure in these years was not the product of defeat at the polls, a fate which overtook President Van Buren alone. Once he had gained admission to the White House a president did not normally go before the people again. Of course, the deaths in office of Harrison and Taylor precluded any possibility of a second term for them, but even had they lived it is extremely unlikely that they would have been re-elected. Martin Van Buren was the only incumbent ever to be renominated by his party. President John Tyler, anxious to be elected in his own right, was disowned by both parties, and President Millard Fillmore, who allowed his friends to present his name to the 1852 Whig convention, found that while his role in the Compromise of 1850 had won him some southern admirers it had lost him critical support in the North. After the ending of the second party system Franklin Pierce also sought renomination, but he, too, had lost his northern supporters while in office. James K. Polk was cannier in not even trying to secure a second nomination.

This failure to win renomination is in some measure a reflection of the weak political authority of the president in these years. The towering and wilful figure of Andrew Jackson has sometimes led scholars to conclude that executive power was substantially enhanced after the constitutional monarchies of Madison, Monroe and John Q. Adams, but Jackson's accomplishment in this respect was personal and ephemeral. Andrew Jackson alone succeeded himself and Andrew Jackson alone was able to designate his successor. Opposition politicians carped endlessly about the powers of patronage in the hands of the executive, but such patronage was not enough to give a president a secure command over his party and was not enough to win an election. With the passing of the Jackson – Van Buren hegemony (which, in any case, had little to do with patronage), a president could not deliver his party's nomination either to himself or to anyone else. Incumbent presidents, indeed, notably Fillmore in 1852 and Pierce in 1856, were even unable to prevent their party conventions from nominating candidates deeply distasteful to them. The ineffectiveness of executive patronage was vividly illustrated by John Tyler in 1842–44, when, rejected by both major parties, he attempted to create his own party by using the federal offices at his disposal, only to fail miserably. The political authority of the president during the era of the second party system, then, was limited in the extreme, despite the misleading example of Andrew Jackson. *Antebellum* presidents were the victims of a pervasive suspicion of executive power, of the state-oriented structure of the party coalitions, of inadequate powers of patronage, and of all the fears, divisions and jealousies which riddled the American political system. The one potential contender for the presidency in these years who could *not* assume some variation of the stance of the Mute Tribune was the man with whom the buck stopped.[21]

Presidential tenure was also limited by personal and party commitments to a single term. After his defeat in the House election in 1825 Andrew Jackson had come to the conclusion that presidents should be confined to one term, and in each of his annual messages to Congress as president he urged a constitutional amendment to restrict the Chief Magistrate to a single term of four or six years (which was one reason why his re-election had to be presented as demanded by the people). A few years later, in February 1838, William H. Harrison became the first contender to give an explicit one-term pledge, writing to James H. Birch of the *Missourian* that if 'elected President under no circumstances would he again be a candidate'. James K. Polk, in accepting the Democratic nomination in 1844, assured his fellows of his 'settled purpose of not being a candidate for re-election', and his successor four years later made the same promise. The Whig platform of 1844 committed the party to 'a single term for the presidency', a principle Henry Clay pledged himself to uphold. These pledges in some degree tended to turn incumbents into lame ducks. Although Jackson was able to circumvent his professed belief, James K. Polk certainly felt himself obliged not to seek renomination and did not attempt to do so. Millard Fillmore's apparent reluctance to seek the Whig nomination in 1852 may have owed something to his party's avowal of the single term, and his unenthusiastic colleagues reminded him of his own anti-Tyler declaration of 1842 that 'our only security against treachery and inordinate ambition is found in the ONE-TERM PRINCIPLE'.[22]

The one-term principle was the product of a mixture of expediency and ideology. The early Jacksonian espousal of the doctrine was probably not unrelated to the inchoate structure of the party, which in 1828 was still largely a coalition of factional chieftains who had been in national politics longer than Jackson. Calhoun's allegiance at least probably owed something to the thought that he might soon follow Old Hickory into the White House. Harrison's one-term pledge, issued in 1838 as Whig politicians were plotting their strategy for the national convention, was a more blatant attempt to buy off the Clay men, one of whom sourly commented that he would have been better pleased if Harrison had not declined the second term before obtaining the first. 'The people are thinking more about who should be president, than how long he should serve, and well they may.' As in 1828, the Democrats used the threat of a Clay succession against their opponents: 'The Whig game is, for Gen. Harrison to come in now... – and Mr. Clay is to lie by on an understanding, that the General is to serve but one term.' But the Democrats were soon obliged to play the same game themselves, for Polk in 1844 was clearly seeking to placate his better-known rivals by promising to vacate the White House four years hence. Indeed, it is impossible to escape the conclusion that his lieutenants at the convention had come to such an understanding during the manoeuvres which preceded his nomination, for they wrote immediately to Polk to urge him to 'express yourself in favor of the one-term system –

This is important – I might say all important . . .'. It was right upon principle, 'And further It would bring asperants [sic] and there [sic] friends more cordially into your support.' If the same calculation was behind Cass's one-term pledge in 1848 it was confounded, for many northerners on the Van Buren wing of the party bolted to the new Free Soil ticket. All parties at this time were relatively new creations and were uncertain of their own capacity to survive their internal divisions. The one-term pledge offered the party a renewed lease of life by holding out the prospect of an early succession to its more ambitious chieftains.[23]

Although a contender undoubtedly offered the one-term pledge primarily with his own immediate interests in mind, it could be justified on the grounds of the unity it would bring to the party and the country. In a polity constantly struggling to contain the strains of sectionalism, it promised to function as one small mechanism for survival. This consideration had been present in the various constitutional amendments to restrict the presidency to one term which had been submitted in such abundance in the 1820s, as it was also in the bizarre proposals to choose a president by lot which also surfaced from time to time. Thomas Hart Benton applauded Polk's one-term pledge in 1844 on the grounds that it would serve to reduce sectional conflict and declared himself 'in favour of seeing the democratic candidate for 1848 taken from the North'. Another Democrat remarked privately to Andrew Jackson that 'as our population increases and the various interests of different sections of the country become more fully developed' the number of presidential contenders would naturally grow, and 'except in extraordinary cases, I incline to think that it may be best, to limit the incumbent to a single term'. A short presidential tenure would keep the Union as well as the party together.[24]

The one-term principle also drew upon ancient critiques of executive power. In eighteenth-century England the Country critics of the Court party had inveighed against the Septennial Act (which allowed seven years between general elections) as a step towards tyranny, especially when the administration had so much patronage at its disposal. The fears that a corrupt executive would use its financial instruments and its powers of patronage to arrogate power unto itself, at the cost of the people's liberty, had long been present in America, and opposition groups periodically exploited this unease by pointing to the way in which a president might buy his re-election. 'At present the first four years of an administration are past [sic] in efforts to CONFIRM THE BARGAINS and pledges, as to the RIGHT OF SUCCESSION', complained some partisans of Jackson in 1828. But it was the Whigs, in resisting what they regarded as the usurpations of the Jackson and Van Buren administrations and the infuriating vetoes of John Tyler, who really invoked all the old warnings against executive tyranny and offered the single term as one remedy. The first of the great Whig mass meetings of 1840 proposed the one-term limitation as one means of preventing 'the attainment of absolute power by the National Executive'. The banner 'One Presidential term, and the good of the people' was hoisted at Whig parades. 'The history of the last twelve years of Executive misrule', instructed a Whig editor in 1844, 'demonstrates that the patronage of the Executive "will be brought into conflict with the freedom of elections", whenever that power is wielded by a person tenacious of office.' The Whig predilection for a single term was consistent with the streak of anti-partyism which ran through the Whig persuasion, for it would mean that the president 'will have no possible inducement to do otherwise than devote his whole constitutional power, his official influence and personal energies, to promote the public good, as a means of obtaining the approbation – not of a PART or a PARTY, but of the WHOLE American People'. This patrician conviction that the good of the whole demanded a curb on executive influence also moved Horace Greeley, who argued against Fillmore's renomination in 1852 on the grounds that 'a Presidential place-hunter must ever be strongly tempted to abuse his patronage to subserve personal ends'. The Whig evocation of the Country diatribes against Walpolean corruption in eighteenth-century England was made explicit by another editor, who insisted that it was one of the main objects of 'the Whigs – the country party – the people, for the terms are synonymous – to eradicate this fruitful source of corruption . . .'. The Whigs never got much opportunity to implement the principle of the single term themselves, but at least they committed a substantial part of the political nation to it.[25]

The one-term principle did achieve a measure of respectability, or at least of inevitability. Although the federal Constitution was not amended in these years, there was a trend towards shorter terms and more frequent elections in the state constitutions. 'As the democratic creed spreads, the tendency is to abridge the duration of official power', wrote one Cass Democrat who believed that the popularity of the one-term principle would militate against Van Buren's election in 1844. 'Rotation comes more and more into favor.' Harrison's one-term pledge was said to be a cause of his success, for the 'public mind had been tending that way'. A Whig editor in 1840 had also believed that 'The *one-term* men are an immense party in themselves, and they all go for Harrison.' But the promptings of democracy apart, the series of single-term presidents in time served as a caution against running an incumbent again. The Whigs did not formally introduce the one-term principle into their platform in 1852, but the *New York Tribune* considered it 'established by the failure to re-nominate President Polk on the one side and President Fillmore on the other'. 'Our own impression is, that the time has passed by for-ever for *second* terms', agreed a southern Whig editor. 'The *outs* are so much more numerous than the *ins*, that neither party will any more nominate a Presidential incumbent for re-election. The certain-ty of overwhelming defeat will deter them from it.' The single-term dogma was beginning to acquire an inertial weight of its own, and it required a Civil War to dispel it.[26]

The one-term phenomenon pointed up the difficulty of maintaining anything like a consensus in *antebellum* America. An electoral major-ity could periodically be forged behind an available candidate, but such coalitions were necessarily precarious. Once elected the new president rapidly lost the ambiguous qualities which had helped raise him. Offices had to be distributed, state papers written, bills signed and perhaps vetoes exercised. Jackson alone was able to do all these things and yet win re-election, albeit with a marginally smaller pro-portion of the popular vote. Martin Van Buren's economic and poli-tical policies retained for him the support of the radicals in his party at the cost of alienating the conservatives, who helped to put Harri-son in his place. Later, his sensitivity to the pressures of his New York and other northern constituents, together with his concern for the Union, lost him crucial support in the South and the West. Presi-dent Tyler's obstinate bank vetoes alienated the bulk of the party through which he had ascended, while Polk was too beholden to his party rivals even to seek renomination. President Fillmore's consci-entious attention to southern interests lost him his old constituency in the North, a fate which was also to befall his successor. In contrast to the twentieth-century situation, it was then a distinct disadvan-tage for a man to be an incumbent if he desired the prize for himself or for a chosen successor. The twin forces of sectionalism and anti-partyism militated against him, as they militated in favour of the Whig military hero and the Democratic dark horse.

It was ironic that the major parties expended so much energy and ingenuity in seeking to capture an office which possessed little effective political authority and which offered so little security of tenure. Its importance lay not so much in the positive power wielded by the incumbent as in its strategic position in the electoral battlefield. It was the one office (with the vice-presidency) which was contested throughout the Union, the one conspicuous objective for which a party could be mobilized nationally. In the fractious political world of *antebellum* America the possession of the presidency could offer some comfort to sectional, factional or other interests, for at least the president could deny aid to one's enemies. The president was not merely a figurehead, for his power of veto (of both legislation and appointments) gave a measure of security to those who enjoyed access to the White House. But his ability to further his own fortunes was limited, for much the same reason as the distinguished party leaders of the day found that their prominence availed them little when they sought the republic's most glittering prize.

The insecurity of tenure in the White House, the dark horse and the military hero, perhaps all served to testify in their different ways to the low regard in which politicians were held. Once they assumed office and began making decisions presidents ceased to be statesmen and became the parochial creatures of sectional and factional interests, at least in the eyes of their enemies and erstwhile admirers. Long-serving politicians had already gained such reputations, so that military chieftains and dark horses came to have an electoral lure often denied their party seniors. The unpopularity of the country's political leaders, compounded of traditional anti-power values and sectional and doctrinal animosities, helped to raise to the highest office men whose qualifications would have been dismissed by an earlier generation. The divided and fractious nature of American politics, the insecurity felt by each of the many elements which made up the political spectrum, probably served to encourage the tendency to oppose rather than to propose, to react against a possible threat rather than to act for a distinct cause, and this phenomenon of 'anti-voting' both prompted parties to protect their fragile coalitions by selecting unexceptional candidates and added to the constraints on the presidential office itself.

If the one-term phenomenon was the product of a complex interaction between political structure, ideology and expediency, so were the military hero and the dark horse. The recourse to the principle of availability cannot be dismissed as mere political opportunism. Each party was accommodating itself to the practicalities of the American political process, but in a way which was compatible with its own character and political beliefs. The Democratic party's will-

ingness to nominate dark horses was the product of its party structure and convention rules, of electoral considerations, and of an
assumption that any man of reasonable intelligence might legitimately hold high office. The Whig party's preference for military heroes
was a reflection of its distaste for mere party politicians and its in-
stinctive deference to rank, as well as of its need to attract votes. The
two parties in their different ways were also seeking to allay the
ancient fear of executive power, the Democrats by making the president the obedient servant of party, and hence of the people, and the
Whigs by placing an attested patriot in the White House. They thus
continued to differ over the nature of the leadership appropriate to a
republic, for not even their resort to availability completely eroded
their political faith.

CHAPTER EIGHT
# The presidential image

'The language of images', Daniel Boorstin has written, '... is the only simple way of describing what dominates our experience'. The substitution of the image for the idea, it is sometimes suggested, has been related to the emergence of the mass society, to the need to communicate with a host of anonymous individuals. Images of a kind have no doubt existed for as long as human society, but in recent times they have come to be consciously created and they have come to perform an important mediating function between the complexities of the modern world and the individual person.[1]

In the United States the mass political society emerged around the 1820s, at least as far as presidential politics are concerned. It was then that the vote for president came effectively to be invested in the people, that serious efforts were made to mobilize popular opinion on a substantial scale, that voters began to turn out in vast numbers to exercise their prerogative. In the election of 1828 some 1,156,328 men, scattered across the immensity of the American Union, performed a common political act in voting for president. It was in the 1820s, too, that the deliberate projection of images of the candidates became central to presidential campaigns. The popular political culture of the United States today in no small measure had its origins in the electioneering of the Jacksonian era.

The task of fashioning the popular image of a presidential candidate fell on his designated biographer, and on his political intimates and on friendly editors throughout the country. Sectional issues, party measures, political scandals and governmental policies had long received their share of attention and continued to do so, but increasingly in the eye of the storm was the figure of the candidate, whose merits and qualifications were now shamelessly broadcast in campaign biographies, pamphlet sketches, newspaper articles and broadsheets. Lithographs, cartoons, buttons, bandanas, and totems of all kinds, from hickory sticks to miniature log-cabins, also began to make their appearance and to convey their symbolic messages. The images were already beginning to overshadow the men.

As we have seen, in some measure this growth in promotional literature was initially the product of the highly personal presidential campaigns of the 1820s. In that brief period between the ending of the first party system and before the advent of the second, contenders for the presidency had little alternative but to seek the prize in their personal capacities, and their partisans were not slow to draw their merits to the attention of the public. Although John C. Calhoun had been the first presidential contender to resort to a campaign biography, it was the candidature of Andrew Jackson which really gave rise to the expansion of promotional techniques of this kind. At first widely dismissed as a serious contender and then denounced as a potential Military Chieftain, the sustained propaganda campaign by his friends sought to show not merely that Jackson could be safely entrusted with the republic but that he was necessary to save it.

As the Jackson campaign rose to a crescendo in 1828, the backers of his rival John Quincy Adams remained more circumspect, concentrating on disseminating a favourable image not in special promotional literature so much as in the press. By the 1830s, however, such patrician inhibitions had gone, and candidacies were invariably launched with the aid of book-length campaign biographies, accompanied by a score of pamphlet sketches, party handbooks, campaign newspapers featuring serialized lives, broadsheets, banners, pictorial portraits and an imaginative array of emblems. James K. Polk, who conducted a very low-key campaign in 1844, was something of an exception in deciding against a full-length biography. A seventeen page sketch did appear, apparently vetted by Polk's friends in Washington, and the candidate agreed to a serialized version of his life in his local newspaper, but Polk's reticence did not start a new fashion. The campaign biography had arrived to stay, as Nathaniel Hawthorne recognized in 1852 when he wrote to his old classmate Franklin Pierce with an offer to do 'the necessary biography'.[2]

The formal biographies, together with the innumerable pamphlet and newspaper sketches which fed off them, played an essential role in the campaigns of this period. It was in this way that the character and qualifications of the candidate were transmitted to the electorate by his promoters. Parties and partisan allegiances, of course, had acquired the strength by the 1830s to draw many voters to the polls irrespective of the candidate, but in an age when parties were still both immature and suspect organizations, finding and merchandizing the right man was important. To some extent different publications were intended for different audiences. As early as 1824, for example, a defence of Jackson's behaviour in the Seminole War was published in Frankfort, 'written for the benefit of the People of the U. States, but particularly for those of the State of Kentucky'. In 1844 an 'Irish adopted citizen' reached for immigrant votes for the Whig candidate with his *Fifty Reasons Why the Honourable Henry Clay Should Be Elected President of the United States* (Baltimore 1844). Sometimes brief biographical sketches were published in a foreign language, most notably German, while more specialized apologies occasionally appeared, such as *An Answer to the Charge Against Gen. Taylor and His Friends, of Opposition to Naturalized Citizens, and Hostility to Catholics* (Washington 1848). With the growing sensitivity over slavery and related issues in the middle of the century the temptation to produce different sketches for different parts of the country increased. In 1848 the Whigs charged the central Democratic committee at Washington with producing two lives of Lewis Cass, one designed for the North and the other for the South. The Democrats blandly replied that there were as many as fourteen different lives of Zachary Taylor in circulation, each intended for a different audience.[3]

Yet while the party publicists did edit their multifarious effusions with specialized interest groups in mind, what is remarkable about the biographies, memoirs and sketches of the candidates is the degree of duplication. Once a *Life* had been published, it was quarried shamelessly and repeatedly by other authors and editors. The same material, the same presentation, the same anecdotes, even the same paragraphs, sentences and phrases recurred endlessly. Biographers of Jackson never tired of telling the celebrated story of how the Hero, as a doughty teenager in the revolutionary war, had defiantly refused to clean a British officer's boots. William Henry Harrison was forever being extolled for introducing the Land Act of 1800, young Jimmy Polk never failed to shine both in classics and in mathematics while at college, and Zachary Taylor each time had his 'brown coat tail' shot off at the Battle of Buena Vista. The same words appear in sketch after sketch: a 'blazing and coruscating' flash repeatedly 'went forth' from Henry Clay in 1812 to summon his countrymen to war, Polk's serious expression was often relieved 'by a peculiarly pleasant smile', Zachary Taylor was possessed of 'remarkably short legs' (and hence looked better on a horse), and Franklin Pierce was forever being presented as 'a politican of the Virginia school'. Unoriginal and repetitive, these derivative sketches had at least the virtue of presenting reasonably consistent pictures of their subjects. While northern and southern voters may have been wooed with somewhat differing impressions of a candidate's views on such measures as the Wilmot Proviso, most of the biographical sketches that appeared offered only minor variations of the image established early in the campaign. Reasons of economy probably explain this phenomenon more readily than a calculated conspiracy; plagiarism was cheap in time and money (and widely-practised in other respects in the United States, as irritated foreign writers discovered). Nevertheless, whatever the reasons, once an image of a candidate had been presented in a broadly-distributed biographical memoir, that was the image which continued to be purveyed.[4]

The creation of a political image via the printed page, then, became a major preoccupation of presidential candidates and their partisans in the second quarter of the nineteenth century. In part, clearly, this phenomenon was a response to the democratized nature of presidential elections – as the choice of president moved out of the hands of national and state legislators and into those of the people at large, candidates had to find ways of reaching a wider, indeed a mass electorate. The process was given a boost when an unconventional or untraditional candidature needed to be justified, or when the political aid of 'the people' needed to be invoked against 'the administration', as with both Andrew Jackson and William H. Harrison. The cheap publication, whether pamphlet or party press, was the most effective means of reaching a mass – and generally literate – audience. Indeed, the tradition of the Mute Tribune virtually enjoined candidates to have literary images manufactured for themselves. If convention (and political calculation) discouraged them from barnstorming through the states, addressing mass meetings and relying on friendly newspaper editors to broadcast their speeches further, they had little alternative but to reach the public through some other medium. A number of candidates, of course, did write letters for publication, but this was an inadequate and hazardous means of projection. The campaign biography was more consistent with the self-effacing role prescribed by tradition, for it was not the work of the candidate himself – ostensibly at least – and it could be presented as the unsolicited testimonial of a knowledgeable admirer. As the candidate secluded himself in his office or in his home, his literary partisans went to work; in his absence from the campaign, the image served in his stead.

The image, of course, enjoyed certain advantages over the man himself. It simplified and idealized him, tailoring him as far as possible to the expectation of a mass and highly diverse electorate. But presidential images were not empty artifices. On the contrary, they were designed to carry messages. Where a candidate's thoughtless word might ignite a storm of sectional controversy, his literary image conveyed soothing reassurances about his nationalism and commitment to the Union. It also simplified issues for the people at large. Where complex questions might be discussed with some authority in the cabinet, Congress and the weighty journals, they needed to be presented in a different form for a popular audience. By casting William H. Harrison as 'the people's candidate' or James K. Polk as 'Young Hickory', the image-makers were seeking to convey messages about executive usurpation and corruption and about the perils of a financial aristocracy. Images served to simplify and to make more intelligible the strange world of politics, and in that sense helped to provide the voter with a clearer choice. Thus they did not necessarily serve a consensual function, as is often the case today; images could also sharpen political differences. The campaign image was also used to counter opposition propaganda, as when Jackson's partisans had to refute the allegation that he was a potential military tyrant and Clay's had to defend him on the corrupt bargain charge. Further, images were designed to energize a party's supporters, so that the partisans of Polk and Pierce tried to summon the faithful to battle by invoking memories of Andrew Jackson and his war against the financial aristocracy, while the Whigs repeatedly attempted to trigger old resentments against the 'officeholders' with their succession of apolitical military heroes.

The recourse to campaign biographies and presidential image-making could be defended as necessary to the functioning of democracy. When Calhoun's friends affronted tradition by displaying him in the public prints in 1822, they coolly pointed out that in a great republic such as theirs, 'a faithful delineation of the conduct and character of living statesmen is one of the most important functions of a free press'. Power emanated from the people, yet the overwhelming majority were personally unacquainted with the leading public figures. In a mass political society, it was being implied, candidates for high office could no longer passively rest their claims on their reputations. They had to permit their friends to present them to their electoral masters.[5]

The images thus created can be examined on at least three different though interconnected levels. First there was what might be called the primary or archetypal image, the basic conception which informed virtually all the promotional portraits of this period. The images of candidates of every kind, from Andrew Jackson to Franklin Pierce, from Henry Clay to Winfield Scott, did share certain characteristics, which reveal something of what Americans sought in a president. At the other extreme was the personal or individual image, the image fashioned around, say, Martin Van Buren or Zachary Taylor, and fitted to his particular specifications. An image did have to bear some relationship to the man if it was to have any plausibility, but it could hope to lessen his blemishes and to enhance his virtues. Finally, there was the party image, for once the Democratic and Whig parties had taken coherent shape, the candidates of each tended to acquire distinctive party characteristics. They became the embodiments of their party, means by which something of the party's character (or affected character) could be projected to the public. These three types of image, the primary, the personal, and the party, each had its own function to perform and an analysis of each tells something about the political culture of *antebellum* America. The first is best examined on its own; the other two will be taken together.

The portraits which were sketched out in the biographical memoirs naturally conformed to the norms and values of the political society which gave rise to them. The images shaped around the several candidates overlapped to a surprising degree, their creators instinctively moving together in their search for the perfect presidential candidate. The images early became stereotyped as the same qualities and qualifications recurred. Out of this process there emerged the archetypal presidential candidate, an image which was created as much by the popular political culture of the period as by the writers who sought to define the aspirations of that culture. This primary image did reflect its creators' assumptions about what the public wanted, but its creators were part of that political world themselves and necessarily shared its language and values. The primary or archetypal image of the presidential candidate in some degree encapsulated this generation's conceptions of the republic and the leadership it deserved.

The idealized image was that of a republic which was still young. The candidate was everywhere and always the dedicated patriot, unstinting in the service of his country and committed above all to the novel American experiment in liberty and self-government. Whig or Democrat, soldier or civilian, the aspiring president had to be identified with the cause of the republic itself. In this sense, the patrician respect for public service lived on, though service might now be displayed in new ways. Americans were still nervously conscious of the uniqueness of their novel form of government and uncertain as to its fate. In presidential campaigns they were searching not only for a chief magistrate but for a leader for their cause.

The first qualification for a would-be president, it seemed, was a patriotic ancestry. His family need not be well-born, indeed a measure of humility was probably an advantage, but it should have made its mark in the Revolution. Andrew Jackson himself, of course, had joined the revolutionary cause as a boy soldier, though he was 'encouraged by his patriotic mother'. His successors could lay no such claim to a revolutionary career, but Martin Van Buren could boast a father who was 'a firm whig in the Revolution', William Henry Harrison was the son of a signer of the Declaration of Independence, and Zachary Taylor's father had fought alongside Monroe and attracted George Washington's attention. Lewis Cass's father managed to enlist in the revolutionary army 'the day after the battle of Lexington', but the exemplary Franklin Pierce was not to be outdone, for his father was a 17-year-old farm-boy when news of Lexington reached him, whereupon he 'immediately . . . left the plough in the furrow' and repaired to the scene of action, in time for the engagement at Bunker Hill. The ardent search for a patriotic ancestry sometimes lapsed from the ingenious to the incongruous, as when a partisan of Winfield Scott paid tribute to his candidate's Scottish grandfather for participating in the 1745 uprising against the King of England, oblivious of the fact that the '45 was an attempt to restore the Stuarts, those papist and absolutist arch villains in the rogues' gallery of Anglo-American Whiggery.[6]

Parents, indeed, were attributed an important role in shaping the characters of presidential candidates. Fathers and mothers who raised their children to respect the flag and praise the Lord were a standard feature of campaign biographies. Jackson's mother would spend the winter evenings telling her sons of the oppressions their family had suffered in Ireland, 'impressing it upon them, as a first duty, to expend their lives, if it should become necessary, in defending and supporting the natural rights of man'. William Henry Harrison had learned devotion to freedom and to his country from his distinguished father and from the other leaders of revolutionary Virginia. The early loss of his father meant that Henry Clay 'started in life with no other patrimony than a pious mother's prayers!', a potent inheritance indeed. In a remote Kentucky log cabin Zachary Taylor's mother 'instilled into the youthful minds of her sons those Christian virtues which she practised with exemplary devotedness, and in the long winter evenings . . . their father would tell them of the Revolution'. So, too, with Franklin Pierce: 'Patriotism, such as it had been in revolutionary days, was taught him by his father, as early as his mother taught him religion'. By the end of the Jacksonian era the functions of the parents of presidential candidates had become clear – the father was to bequeath a love of country and of liberty and the mother the principles of morality and religion. This conformed with the cultural patterns of the age, when politics and war were very much male prerogatives while religion was largely a female domain – as witnessed by attendance at church and revival meetings and by the assumption that women were 'naturally' religious and that their piety would help to redeem a sinful world.[7]

Patriotism and religion were often learned in living conditions which were far from comfortable. The rugged life of the frontier helped to shape too many presidential candidates, thanks partly perhaps to Andrew Jackson's towering example. While not yet 20 William H. Harrison 'abandoned' a comfortable upbringing in Virginia 'for the rude fare of a frontier camp, and exchanged his books for the sword'. Polk's family moved from North Carolina to Tennessee when James was a child, to his everlasting benefit: 'The hardy life of a western pioneer is eminently fitted to give strength of character, and the true democratic feeling.' Similarly with Taylor, 'an inmate of a humble log cabin, the character of young Zachary was formed amidst the hardships and dangers of backwoods life'. Quite apart from the strength and self-reliance which a frontier upbringing guaranteed, life in the West often invested a candidate with a special significance, because it associated him with the process by which the wilderness was replaced by civilization. Andrew Jackson was celebrated for removing Indian savages, as was William Henry Harrison, who, in addition to serving as Lieutenant-Governor of the Northwest Territory and Governor of Indiana Territory, had played a major part in securing the Land Act of 1800. This had reduced the size of the lots in which public lands were sold and enabled them to be bought on credit and Harrison's promoters made the most of it: 'Emigrants poured into the west, the population expanded, the forest gave place to smiling cultivated fields; and the great valley of the Mississippi, instead of being the haunt of the savage, has (THANKS TO HARRISON!) become the abode of millions of men PROSPEROUS, HAPPY, FREE AND INDEPENDENT.' The pioneer father of James K. Polk had helped to turn 'a wilderness' into a 'flourishing' region, which prompted the reflection that 'The magical growth of a country which was but yesterday redeemed from the sole dominion of nature, is a phenomenon of great moral and political interest.... '. Of Henry Clay it was said that 'No man has contributed more towards bringing the agricultural interests of his State, and of the Union, to perfection', while Zachary Taylor's father was 'one of the leaders of those hardy pioneers who attained such brilliant victories over their savage opponents, and the wild luxuriance of untamed nature'. Lewis Cass emigrated to the Northwestern territory at the age of 17 and shared in 'its conversion from a primitive forest to the happy abodes of civilized man'. Even the backwoods of New Hampshire had been 'almost a wilderness' when first settled by Franklin Pierce's father, who had 'contributed as much as any other man to the growth and prosperity' of the area. The archetypal presidential candidate, either directly or vicariously, had played a part in the momentous drama in which savagery was replaced by civilization, in which the forest was claimed for cultivation. He was thus identified with the cutting-edge of American destiny, with the expansion of the great experiment in republican liberty.[8]

In this historic epic the frontier gave way to the farm, and the presidential candidate was almost always identified as a farmer, or at least as of farming stock. Andrew Jackson as the 'Farmer of Tennessee' again perhaps provided the archetypal model, though William H. Harrison was probably the better Cincinnatus, laying down his arms to return to the banks of the Ohio, where 'he cultivated his farm for his support, beloved by his friends and honoured by his country'. James K. Polk's father was 'a farmer of unassuming pretensions', while his rival was celebrated in song as 'Honest Farmer Harry' and 'The Farmer of Kentucky'. Zachary Taylor had been 'reared by his father to his own profession – that of farmer', while Pierce's father, too, was 'a practical farmer..., not rich, but independent...'.[9]

The candidates derived certain essential qualities from their lives on the frontier and on the farm. John William Ward has shown how Andrew Jackson came to personify Nature for his fellow-countrymen. 'He is artificial in nothing', wrote an early admirer. 'His reading cannot be supposed to be extensive, nor his application to books very frequent.' From the 'privations and toils' consequent upon settling the wilderness, wrote a Harrison biographer, 'none were exempt'. 'It was in this school that Mr. Harrison became intimately acquainted with the character, the wants, and the wishes of his countrymen. He learned the lessons of political economy out of the great volume of human nature.' The process of subduing the wilderness, wrote an admirer of the Polk family, 'cannot fail to impress a character of strength and enterprise upon the authors and participators' of the wonderful result'. Zachary Taylor's youth was spent 'working with his own hands', laying the foundation of his 'robust health, hardy habits, and persevering industry', and 'His education . . . was necessarily limited – practical, rather than finished or classical.' It was never too late to draw virtue from the land, for a Clay partisan was ecstatic about his Hero's decision in 1842 to retire from the Senate and return to farming: 'There is a purifying influence in the cultivation of the soil, that as seldom fails to reach the heart as it does to invigorate the frame of man; and he who delights to till the ground will find himself not less favored than the fabled Anteus, to whom was given new strength and energy as often as he touched his mother earth.' From their experiences in the West and on the land the presidential candidates derived a natural wisdom, a strength of character, and a simple and virtuous morality.[10]

The sturdy natural qualities and love of freedom nurtured by life in the West, as well as an identification with the advance of American civilization, could also be demonstrated by military service, which in itself was closely associated with western expansionism at this time. A high proportion of presidential candidates were either distinguished generals like Jackson or Taylor, or had served in military campaigns like Cass or Pierce, or were prominently identified with the prosecution of a war, like Clay and Calhoun in the War of 1812. The military exploits of their subjects were dwelt on at indulgently excessive length in the campaign biographies. Andrew Jackson again provided the overpowering model of the soldier-statesman, and the sketches of his successors reproduced the features which had worked so well for the Hero: tales of courage and heroism; episodes designed to demonstrate the subject's transcendent patriotism and remarkable gifts for leading men; stories of compassion for the sick and hungry. The aspiring candidate was expected not merely to have committed deeds of bravery in the face of the enemy, but to have shared the privations of his men as well. General Harrison's troops had the utmost confidence in him, according to one improbable officer: 'They knew that if they were sick, he would see them taken care of; if wounded, they would not be left to suffer. If there was only a crust of bread, their general would share it with them.' Similarly, Zachary Taylor was depicted as bedding down with his men in the mud and rain, Lewis Cass as giving up his horse to a sick private, Franklin Pierce as sharing his water ration and his private funds with his men in Mexico. Military service afforded an opportunity to display humanity as well as heroism, an empathy for the common man as well as a self-sacrificing love of country.[11]

As the lyrical descriptions of rugged childhoods on the frontier and courageous acts on the field of battle helped to emphasize, the archetypal candidate enjoyed few privileges of wealth or birth. Like Jackson, he was a self-made man. Jackson as a youth had inherited a small estate from his father, but his impulsive generosity had soon scattered it, 'which threw him at once upon the resources of his own mind, and compelled him to become the architect of his own fortunes'. Martin Van Buren, too, had been 'Thrown upon the resources of his own industry' at an early age: 'Humble and poor; ... having no patronage of connexions or friends, and born in a country village, but possessing sound principles, pure morals, and an upright heart.' Even Harrison, the scion of Virginia gentry, was said to have 'inherited from his father little save his noble example' and hence was 'Dependent on his own exertions ... '. It was possible indeed to be a second-generation self-made man, as was James K. Polk, a 'self-made American' who had inherited his father's capacity to be the architect of his own fortune. Henry Clay, of course, was celebrated as the quintessential self-made man, to whom 'the "bar of poverty" ... was regarded merely as a difficulty over which he was, OF COURSE, to achieve a triumph'. Even Winfield Scott, whose biographers encountered problems in forcing him into the archetypal mould, made his own fortune in that his father died young and Winfield 'came into the world the hardy child of difficulty and fortitude, and no nursling of ease and indulgence'.[12]

Once the candidate had made his own life he devoted it selflessly to his country. Every presidential aspirant was a transcendent patriot who would die for the cause of liberty. The very act of enlisting in the army was invariably attributed to the surging patriotic emotion felt by every true American when his country met danger, as when Jackson, 'an intrepid and ardent boy', joined the revolutionary army at the age of 14, when both Zachary Taylor and Winfield Scott were allegedly moved to enlist by the outrage they felt over the *Chesapeake* affair, and when the outbreak of the Mexican War induced Franklin Pierce to leave his family retreat and sign on as a private. The civilians among the presidential candidates exhibited the same ardent love of country in the legislative chambers. Van Buren, living down a vote for Clinton in 1812, was depicted as an energetic supporter of the War of 1812, while Henry Clay was no less than 'the guiding genius of the conflict, which ended, not less by his instrumentality, for the honor and enduring good of the republic'.[13]

The patriotism of the archetypal candidate was compounded of a love of liberty and a devotion to the Union. In his youth among Virginia's revolutionary leaders, William H. Harrison 'imbibed that devotion to freedom and his country which has since ranked his name among the most illustrious of America's champions'. As evidence of Clay's commitment to liberty his admirers cited his early support for the gradual emancipation of slavery in Kentucky, his denunciation of the Alien and Sedition Acts, and his part in the War of 1812, which placed him 'in that scroll where Freedom inscribes the names of her worthiest champions... '. Similarly, Clay's American System and his role in the compromises of 1820 and 1833 showed that 'His noble heart throbbed with the highest love for every portion of the Union.' Harrison had held civil as well as military offices, and in them 'his views were at once national and deeply imbued with the love of liberty'. The principles of nationalism and freedom became identical in the war against Mexico, which Pierce joined because he 'believed that it was the destiny of the American people to extend the empire of republican principles throughout the western world'.[14]

The primary or archetypal candidate, then, was the quintessential American republican: self-reliant and self-made, a transcendent patriot, a staunch nationalist, a champion of human liberty. As befitted an American republican too, he was close to the people, simple and unaffected in his ways. 'The ease and frankness of his manners', said a biographer of Martin Van Buren, 'his felicitous powers of conversation, and the general amiableness of his feelings, render him the ornament of the social circle'. The Whigs praised Harrison for accepting a humble county clerkship after he had retired from the service of his country, proof of his self-effacing character and his determination to support his family through honest labour. 'Frugal and simple in his personal habits', it was said of Polk, 'he has been anxious that the same great republican virtues should pervade the administration of the affairs of state.' Like Andrew Jackson, 'he had little affection for the fopperies of public station and the cozening subtleties of diplomacy'. Zachary Taylor had had little opportunity to display his simple republicanism in civil life, but his military victories revealed him to be 'great in all those republican characteristics, those virtues, at once homely and lofty, unpretending yet impressive, natural yet heroic, which... go to form the truest pattern of an American citizen... '. In the presidential candidate, a love of country blended with an empathy with the people. As Jackson had demonstrated, in the American republic the guardian of freedom needed the common touch.[15]

The image of the archetypal candidate was tailored to the expectations of *antebellum* Americans. In placing someone in the White House, commented Abiel Abbott Livermore, 'We virtually . . . say by such an act, *that* is our highest ideal of what a great and good man is; *that* is the American man.' The idealized candidate was in large part shaped by the hopes and fears that Americans had for the republic. He was evidently closely identified with the American mission itself. His ancestry was patriotic, illustrated frequently by a father who had enlisted in the revolutionary cause. From his father he had imbibed a love of liberty and of country, and from his mother he had learned the principles of virtue and religion. The life of the farm and the frontier had continued to shape his American character. This experience had served to identify him with the American cause, with replacing barbarism with civilization, it had given him courage and strength, it had taught him a natural wisdom, and it had helped to endow him with humanity and a simple code of morality. Participation in a patriotic war further served to identify him with the great experiment in liberty and further developed these manly yet homely qualities. These were the qualities needed to make his own way in the world, and the archetypal candidate was the unquestioned architect of his own fortune. Thrown onto his own resources, he was the supreme American individual, beholden to no one and owing his achievements entirely to his own talents and will-power. The candidate's self-reliance was underlined by an otherwise curious omission from the biographical sketches – there was rarely any mention of his wife or children, and pictorial representations invariably showed him standing alone. Yet beyond himself, he recognized a larger duty to his country, and he was prepared to risk his all for the liberty and Union he so revered. He was indeed an embodiment of his country, his unpretentious ways serving as a reminder that this was a people's republic.[16]

The man who occupied the White House was the Chief Magistrate of the republic, and as such was invested with great symbolic significance. He was the young nation's representative to the outside world, as he was the first servant of the people and the guardian of their liberties. The primary image of the presidential candidate encapsulated the ideals of mid-nineteenth century America, which was still conscious of the distinctiveness of the republican experiment, with its commitment to liberty and equality, with the strength, vigour and virtue it acquired from its closeness to nature, with its capacity to nurture self-reliance and self-government. But the republic, while distinctive, was still young, and the archetypal image seemed also to betray a fear that the republican mission could still go astray. The very strength of the identification of the candidate with the cause of the republic suggested that Americans were still seeking a leader, someone who would spring to the defence of the republic when it was in peril. It is little wonder that Cincinnatus was invoked at every opportunity. While the Cincinnatus figure was in large part created initially to counter the Caesar image, non-military candidates were also cast in the Cincinnatus mould. Even the unlikely nomination of that darkest of dark horses, Franklin Pierce, seemed to one biographer to recall the occasion when 'the ROMAN SENATE laid aside their quarrels, and buried their factions, which were tearing the state to pieces . . . ' and called the 'plain old farmer' from his plough. The time had apparently come when the American republic, nearly ruined with a surfeit of 'statesmanship, and demagoguism', had need of the services of its own Cincinnatus from New Hampshire. The ever-imperilled American republic as always needed a saviour, and one who would retire once more to his plough when the danger was passed. In the archetypal presidential candidate, Americans were offered a symbol of reassurance, a quintessential American in whose hands the great republican experiment would be safe.[17]

Complementing the primary or archetypal image of the candidate were the personal and party images. From the 1830s, as contests for the presidency effectively became contests between the champions of the two major parties, there emerged both Whig and Democratic versions of the ideal presidential candidate. The respective parties sought to communicate something about themselves through the medium of their candidates. The presidential candidate in no small measure came to embody the character of his party, at least as party publicists wanted the electorate to perceive it. But each candidate was also provided with his personal image, with a portrait which conformed to the known facts of his life and career, which drew attention to his merits and achievements and which disguised or explained away his weaknesses. The personal and party images are not easily separable, and the former may be used to illustrate the latter.

Old Hickory inevitably cast his long shadow over his Democratic successors, and one feature of the Democratic variations of the presidential candidate was the constant evocation of the spirit of Andrew

Jackson. Yet in one important respect Jackson's successors emphatically departed from his example. They were not military heroes. While Jackson's military glory had helped the Democratic party to win a narrow ascendancy in the nation at large, once its organization was complete it avoided harnessing its fortunes to such mythic figures. Occasionally a colourful military man or frontiersman offered his services, such as Sam Houston of Texas or Joseph Lane of Oregon, both of whom could have been cast in Jackson's heroic mould, but the Democrats preferred loyal party servants as their flagbearers.

Unlike their Whig opponents, the Democrats never played down the party identification of their nominee. On the contrary, they made it clear that their candidate was a true Democrat, committed to Democratic doctrines, as he was able to demonstrate by many faithful years in the party's service. Of course, he partook of the characteristics of the archetypal candidate, sharing a patriotic ancestry, a practical wisdom and a humble demeanour. But in addition to being an authentic republican, he was a Democrat too.

Andrew Jackson was not a typical Democrat, but Martin Van Buren was. In a sense, Van Buren's presidential candidacy was more of a break with the past than Jackson's, for Jackson at least had served his country outstandingly on the battlefield, while Van Buren had little to commend him beyond his party services. He had served briefly as secretary of state, his critics would say without distinction, and his elevation to the vice-presidency had been for reasons of party politics. He had originated no distinguished pieces of legislation, had been the author of no great principles or measures, and was not even a competent orator. More than any previous presidential candidate he was the creation of a party. This point was not missed by his enemies, and, as his biographers ruefully observed, probably no other figure in American public life encountered as much animus. 'At an early age, they selected him as a subject of perpetual and virulent abuse', complained William Emmons, 'and for nearly twenty years, this abuse was persisted in, to a degree rarely paralleled, and never surpassed, in the history of our politics.' Emmons and others were inclined to attribute this hostility to Van Buren's lack of wealth and social standing, and there may have been an element of truth in this explanation, for those conservatives who regretted the passing of the old order were inclined to see Van Buren as the personification of the new style of party politics. Party rather than public service had raised him from obscurity.[18]

Van Buren's promoters, then, had to put across a candidate who

lacked the traditional qualifications, who was regarded as the creature of Andrew Jackson, and who had a reputation for non-
committalism. They sensibly avoided the temptation to present him
as a statesman, and cast him instead as the agent of democracy. (It
was implied that the Democratic party embraced the whole people.)
The candidate was introduced as of humble beginnings, 'not indebt-
ed for his eminence to the wealth or distinction of his family.' He
had been reared as a 'democrat' by his democratic father, in a county dominated by well-to-do Federalists, whose enmity he earned by
refusing to seek their patronage. Once in politics he proved a faithful
Jeffersonian and Jacksonian, the one embarrassment in his career
being his vote for De Witt Clinton in 1812. Even this was turned
into a virtue – Van Buren was simply said to be acting as a regular
New York Republican, a loyal party man. Thereafter he is depicted
as a true strict constructionist, an opponent of the Maysville Road
and the Bank and an unwavering Democrat. Van Buren, it was said,
possessed 'the good fortune to reflect as in a mirror, the sentiment
and spirit of the nation and the epoch'. The charge that he was the
blind tool of party originated with those who had no feeling for the
mass of their fellow men. Thus Van Buren was projected as an unpretentious but persevering man who had made his own way in the
world against great odds, a life-long Democrat who had devoted his
energies to the party and hence to the people. The quality of his
mind was not stressed and relatively little was said about his public
services. Candidate Van Buren was the reliable agent of the (Democratic) people.[19]

The formula used for Van Buren was employed with variations
for other Democratic candidates. One of its advantages was that it
did not require the candidate to be well-known. Indeed, a degree of
obscurity aided the identification with the democratic people, for it
made the candidate one of them. This was the case with James K.
Polk, who was projected as a plain Jeffersonian republican, a hard-
working Democrat of the old school who remained close to plain
folks. His biographers paid the customary homage to the revolutionary services and Jeffersonian heritage of his family and to his father's
civilizing efforts on the Tennessee frontier. James K. himself was
introduced as an able and assiduous scholar, his 'ambition to excel'
being 'equalled by his perseverance alone'. He resisted his father's
encouragement to become a merchant, the budding Jacksonian
finding the business life uncongenial to his tastes, and eventually
embarked on a political career in which he displayed himself as 'a
republican of the "straitest sect"'. 'He has ever regarded the Con-

stitution of the United States as an instrument of specific and limited powers', it was said, 'and that doctrine is at the very foundation of the democratic creed.' Much was made of his friendship with Jackson, and he was shown to have adopted a true Democratic course on the issues of the Jackson presidency, even to the extent of standing by Van Buren in 1835–36, when many Tennessee Democrats deserted to White. 'A self-made American', it was said of him, 'his sympathies have been at all times with the humble, the enterprising and the patriotic.' Polk's publicists seemed unconcerned about his relative obscurity and left unmentioned his recent defeats for governor. They presented him as an Old Republican of the school of Jefferson and Jackson, a self-made, hard-working, strict constructionist Democrat. 'On every measure in Congress, Mr. Polk took strong democratic ground', the party faithful were assured. This was 'Young Hickory', a kind of mixture of Andrew Jackson and Martin Van Buren, with the former's frontier heritage and simple ways and the latter's perseverance and party attachment. 'Duty' and 'integrity' were favourite Democratic words, suggesting as they did something of the stern republican virtues of the Founding Fathers. 'Upon several emergencies, when the current of popular opinion threatened to overwhelm him', it was said of Polk, 'he has sternly adhered to the convictions of duty, preferring to sink with his principles, rather than rise with their abandonment.'[20]

The personal images of Van Buren and Polk shaded into the party image of the Democratic candidate. The Democratic flagbearers from Van Buren to Pierce (and beyond) shared distinctive characteristics. While the archetypal image of the presidential candidate shimmered behind them all, and while each needed a persuasive image of his own, each also contibuted to a kind of composite image of the idealized Democrat. The party image was a reflection of the party itself, and, as has been suggested in the preceding sketches, the Democratic candidate was very much the faithful party servant.

A Democratic variation on the theme of a patriotic heritage was an Irish ancestry. A Scotch–Irish family was usually represented as pure Irish, as likely as not the sufferers of British oppression, though it is not clear whether this was the result of an inability to distinguish between varieties of Irishmen or of a calculated bid for Irish Catholic support. Jackson himself was apt to be presented as of Irish descent, as were James K. Polk and Franklin Pierce (with very little justification in this last case). The identification of the Democratic party with the Irish was thus early made. An Irish ancestry in the candidate managed to suggest both a centuries-old enmity for the hated

British and that he was a deserving and safe recipient for Irish votes.[21]

But whether or not he was of Irish descent, the Democratic nominee was invariably a life-long Democrat. His political principles had been instilled in him in childhood and hardened by his own convictions as he grew older. For their early candidates, of course, the Democrats had to assume a continuity from Jeffersonianism to Jacksonianism. Hence Martin Van Buren's father was represented as 'a democrat in the days of John Adams' and Polk's father, too, was 'a warm supporter of Mr. Jefferson'. Their sons, as we have seen, subsequently gave their unstinting loyalty to the Democratic cause. Lewis Cass, too, was presented as 'in every sense of the word a Democrat', while Franklin Pierce had the great good fortune to be the son of a Democratic governor of New Hampshire, who was reassuringly said to have had 'a rigid, honest looking face, resembling to a degree, the best portraits of Gen. Jackson'. Aristocrats were fond of tracing their ancestry, remarked another Pierce biographer, but to the '*true* Republican' a Democratic ancestry was a far prouder possession: 'Frank Pierce . . . inherited Democracy with his birth – it flows in his blood – it has spoken in every act of his life – it has tinged and shaped his whole character.' Needless to say, Pierce, like his predecessors, loyally supported the Democratic administrations at state and national levels, and 'So true was he to the democratic cause', it was said of his performance in Congress in the Jackson years, '. . . that the president became warmly attached to him, and often invited him to his fireside and hospitable board.'[22]

To this generation of Americans the Democratic cause was the Jacksonian cause, and the blessing of Old Hickory was frequently sought for the party's nominee. Van Buren's debt to Andrew Jackson was so well-known as to be a liability, and his promoters were obliged to emphasize that their candidate was the free choice of the party and of the people. Polk's Tennessee origins also placed him close to Old Hickory, whose initial entry into presidential politics was partly credited to Polk, who himself could be likened to 'his admirable friend Andrew Jackson'. Lewis Cass stumped for Polk in Tennessee in 1844 and was careful to spend some time at the Hermitage with the elderly general, and when they parted 'the tears of the veterans were mingled together as they bade each other a last farewell'. Nathaniel Hawthorne even managed to wring a death-bed benediction out of Old Hickory, a visitor to the dying patriarch reporting that 'the old hero spoke with energy of Franklin Pierce's ability and patriotism, and remarked, as if with prophetic foresight of his young friend's destiny, that "the interests of the country would be safe in such hands"'. As Lafayette's approval during his visit to the United States in 1824–25 was taken as evidence that the republic was remaining true to the faith of the Fathers, so Andrew Jackson's blessing was proof of the fidelity of the party's candidate to the Democratic cause.[23]

The Democratic candidate further demonstrated his party commitment through his political philosophy, which was invariably built around the strict constructionist core of the Jeffersonian – Jacksonian tradition. Andrew Jackson himself in 1832 was lauded for his Maysville Road and Bank vetoes. Extracts from Van Buren's speeches were published to show his soundness on such issues, and in his own term in the White House he 'kept the old republican track manfully and fearlessly'. James K. Polk 'Of course' had always been 'a strict constructionist, repudiating, above all things, the latitudinarian interpretations of federalism . . . .' Lewis Cass, who sought the support of the expansionist and commercial interests in the Democratic party, was a little more ambiguous in his political faith, but he was careful to avow himself 'against a national bank, opposed to the distribution of the proceeds of the public lands, opposed to a tariff for protection' and in favour of keeping the revenue 'to the lowest point compatible with the performance of its constitutional functions'. More reassuring were the speeches and votes of Franklin Pierce, which 'present him as a politician of the Virginia school, in favor of an economical administration of the general government, of a strict construction of the constitution, and as a republican of the Jeffersonian cast'.[24]

The quintessential Democratic candidate, then, had been born and bred a Democrat, had fought staunchly for the party's measures, had won the approbation of Old Hickory himself, and was a strict constructionist of the Old Republican school. He had also made his own way in the world, albeit within the virtuous confines of the Democratic party. An iron will, perseverance, determination – these were the qualities frequently ascribed to the rising Democratic politicos. Unlike their Whig opponents, it was not normally suggested that they possessed exceptional intellectual powers or outstanding talents. As with Jackson, it was will-power which drove them on.

If Jackson himself had been projected as a larger-than-life (though human) figure, his successors were depicted as rather ordinary mortals who turned themselves into self-made men through doggedness rather than brilliance. Much was made of Van Buren's early career, when he had obstinately resisted the wiles of his richer and more powerful Federalist neighbours and triumphed against the odds. The young Polk displayed many of the same qualities of determination at college, where he graduated first in his class, though not apparently because of exceptional native wit. 'His course . . . was marked by the same assiduity and studious application which have since characterized him', it was reported; indeed, such was his perseverance that 'he never missed a recitation, nor omitted the punctilious performance of any duty'. Nathaniel Hawthorne cannily appended to his biography of Pierce an anecdote of how Frank as a student had been at the bottom of his class in his junior year. Then, eventually taking hold of himself, he had risen at 4 a.m. each day and worked until midnight and finally graduated third in his class. 'The moral of this little story lies in the stern and continued exercise of self-controlling will, which redeemed him from indolence, completely changed the aspect of his character, and made this the turning point of his life.' It was will-power, not birth, wealth or intellect, which was the key to Democratic success. There was a strong anti-élitist streak in the Democratic ethic. The Democratic party prized industry above genius.[25]

Industry and perseverance might be possessed by anyone, and through its presidential candidate the party was stressing its identification with the ordinary man. Its egalitarianism was also attested by its emphasis on service, another quality the Democrats greatly prized. If the people were the best judges of the public interest, as Democrats liked to say, then the function of the party was reduced to translating the will of the majority into government action. In this perspective a Democratic president was a servant rather than a leader, dutifully carrying out the wishes of his electoral masters. A lifetime spent loyally in the service of the Democratic party, then, was a powerful qualification for a presidential aspirant. The Democratic party, said Van Buren's biographer, wanted 'agents who will execute their will and not dictators to control it'. Another biographer countered the charge that Van Buren was a master of intrigue with the argument that he saw it as his duty to reflect the popular will, and that he possessed 'in an eminent degree the talent of harmonizing, concentrating and directing the feelings and exertions of those with whom he acts'. The agent of the people rapidly became the servant of party, particularly since that party saw itself as encompassing the whole people, and the partisans of later candidates stressed their subjects' faithful and constant devotion to the party cause. Franklin Pierce, for example, 'stood by Gen. Jackson from the first to the last hour of his administration. When others deserted him, Pierce alone clung to him closer'. The Democrats – unlike their opponents –

accepted no shame in identifying their champions with party measures. 'It is true that, despising the cant of *no party*, which has ever been the pretext of selfish and treacherous politicians, and convinced that in a popular government nothing can be accomplished by isolated action', it was said of Polk, 'he has always acted with his party, as far as principle would justify.' The Democratic flagbearer was above all a regular and reliable party man, a plain man of humble origins who had made his own way in life through hard work and an iron will, and who as president would conscientiously serve his country as the humble instrument of the people.[26]

This was the image that the Democrats projected of their nominee, and it was their own image of their party character. They did not distinguish very clearly between 'the Democracy', as their party was known, and 'the democracy', deliberately implying that they were the party of the people and that their rivals were aristocrats. Like their candidate, they were plain folks. Franklin Pierce, it was said, 'lives (just as a man ought to live, before he is nominated for the Presidency of a great Republic,) in a small white house, near Main street, in Concord'. Yet this very identification with the people gave the Democratic party an extraordinary potency. The people, after all, had the capacity for self-government in them, had the capacity to triumph against aristocratic cabals or other obstacles to the full exercise of their liberty. As the Democratic candidate demonstrated, all they required was an unwavering determination, the perseverance to see a thing through. By the exercise of will they could be the masters of their own destiny. The Democratic party was to be the vehicle of their will, and as such party officers became the servants of the people, their agents rather than their leaders. Ultimately, the Democrats prized qualities which were – or could be – common to all men, qualities which the people at large could use to master the privileged classes. By enlisting in that brotherhood of equals, the Democratic party, the people would ensure that the majority would rule.[27]

But there was also an agrarian colouring to Democratic radicalism. The party which represented the body of the people was also the party of Jefferson and Jackson, under whose presidencies the majority had clearly repudiated the designs of the monied aristocracy. At heart, it seemed, the people were strict constructionists, for governmental activity was a cloak for the commercial interests and represented a threat to states' rights and individual liberty. There was a strong streak of Old Republicanism in the Democrats' self-image, an invocation of the stern virtues and the republican simplicity of an earlier day. This, it was assumed, was what the people wanted, and the Democratic party was held to be the only safe repository of their hopes. The Democratic party did not shrink from proclaiming its party principles, for ultimately the party was a patriotic association, dedicated to pursuing the true republican mission – which seems ideally to have required a society of independent, equal and self-reliant producers, whether on the farm or in the workshop, and honest professional men.

The Whig party, too, had its own idea of what its presidential candidates should be like. The Whigs shared with the Democrats a preference for candidates possessed of some sort of revolutionary heritage, self-made men who had known something of the life of the frontier or the farm, liberty-loving patriots who had fought for their country. But they did not share the Democrats' enthusiasm for faithful party servants. The Whig heroes tended to be men of some *éclat*, men possessed of a degree of military genius or exceptional powers of mind. Like the Father of his Country himself, they were men who revered the civil constitution, who rose massively above party or sectional considerations, moral and humane men who were reluctantly prepared when called to put their considerable talents to the service of their country. In its gifted candidates the Whig party was groping for a definition of its own character.

The personal image of particular candidates blended into the party image projected by the Whigs, and before examining the Whig image as such two examples may be taken for illustration. Henry Clay was a perennial Whig hopeful. He was the National Republican candidate in 1832, although he won the formal Whig nomination only once, in 1844. But he was clearly the leading figure in the party and was celebrated as 'the embodiment of Whig principles'. More often, as we have seen, the Whigs took a military hero as their nominee, and although William H. Harrison was the first of these Zachary Taylor might be taken as the more representative. Certainly his career was more exclusively military than that of any presidential candidate.

Henry Clay was the candidate as self-made statesman, a man of humble origins but with talents which marked him out from other men. Educated in 'a log schoolhouse', as a youth he 'ploughed in the cornfields, many a summer day, without shoes, and with no other clothes on than a pair of Osnaburg trousers and a coarse shirt'. Clay's transition from such an inauspicious beginning to first statesman of his age never failed to move his biographers: 'The spectacle of the boy working "barefooted" for his mother, touches all hearts;

and when that boy, in riper years, is seen toiling through a like career for his country, the mother of us all, he obeys the instincts, and fulfils the high destiny of his filial piety.' It was, of course, his soaring genius that carried him thus far. 'He was as a general-in-chief over the intellectual power of the country', it was said of his role in the War of 1812, 'and the breath of his mouth moved over it as the wind of heaven sways the forests of an unbroken wilderness.' His vision and nationalism were further affirmed by his role in the compromises of 1820 and 1833 and by his authorship of the American System. Attention was drawn to his refusal of cabinet places under Madison and Monroe, presumably in part to refute the corrupt bargain charge which designated him as an unprincipled office-seeker, but also perhaps to suggest that in good Whig fashion he preferred a seat in Congress, 'with the questions of internal improvement and the Tariff pending. . . . He preferred usefulness to place.' Clay, then, was a humble-born but liberty-loving patriot whose genius had taken him from the backwoods to the highest councils of the nation. Unlike most presidential candidates he was also a man of measures, as his American System made clear. There was little mention of party in the Clay biographies, and he owed his rise to his own talents rather than to party services. Henry Clay, it was confidently averred, 'confessedly the first Statesman of the Nation, and whom posterity will place by the side of the Father of his Country, when recounting the deeds of her purist benefactors, is, emphatically, the architect of his own fortune and fame'.[28]

If Clay was the candidate as statesman, Zachary Taylor was the candidate as military hero. As usual, Taylor's life began with his patriotic ancestors, with a father who had fought with Washington and had helped to subdue the West, and young Zachary grew up 'amid the danger and toil of a frontier life'. His youthful patriotism took him into the army, and there he displayed his courage and, more importantly, his genius, for on the battlefield he seemed repeatedly to be faced with forces larger than his own. One instructive example was the Battle of Buena Vista:

Thus was the greatest battle on record, perhaps, gained by less than five thousand troops, nearly all of them volunteers, against twenty-one thousand – a well-appointed and well-disciplined army. . . . The odds were frightful, and at times the stoutest hearts quailed; but whenever his form was seen amid the roar and shock of battle, hope came back and their spirits rose; for such was the moral power of his name, and such the confidence of his men in General TAYLOR, that so long as he was safe, all felt 'there was no such word as fail'.

But if he was an exceptional leader of men on the battlefield, he was not disposed to arrogate power to himself. As with other Whig military heroes, much was made of Taylor's law-abiding nature and his willingness to yield as president to the will of Congress. President Polk had plunged the country into war 'by his own will' and successive Democratic administrations had undone the laws of Congress by the perverse use of the veto, it was said, but Taylor's Allison letter showed that 'if elected, his purpose is to leave Congress to settle questions of domestic policy, and to circumscribe the Executive power to the limits assigned to it by the Constitution'. Like other military candidates, too, he was represented as above party and as of the people. And, of course, Taylor was presented as 'Old Rough-and-Ready', a kindly, simple and wise old soldier who avoided punishing deserters with death, a respecter of the Sabbath and a strict teetotaller, a figure who could be compared not unfavourably with George Washington himself. Little was said about his political beliefs, save his respect for the Constitution and for Congress. Rather, Taylor was projected as a military hero, a soldier of genius who regularly triumphed over great odds and greater numbers, a patriot above section and party, a second Washington. He was no less than 'an American Cincinnatus', and in 'the hour of peril' his countrymen were sending for him 'in his tranquil home, to offer him the chief command of the Republic'.[29]

The images of Clay and Taylor illustrate several of the features the Whigs expected of their candidates. Both were men of distinction, if in different ways. Their purely party attributes were played down, and they were presented as good-hearted patriots who rose above factional and particularist interests. Where the Democrats unashamedly identified their candidate with the people, the Whigs (except to the extent that a military hero would be pitted as the people's champion against the spoilsmen) tended to identify theirs with the nation. As a patriot, the Whig candidate had a great respect for the Constitution, not in the strict constructionist sense of the Democrats but as an instrument of law and order. His constitutionalism led him to disavow the lawless behaviour of Democratic executives and to acknowledge the right of Congress to legislate for the common weal. The Whigs had a somewhat different conception of the function of the president from the Democrats, as the examples of Clay and Taylor to some extent have indicated and as a fuller analysis of the Whig candidate will show.

The Whig candidate, like the Democratic, was a self-made man, but whereas his rival had made his mark through perseverance and·

industry, it was great talent which had carried the Whig candidate to the heights. Clay, as we have seen, was credited with a mind of the highest order, an intellect which 'can wrestle upon earth, or soar upward to the eagle's home of storms'. He was gifted in other ways, too, for 'Every instinct of his heart bears the stamp of a lofty nature.' A lofty nature was commonplace among Whig candidates. William H. Harrison was chiefly known for his military victories, but his friends denied that they rested his claims on 'the glory of his military renown, brilliant though it be'. Mention was made of his part in the Land Act of 1800 and of his governorship of Indiana territory and of 'the brilliant qualities which distinguish him as a Warrior, a Civilian, and a Statesman'. Zachary Taylor could only plausibly be hailed for his military talents, but these were held to be truly extraordinary. 'At periods of great peril, when the nation held its breath, and when discomfiture and ruin seemed inevitable', went one account, 'the genius of Taylor immerged from the gloom, and relieved the country from apprehensions of disaster and disgrace'. Winfield Scott, too, could be offered as a Whig nominee because he combined 'the fame of a warrior' with 'the glory of a peacemaker'.[30]

With exceptional talents went a patriotic disdain for partisan considerations. As we have seen, this was one of the attractions of the military hero, who appealed to the antiparty streak in Whiggery. Thus it was promised that Harrison as president would 'subdue that baneful spirit of party animosity, which has made the state a political gambling board'. It was difficult to make the same claim for Henry Clay, though much was said about his lack of bigotry and his lifelong devotion 'with single-hearted, unselfish earnestness to the best good of his country'. Zachary Taylor's ambiguous views on party have been amply adverted to. Even Winfield Scott, who had flirted with the Whig party for years, was held to transcend mere party considerations. 'We consider it a strong circumstance in favor of General Scott, that he has not mingled at all in the bitter party strife which has characterized in a marked degree the political movements of the country for many years,' argued one apologist rather weakly. 'He will, therefore, come into the Presidency . . . with his heart uncontaminated, his feelings unblunted, and his views unwarped by faction and all its miserable expedients.'[31]

If the Whigs played down the party identification of their candidates, they also said little about their political views. A man without a party was also a man without measures. Henry Clay was necessarily something of an exception to this, as was the Whig platform of 1844, which possessed rather more specific content than was usual with the Whigs. But while he might be vague about policies, the quintessential Whig candidate did respect the law, the Constitution and Congress. This was a conservative affirmation of the rule of law rather than the Democrats' Old Republican interpretation of the Constitution. 'Although a brave and successful commander,' said one reviewer of Harrison's military career, '*no man can accuse him of one disobedience to the laws, or one violation of the constitution of his country.*' The errant Jackson was not mentioned by name, but his high-handed deeds, as a commanding general and as president, were clearly in mind. The Whig respect for law and the Constitution shaded into the party's opposition to executive usurpation. Henry Clay's youthful hostility to the Alien and Sedition Acts was ingeniously related to his later resistance to Jackson's arbitrary ways: 'Where can be found, in this broad land, a more vigilant sentinel of popular rights, or a more faithful denouncer of Executive usurpations, and the abuses of Executive power?' An incident in the Mexican War, when to his chagrin Zachary Taylor was superseded by Winfield Scott, was cited to establish the former's 'ready and uncompromising obedience to the civil authorities in this most trying and mortifying circumstance', and, of course, it was assured that under a Taylor presidency members of Congress would not become 'the cringing slaves of Executive power'. Winfield Scott was held to be a profound student of the Constitution and of the laws of nations, and his partisans promised that he, too, would confine the federal government to its rightful powers. If the Whig candidates were men of genius, they were not to be given much opportunity to show it in the White House. Other than in the Clay campaigns, the Whigs paid less attention to American System measures than to the issue of the balance between the executive and the legislature in their promotion of their candidates. The typical Whig candidate was not committed to any policies or 'pledges', but he did promise to restore to the people the liberty they had lost as a result of the lawless depredations of the Democratic presidents.[32]

Yet Whig nominees were saved from a literal-minded enforcement of the law by their essential humanity. They were, it seems, charitable men, free of the vindictive impulses which implicitly disgraced the Democrats. An occasion when General Harrison pardoned a black deserter who was suspected of plotting his assassination was said to show 'a heart warm with the finest feelings of humanity, and is in consonance with the whole tenor of his life, in which we find no act of irascible precipitation, military violence, or selfish revenge'. It was rather pointedly added that during his whole term of service Harrison had never caused a militia soldier to be punished. Henry Clay's law career was cited as proof of his generosity of spirit, for it was said that he preferred to defend than to prosecute, that none of his clients ever went to the gallows, and that he was always prepared to represent those who could not pay for his services. Zachary Taylor's biographies were replete with anecdotes of his benevolence, and of Scott it was said that 'he had sought by acts of charity and kindness towards the Cherokees, to efface some little of that hard fate by which they had been driven from their homes'. In a sense, the humanity of the Whig candidate was a natural accompaniment to his stature. With greatness went obligation – *noblesse oblige* – and the Whig emphasis on their candidate's benevolence tended to betray his patrician nature.[33]

There was also a hint of an evangelical as well as a patrician basis to the benevolence of the Whig candidate. He was frequently credited with the somewhat puritanical moral code associated with many Whig voters. As a young officer Harrison had resisted the lure of drink 'and laid the foundation of those habits of temperance, which have characterized him through a long life'. Even during the hard cider campaign of 1840 the vigour of the ageing Harrison was attributed to 'the effects of habitual activity and temperance'. Henry Clay in 1844 was somewhat incredibly represented as a convert to the causes of anti-duelling and anti-gambling. Zachary Taylor's rough-and-ready qualities did not take him into the tap-room, it seems, for he was reported to be a strict teetotaller and a friend of the Sabbath and public worship. With splendid foresight Winfield Scott in 1821 had published an essay entitled a 'Scheme for Restricting the Use of Ardent Spirits in the United States', which was reprinted in his principal 1852 biography. There was no doubt an element of calculation in these attempts to attribute a virtuous morality to their candidate, for in many areas the Whigs looked to the votes of the more evangelical Protestant sects.[34]

The essential Whig candidate, then, was a man of truly exceptional talents, a patriot whose lofty views transcended party and section, a military hero perhaps but in any case a profound admirer of the law, the Constitution and Congress, and a humane man possessed of sound religious and moral principles. This image bore a noted resemblance to the popular view of George Washington (who may have liked a drink but not as recorded by Parson Weems). The first president would have been the ideal Whig candidate, and the Whig nominees were repeatedly likened to him. William Henry Harrison was apparently 'universally known' as 'the Washington of the West'

Henry Clay's lack of a military career made comparisons with Washington more difficult, but his splendid patriotic record placed him 'by the side of the Father of his Country'. There could be no doubt about Taylor's claims: 'The life of this distinguished hero, who has led the armies of his country to a series of triumphs unparalleled in the annals of warfare, will occupy a place beside that of our immortal Washington, whom, in clear-sighted sagacity, judgment, and decision, in perfect self-possession, unassuming merit, and brilliancy of genius, he so much resembles.' If Democratic candidates proved that they were true men of the people by their association with Jackson, Whig candidates derived an authenticated patriotism from their identification with Washington. The Whigs seemed to hanker after an orderly republic held together by the patriotic selflessness of the Founding Fathers.[35]

Such was the Whig character as projected through the images of the party's presidential candidates. The Whigs did seek to identify themselves with 'the people', especially when they were running a military hero as an opposition candidate, but it was patriotism rather than egalitarianism which they invoked most forcibly. The Whig party, it seemed to be implied, was the embodiment of patriotic principles, a genuinely nationalist phenomenon with the capacity to rise above partial, particularist and self-interested views. As such, it was scarcely a party, and the Whigs played down the purely party associations of their candidates, as they said little about what policies they might follow in government. Where the Whigs did associate themselves with political viewpoints, as in their deference to the authority of Congress, those views again tended to reinforce their anti-party character. They were suggesting that the Democratic presidents' use of the veto and of the spoils system had been for narrowly partisan purposes. The Whigs would have liked to have thought of themselves as above mere politics. There was thus an element of nostalgia in the Whig character, an assumption that public affairs should be entrusted to statesmanlike figures, as in the days of old. This rather patrician impulse in Whiggery was reinforced by an evangelical impulse which cast the party as one of religion and morality. Again, this seemed to betray a distaste for mere politics, a suggestion that the manoeuvrings of party were tiresome distractions to the holier cause of achieving the good society. The Whigs were appropriating to themselves the qualities of patriotism, talent and virtue, and implicitly denying those attributes to their opponents.

Despite the hullabaloo of Whig campaigns, the party's self-image revealed a highly conservative character. Their above-party stance was grounded on a holistic view of the good political society, in which men of distinction governed for the benefit of the entire nation. Order was to be maintained by an enlightened leadership, aided by the unifying forces of patriotism, religion and public virtue. The paternalism inherent in this organic conception of the polity was not necessarily self-interested, at least not exclusively; the ideal of public service carried a genuine meaning for many Whigs. But in their celebration of talent the Whigs were marking their leaders – and themselves – off from the common run of men. The reluctance to discuss issues and policies also betrayed an élitist temperament. The people were not to choose the measures to which they were to be subject; rather policies would be formulated after proper deliberation by the leaders in government. The Whig emphasis on the sanctity of Congress was also the product of a conservative character, for its object was to resist the Democratic attempt to turn the presidency into the popular branch of government. The Whigs opposed the levelling tendencies of the Democrats with a creed which was ultimately retrogressive.

Alexis de Tocqueville lamented the absence of 'great parties' in the United States of the 1830s, but he did nonetheless identify differences between the unhappy parties he discovered there. 'The deeper we penetrate into the inmost thought of these parties, the more we perceive that the object of the one is to limit and that of the other to extend the authority of the people.' He added that 'aristocratic or democratic passions may easily be detected at the bottom of all parties, and that, although they escape a superficial observation, they are the main point and soul of every faction in the United States'.

The self-images of the Whig and Democratic parties give some credence to this observation. In his campaign biography of Martin Van Buren, William M. Holland made a similar remark about the differences between Democratic and Whig presidential candidates. The Whigs, he alleged, 'regarding government as a matter too important and intricate to be trusted to the integrity and capacity of common people, cast around for *great men* . . .'. They preferred men 'of splendid talents', for 'they feel great reverence for high birth, wealth and station; and delight to do homage to some political idol'. The Democrats, by contrast, 'want, for public office, servants and not masters; agents who will execute their will and not dictators to control it'. Holland's analysis was a partisan caricature. The Whigs, for example, showed no preference for men of high birth and were as ardent admirers of the self-made man as the Democrats. But there was a kernel of truth in Holland's observations, as the Whigs themselves on occasion came close to admitting. 'The Whig National Convention was no ordinary body', a Whig editor said at the outset of the Log Cabin campaign. 'It was composed of the best men in the Republic. Age, experience, talents, intelligence, and long services, gave dignity and character to the assemblage, and weight to its proceedings.' Whig leaders may have been born low, but they were the personification of every American's right to rise as high as his talents might take him. The Whig view of society was still a hierarchical one, though it was a hierarchy of talent rather than birth which was offered. Whig candidates were commended not for their services as such, for their careers had often not been political, nor for their views, but for their talents and virtues. Their transcendent patriotism and splendid gifts seemed to evoke something of the departed patriarchs of old.[36]

The Democratic flagbearers broke with tradition more decisively. They were presented as unashamed party men, and they were publicly committed to a strict constructionist platform, which arrayed them against the Bank, paper money, a high tariff, and federal aid to internal improvements. It was this commitment to party and to measures which was novel rather than the measures themselves, which in denying commerce and industry the government encouragement they needed made the Democratic candidate the guardian of an Old Republican agrarianism. Yet it was an agrarianism devoid of paternalism, for to the Democrats the president was an equal among equals, a party servant loyally doing the people's bidding. Their candidate remained essentially plebeian, a self-made man who owed his rise not to genius but to will-power and perseverence. These good Jacksonian qualities, with their suggestion of horny-handed self-reliance, helped to identify the Democratic candidate with the people he dutifully served.

As de Tocqueville had perceived, the Whig and Democratic parties *were* offering people a choice, for their presidential candidates embodied differing conceptions of the good republican society. One party conveyed an image of an America where liberty was more to be cherished than equality, where men were to be constrained not by party but by patriotism, where they were to be free to seek status and privilege as long as these things were fairly earned, where statesmen in government were gravely to pursue the public good. In the United States of the 1830s and 1840s this orderly vision could only seem the relic of an earlier age. In striking contrast, the other party looked to a society of sturdy and equal self-reliant producers, whether on the farm or in the workshop, united by the fraternal association of party which would root out privilege and provide the mechanism whereby the majority would rule. The party itself was to be a levelling device, a conception of party which has since disappeared from American politics but which is not wholly dissimilar to that found in some modern one-party states. There is little doubt which party offered the more radical vision.[37]

The ideological divide between the Whigs and Democrats, as revealed by their self-images, was deep and genuine, yet each party was possessed of a fervent commitment to American republicanism. Despite their differences, the two parties did share some assumptions about the social and political world they inhabited. Behind the party images there was a common set of beliefs and values, encapsulated in the archetypal image of the American president. In defining 'the American man', the image-makers were saying something about their country, which was a country with a mission, dedicated to the cause of liberty and self-government, to showing the world that a self-made, self-taught people, whose strength and wisdom had in large part been derived from the ennobling process of replacing the wilderness with civilization, could live together and govern themselves without coercion or corruption. Yet the republic was still young and the future uncertain, and America's republican people still needed a patriotic champion to save them from their foes.

# CHAPTER NINE
# *The anti-image*

Enemies, real or imaginary, have performed an indispensable role in American political life. American causes have frequently sought to define themselves by reference to what they are not. Every crusade, perhaps, needs an enemy to give it direction and legitimacy. Americans have been an ideological people, and commitment to a thesis implies a rejection of its antithesis. Many Americans have demonstrated their own commitment to their republic by identifying its adversaries and enlisting in an assault upon them.

The extent to which *antebellum* Americans were often mobilized against something is revealed in the very names of their movements. In the early days there had been the Anti-Federalists, and later came the Antimasonic party and the American Anti-Slavery Society. Then there was the phenomenon of anti-Catholicism, propagated through such journals as the *Anti-Romanist*, and a variety of other movements which have been defined by titles bestowed by modern historians, such as anti-Mormonism, antipartyism, anti-Missionism, and anti-southernism. And even where a movement was not bedecked – either in its lifetime or posthumously – with the proclamatory prefix of 'anti', its purpose may still have been to mobilize the citizenry against some perceived subversive design, such as the Monster Bank, the Demon Rum, the immigrant hordes, or the abolitionist conspiracy.

Political expediency as well as ideological fervour may also play a part in the creation of the anti-movement. In a political system in which two major coalitional parties are in competition with one another, a party may find it easier to achieve unity and vigour by focussing on the evils of its opponents than on its own virtues. Both the major components of the second American party system in a sense were first created as 'anti-parties'. The Jacksonians grouped in

1828 to turn the Adams men out of office, united by their conviction that the republic was imperilled by the perpetrators of the 'corrupt bargain'. The Whigs took shape in the 1830s in outraged resistance to Andrew Jackson and all his works. The disparate elements in each coalition were welded together by their determination to vanquish the enemy, a determination which went deeper than any differences over policy. In mobilizing against its detested opponents a party could combine pragmatism with principle.

Perhaps the political leaders of this era sensed that many Americans possessed a propensity for anti-voting, as modern scholars have dubbed that phenomenon in which a voter casts his vote not for but against something or someone. Anti-voting operated at a variety of levels. Catholics and Protestants appear frequently to have entered opposing political parties because of their mutual antipathy, and such 'negative reference group' activity may explain the voting patterns of a wide range of ethnic and religious groups at odds with their neighbours. It is difficult to escape the conclusion, too, that sectional antagonisms played some part in voting alignments, that, for example, many Yankees in 1828 cast ballots against the slaveholder Andrew Jackson because he seemed to them to personify the South. Economic and class grievances probably also contributed to anti-voting, and there were almost certainly men who voted against Henry Clay because of his close association with the Bank, that symbol of plutocracy. For many of those conservative Americans who voted for Whig candidates, the Democratic party itself was no doubt a potent negative reference group.[1]

If voters were induced to go to the polls in significant numbers primarily to vote against the enemy party, it is relevant to consider how they saw that party. The 'anti-image' may have been mightier than the image in the process of party formation. Certainly many *antebellum* editors and politicians considered the voters' perceptions of the enemy to be electorally important, for they devoted considerable energy to fashioning hostile images of the opposing party and its political candidates. Countering the presidential image, then, was the anti-image, the work of the candidate's political opponents. Whatever impact the anti-image may have had on electoral behaviour, it served to define the kind of president that Americans did *not* want, or at least the kind that propagandists believed their fellow citizens would find unacceptable. If the president was expected to personify his country, the presidential anti-image delineated the reverse, the quintessential un-American of his day. But the act of designating un-American qualities implied something about American qualities. A political movement reveals much of itself in its perception of its enemy.

Anti-biographies did not appear in the same abundance as biographies. Indeed, the anti-image relied less on hostile biographies as such and more on newspaper articles and *ad hoc* pamphlets and leaflets. Newspapers attacked the opposing candidate endlessly and bitterly, but only occasionally was a full biographical sketch attempted by a hostile press. The anti-images were thus constructed in a piecemeal and accretive fashion. Their manufacture was also more erratic than that of the images in that some candidates seemed to attract more venom than others. Andrew Jackson and Martin Van Buren in particular, those undecorous disturbers of gentlemanly order, provoked an abnormal number of poison-pen portraits. Thus the anti-image lacked the complexity, completeness and balance of the image and is less readily subject to analysis. But politicians can usually be relied upon to abuse their opponents and *antebellum* politicians were sufficiently abusive for our purposes. As with the image, the anti-image functioned on three main levels: first, the primary or archetypal anti-image, which defined those attributes which Americans of all persuasions apparently found unacceptable in a potential president, secondly, the personal anti-images constructed around particular candidates, and finally the party anti-images through which a party revealed its distinctive perceptions of its opponents. Anti-images, like beauty, were in the eye of the beholder, and a party probably betrayed more about itself than it divulged about its rivals in its rhetorical assaults upon them.

Because the construction of anti-images was less deliberate than the construction of images, their common characteristics are more difficult to define. The touching devotion that the image-makers gave to the ancestry and upbringing of their candidates is not so evident in the hostile portraits, which were fashioned speedily in the heat of the campaign. But certain themes do recur in the anti-images, enough to make visible the archetypal anti-image which hovered behind them all. It was this construction which embodied the very antithesis of the model presidential candidate, possessed as it was of those characteristics which Americans were presumed to consider inexcusable in their president. In defining the sort of person who should *not* be president, the primary or archetypal anti-image both defined those qualities which were held to be pre-eminently un-American and, by implication, those qualities which were held to be pre-eminently American. The primary anti-image was the mirror image of the quintessential republican citizen.

There were perhaps three principal aspects to the primary anti-image of the presidential candidate. The anti-president, as we might call him, was first possessed of a despicable personal character. Consumed with insatiable ambition, he grossly subordinated the public interest to his self-serving ends, changed his principles when he deemed it expedient, and resorted to fraud for personal gain. Secondly, the anti-president was never genuinely the representative of the people, but was either the agent of some noisome faction or cabal or else was an incipient (or actual) Military Chieftain or despot, sustained in practice or potential by force and corruption rather than by public opinion. And finally and inescapably, the anti-president was the very embodiment of un-Americanism and anti-republicanism, often of Tory or Federalist descent, riddled with aristocratic pretensions, an admirer or even an agent of England, and unpatriotic to the point of treason. The anti-president was the creation of an imagination touched by uncertainty, of a consciousness which still searched for threats to the American body politic. The republic was still vulnerable, or so the architects of the anti-images seemed to imply, and the election of the wrong man to the White House could swiftly undo the patriotic labours of the Founding Fathers. The security of republican institutions, it was still insisted, rested on who was elected president.

Ambition in its more sinister forms was a characteristic vice of the anti-president. Much was made of Andrew Jackson's reputation for violence, wilfulness and high handedness, and it was alleged that his desperate ambition would drive him on to establish a military tyranny. After four years of his administration it was being claimed that he had indeed become an 'EMPEROR or AUTOCRAT'. Ambition was a favourite charge levelled at John Quincy Adams. A campaign song of 1828 entitled *Johnny Q!* lamented its subject's 'growing passion' and his fateful tendency to 'leuk wi' scorn . . . on ither folk', while for others the corrupt bargain affair was proof enough that 'ambitious and selfish passions have been the governing impulses of Mr. Adams and Mr. Clay'. But it was Van Buren, who had emerged out of an obscure background to rise to the heights without any great public achievements to commend him, who really attracted the venom of his critics. His boyhood political activity first aroused distrust, for 'The most disagreeable animal on earth, in our humble judgment, is a pert, pushing, self-sufficient boy of the precise age of sixteen.' From early youth, another critic echoed, 'he has been distinguished for the most inordinate ambition'. The self-serving character of the anti-president was best exemplified by his vacillating and inconsistent conduct in public life, as he calculated which stance would serve his interest best. Van Buren, of course, 'from his cradle . . . was of the *non-committal* tribe' and 'had always two ways to do a thing'. As an infant, according to Davy Crockett, Van Buren could laugh on one side of his face while crying on the other, while by the age of 12 he had mastered the art of reading a book upside-down 'to acquire a shifting *nack* for business, and a ready turn for doing things more ways than one'. Henry Clay, too, was known to change his views and his enemies in particular liked to remind the public that he had once been an opponent of the Bank, before becoming its advocate and a beneficiary of its financial favours. The Whigs in turn pounced on the Kane letter and its promise of 'incidental protection' to charge the formerly free-trade Polk with 'hypocrisy' and 'tergiversation'. Lewis Cass played 'the demagogue instead of the statesman' because he had 'occupied adverse positions' both on Texas annexation and the Wilmot Proviso, and a few years later, too, Winfield Scott was accused of having 'no fixed principles' and old letters of his were reproduced to illustrate his inconsistent and self-contradictory views on naturalization.[2]

Sharpening the charges of ambition and self-serving vacillation were queries about the probity of the opposing candidate. A man who manipulated his government expense accounts was evidently in public life for what he could get out of it. Allegations of this sort were raised against Andrew Jackson, who while a major-general in the regular army was said to have charged the government for rent, fuel and subsistence even when living on his own plantation. (It was also alleged that he had obtained land by fraud and that he had made personal gains in Indian treaties.) His opponent, John Quincy Adams, was charged with having padded his expense accounts while a peace negotiator at Ghent in 1813–15. Martin Van Buren, while not exactly venal himself, could be accused of lavishing 'the public treasure upon baubles and trinkets adapted to the effeminate court of some degenerate Oriental Nabob'. More unfortunately his administration had been bedevilled by a number of celebrated cases of embezzlement by government officers, most spectacularly by Samuel Swartwout, whose accounts as collector of customs for New York were found to be over $1 million short in 1837, and the president was accused of countenancing such corruption. Henry Clay in turn was accused of receiving $17,000 from the Bank for espousing its cause, while Lewis Cass was said to have used his position as Governor of Michigan Territory to accumulate 'a splendid fortune from the public Treasury'. Winfield Scott, too, was alleged to have used his army position to claim extravagant extra allowances. Such suggestions of venality in the presidential hopefuls lent some plausibility to the accusation that they were self-serving men, more interested in advancing their own fortunes than the republic's.[3]

As befitted ambitious, selfish and dishonest men, too, they also tended to be vain, pretentious and cowardly. Davy Crockett accused Van Buren of forgetting 'all his old companions and friends in the humbler walks of life', and of lacing himself up in corsets before appearing in the Senate chamber, where 'he struts and swaggers like a crow in a gutter'. Further, while others had been risking their lives in the War of 1812, Van Buren had been 'snugly and safely standing up in the senate of New York, branding the war as unjust, unnecessary, and unwise'. Another critic of his war performance had it that Van Buren had been 'Snugly seated at Kinderhook, warming his feet by the fire'. Polk was said to be vain enough to have had a splendid official chair made for himself when Speaker of the House of Representatives. William Henry Harrison's war career was not enough to protect him from imputations of cowardice, one story which went the Democratic rounds being that the women of Chillicothe had been so disenchanted with Harrison's timid defence of the town that they had made up a petticoat for him. Lewis Cass was also charged with having greatly embroidered his exploits during the War of 1812, while his real character was revealed as Minister to France, where he spent his time 'rosying his gills with "bewitching Burgundy", swelling his portly dimensions with frogs, filets, and Perigord pies, stretching his legs under Louis Phillippe's mahogany, familiarly hob-a-nobbing with his Majesty in the eyes of all Europe'. Franklin Pierce failed to display the manliness expected of a president, too, his falls from his horse in the Mexican War being variously attributed to fright or drink. The very nickname of Winfield Scott, 'Fuss and Feathers', as James Buchanan happily pointed out, was evidence that he was 'vain-glorious to an excessive degree'. Vanity, pretentiousness and an occasional lack of martial valour were not serious indictments, perhaps, but the imputation of characteristics of this sort to presidential candidates served to belittle them, to suggest that they lacked the manly dignity expected of the first officer of a republic. Americans evidently preferred to see in their public men such qualities as disinterested statesmanship, a firm resolve, a disdain for personal mercenary considerations and an empathy with plain folk.[4]

The anti-president's weaknesses of personal character made possible more fundamental defects in his political régime. The anti-president characteristically did not properly reflect the popular will and relied on force or fraud to sustain himself. John Quincy Adams no less had been raised to the presidency by a species of fraud, by the 'corrupt bargain', and was not the choice of the people, as the Jacksonians never tired of pointing out. Andrew Jackson, of course, was accused of subjecting the country to 'the DOMINION OF ONE MAN' and of promising the succession to Martin Van Buren. The latter allegedly reinforced this dictatorial tendency by approving Secretary of War Joel Poinsett's plan to reorganize the militia, 'which would CREATE A STANDING ARMY OF TWO HUNDRED THOUSAND MEN, *whose bayonets would be at the control of the President*'. The Democrats' brazen use of the spoils system cemented their control: 'The offices and salaries of the government are assumed to be the property of Mr. Van Buren, to be used by him for the purpose of entrenching himself in power, and rendering himself secure against the remonstrances of public opinion.' Henry Clay, however, offered no relief, for his 'dictatorial conduct in Congress . . . is stamped with all the characteristics of a tyrant and dictator'. His American System was no better than his character, since 'The natural tendency of his measures is to a consolidated despotism'. Winfield Scott, too, 'would clothe the national government with dangerous powers'.[5]

A president who used corruption or governmental or military power to consolidate his position was evidently not the genuine choice of the people. Like the despots of Europe, he was being sustained by something other than public opinion. His unrepresentative nature was further underlined by his tendency to turn for aid and advice to some disreputable faction. A president who was not the agent of the people was likely to be the agent of someone else, a sinister group who could not reach the levers of power through the open system of election. 'Perhaps the worst evil of monarchies is their liability to be influenced by favourites around the throne', warned a cynical critic of King Andrew, creatures whose 'lives are spent in eating their corrupt way into the root of a noble empire, and their highest ambition is to leave the nation, which they found powerful and flourishing, prostrate and blasted.' Jackson's unofficial advisers, the so-called Kitchen Cabinet, admirably fitted this description, 'a cabal thus sordid, grasping and powerful, who control our executive, direct our government, and constitute in fact our rulers'. The Democrats sometimes implied that there was a similar sinister cabal behind the campaigns of William H. Harrison, who was 'known to be in the imbecility of age', one opponent alleging that he was the candidate of the 'British Whigs', who ultimately seem to have been the bankers and aristocrats of England. James K. Polk's unexpected nomination aroused Whig suspicions that it was the work of 'a set of *Texas Speculators*', men with large holdings of '*Texas Scrip*' which would rise markedly in value if Texas were annexed, operating in league with the 'slave interest of the South'. The candidature of Polk's fellow dark horse, Franklin Pierce, also needed explanation, Pierce apparently being the modern equivalent of the horse which was made a Roman Consul, a beast of burden who 'if elected, will carry his *backers* of the Convention'. Even more sinister were the advisers of Winfield Scott, who were 'more intolerable even than his political heresies. . . . For years he has been under the control of William H. Seward, Thurlow Weed, and their followers.' In the somewhat paranoid atmosphere of *antebellum* America it was easy to espy conspiracies lurking behind the candidacies of available men. If the anti-president was not a domineering dictator he was the hapless agent of a shady and unrepublican cabal. Either way, he was not the authentic spokesman of the people.[6]

But the anti-president was much more than untrustworthy and unrepresentative. He was also distinctly un-American, a witting or unwitting foe of the people's republic. This was sometimes revealed in an unpatriotic ancestry. John Quincy Adams, of course, was encumbered with an ill-starred lineage, with a father who had been 'among the highest toned of the monarchical party', as extensive quotations from John Adams's *Defence of the American Constitutions* were deployed to show. (John Quincy Adams was also much distressed during the 1828 campaign by a story that his wife was an Englishwoman.) Quite dumbfounding was Charles Hammond's allegation that 'General JACKSON'S mother was a COMMON PROSTITUTE, *brought to this country by the British soldiers!!!*' More damning, perhaps, than her venerable profession was her British identity, for the implication was that Andrew Jackson was half English. (She later confirmed her un-American character by marrying a mulatto and giving birth to Andrew, who was thus not merely an Englishman but a black Englishman!) Davy Crockett conjured for Martin Van Buren a Tory uncle, who was said to have occasionally guided British scouting parties during the revolutionary war. James K. Polk was vastly disturbed by Whig charges that *his* long-dead grandfather had been a Tory supporter of the King, while Franklin Pierce was said to be a descendant of the Percy family of medieval England. More often the unpatriotic tendencies of the anti-president had first been revealed by his espousal of Federalism. Van Buren's support of De Witt Clinton's candidacy during the presidential election of 1812 was enough to brand him with this heresy, and with a little imagination it was possible to charge him with having been 'in league with the abettors of the Hartford Convention, plotting the overthrow of the administration of Mr. Madison'. William H. Harrison's political record was carefully scrutinized in order to sustain the charge that 'he is a Federalist in his Creed, and in his measures', and an old associate was produced to testify that in John Adams's administration Harrison had been 'a Federalist, and wore the black cockade'. The young Lewis Cass had similarly erred in the late 1790s, when he had 'always appeared with a black cockade in his hat'.[7]

Such British, Tory and Federalist antecedents invariably spawned a character which yearned for an aristocratic order and nursed an unpatriotic regard for the Old World, sometimes to the point of treason. John Quincy Adams's 'Publicola' letters were cited as proof of 'a disguised hostility to republican principles, and the same devotion to monarchy which is found in the writings of his father...'. Even President Jackson's foreign policy was said to be marked by 'a mean prostration of the honor of the country at the feet of the British Ministry...'. The questionable trade treaty referred to was often attributed to the unpatriotic influence of Van Buren, who in 1836 was castigated for using an expensive English coach: 'We do not like to see a proud, rich nabob, who dashes through our streets in a fine coach, with all the pomp and parade of an heir apparent, and who is attended by English waiters, *dressed in livery* after the fashion of a British lord, attempt to pass himself off as a true workingman's democrat.' But no one had a monopoly of undemocratic sentiments. 'Every man who wishes for an aristocracy', wrote one editor in 1844, 'and thinks he would or might belong to it, will vote for Clay.' While a minister in Paris, Lewis Cass could be found 'basking in the sunshine of royalty, and revelling in all the splendors and luxuries of that voluptuous metropolis.... – a pretty spectacle he exhibited, to be sure, of a Republican minister at the court of a European sovereign!' He had even 'signalized himself in the publication of a fulsome eulogy on the despotic and profligate Court of Louis Phillippe'. The imputation of an un-American character to the opposing presidential candidate sometimes merged with the suggestion that he was the dupe of alien interests. Thus Old Tippecanoe himself was projected as a front for a conspiracy of British and American capitalists who wanted to re-establish the Bank: 'It is now no longer a matter of doubt that the Whig party, in their attempt to elect Gen. Harrison, do receive the aid, the countenance and the support of the British bankers and fundmongers, if not of the English Government itself.' The anti-president was a potential traitor to the republican cause, a man who would gladly trade democracy for aristocracy and who would betray his countrymen to the decadent monarchies and capitalists of Europe.[8]

The primary anti-image of the presidential candidate, then, projected a creature of inordinate and self-serving ambition, lacking both probity and principle, who was vain and unmanly to boot. He lacked real legitimacy and was apt to resort to force or corruption to sustain himself, was perhaps possessed of an authoritarian temperament and was often the conscious or unconscious dupe of some sinister cabal. His Tory or Federalist lineage, aristocratic leaning and obsequious regard for the Courts of Europe rendered him an unsafe guardian of his people's liberties.

The opposition's candidate was thus cast as fundamentally un-American. To that generation to be un-American seems to have meant to be pro-British, or at least pro-European, and candidates themselves spent a remarkable amount of energy in disavowing an English connection, as when John Quincy Adams bestirred himself to scotch the rumour that his wife was an Englishwoman and James K. Polk collected evidence to disprove his grandfather's Tory sympathies over half-a-century earlier. In 1776 the United States had cast off British rule, and any Anglophilia in her citizens seemed to imply a lack of support for the alternative course upon which she had embarked. This tendency to define 'Americanness' by identifying what it was not – British, European, monarchical, aristocratic – betrayed a chauvinistic desire to create a different and distinctive American identity, an unnerving uncertainty as to what that identity really was, and a fear that it might not after all prove possible to escape the clutches of the Old World. That, at any rate, was the message of the anti-image, that under the wrong president the American people might once more fall victim to British or European wiles. The propagators of this warning were saying that the young republic was still in peril, that the invulnerability of American institutions could not even yet be taken for granted. The American experiment was still new, isolated and fragile, and would be safe only in the hands of a president truly dedicated to the cause.

But to be 'American' did mean something more than being 'un-British'. Americans identified the full application of the representative principle as being central to their distinctive political institutions, and the un-American nature of the anti-president was confirmed by his failure properly to represent the popular will. His dictatorial impulses, his willingness to use corruption or even force, and his role as the instrument of an illicit cabal, exposed the hollowness of his claim to be the chosen agent of the people. Even a president who was not seduced by the aristocratic régimes of Europe could render a death-blow to the republic by concentrating power in his own hands or in those of a faction which was not responsible to the sovereign people. It was for these reasons, said Jackson's enemies, that his re-election 'would be fatal to the Union'. The president was held to possess the capacity to destroy the republic, and for this reason it was essential to find a man of honesty, of firm resolve, and of unwavering devotion to the public good. Thus the primary anti-image ultimately invoked the traditional conception of the president, insisting that ambition, self-serving vacillation and intrigue were fundamental disqualifications. Those who fashioned the anti-images of the *antebellum* decades shared with an earlier generation the assumption that the republic could be mortally wounded by an ambitious and corrupt executive. American liberty and democracy would be rendered secure only by virtue in the White House.[9]

The primary or archetypal anti-image informed all the hostile images fashioned around presidential candidates, both the personal anti-images fastened on particular men and the party anti-images which each party projected for the candidates of the other. But, of course, the personal and party anti-images were subject to variations of their own. Whigs and Democrats each perceived rival candidates in somewhat different ways. Their perceptions further revealed something about the beholder as well as the beheld. The Whig portrayal of the typical Democratic candidate, for example, was in part the product of *Whig* party character. The evils that partisans espied in their opponents were those they were disposed to espy. Further, in identifying the distinctive sins of the opposition, each party was attributing the contrary virtues to itself. Each party was defining itself by its characterization of its enemy, by making it clear to the electorate what it was *not*. And it was, among other things, attempting to harness to its own purposes the instinct in the American electorate to vote against, rather than for, something. The personal and party anti-images reveal what their architects believed would stir the active hostility of important elements of the American people.

The Democratic critiques of Whig candidates tended to focus less on their personalities than on their policies. As a result, no very clear Democratic definition of the Whig presidential personality emerged. But enough insults were levelled to make some sort of Whig profile visible, even if not a very complete one. As with the presidential images, the personal and party anti-images were woven inextricably together, and before examining the Democratic conception of the

Whig candidate as such, a brief examination of the Democrats' perceptions of particular opposing candidates may serve as illustration.

The Democrats were probably happiest when Henry Clay was the Whig candidate. Their denunciations of him, at least, revealed imagination and enthusiasm. By 1844 Clay's long and highly public career provided the Democrats with ample evidence to discredit him. Clay's lowly origins were passed over lightly, but the character that he bore seemed almost to mesmerize horrified Democratic editors. His nights in Washington, it seemed, were spent in 'gambling, revelry, and debauchery' and even in the daytime he had been seen 'riding through Pennsylvania Avenue with public prostitutes'. Sporting men apparently regarded him as 'the best brag player in the Union' and it was said that 'the principal part of his fortune had been won at cards'. More serious, however, was the part he had played in a number of duels, both those in which he had been a principal himself and the so-called 'Cilley murder' of 1838, when Clay had allegedly encouraged a duel which resulted in the death of a young congressman. He had compounded this life of crime by quarrelling with Senator King of Alabama as recently as 1841, when at the age of 64 he had been compelled to give a bond of $5,000 to keep the peace: 'Five thousand dollars restrain the passions of decrepid old age, and save the life of a human being.' A tyrannical disposition further detracted from his personality. Clay's political career was little more edifying. He had corruptly delivered the presidency to John Quincy Adams in 1825 in return for the secretaryship of state and the promise of the succession; political ambition had also led him to change his view on the Bank and to equivocate on the tariff. Yet despite his inconsistency, he was clearly a Federalist, and as such favoured the Bank and internal improvements and was hostile to the executive veto and to immigrants. The Whigs often toasted Clay as 'the embodiment of Whig principles', and one Democratic newspaper sketch of him entitled 'The "Embodiment"' was printed so that the print formed the outline of a man's body. Its contents recited all the old charges: Clay's duels, the Cilley affair, the $5,000 bond to keep the peace, Clay's gambling and sabbath-breaking, and his Federalist-Hartford Convention views on politics. 'His election would be in contradiction of the moral lesson, that infamy and disgrace follow a life of wickedness;' concluded another editor, 'and would be a poor incentive to the rising generation to walk in the paths of virtue.'[10]

The emphasis on Clay's immoral character no doubt reflected a Democratic attempt to prise away from the Whig camp some of

199

those voters of 'evangelical' or 'pietistic' religious persuasions who normally voted against the Godless Democrats. Whig politicians occasionally expressed between themselves a private fear that the stories associated with Clay were 'enough... to kill him, or any other man, among the moral & religious community, of the American people...'. This careful delineation of his dissolute nature was very much the personal anti-image assembled around Clay, since the Democrats normally said little about the moral standing of the Whig candidates. When Clay was not the nominee, of course, they were confronted with a military man, and apart from lack of evidence they were probably reluctant to denigrate the personal character of a popular hero. What the Democrats could suggest was that the old soldier, whatever his military prowess (which was sometimes called into question), would not be competent at presidential duties. Hence Harrison was sniggered at as 'The Old Granny' (and one Democratic campaign paper was published under that title), a senile old duffer who could not be trusted even to write his own letters, and Taylor was assailed for his tiresome capacity to write innumerable letters without disclosing his political views. Taylor evidently owed his nomination 'to no political sagacity', commented one caustic Democrat, 'because he confesses himself unacquainted with political questions'.[11]

Winfield Scott presented a more tempting target for Democratic abuse than the apolitical and genuinely popular Taylor. Compared with Clay, he escaped lightly in the sketches of his personal character, although his vain struttings as 'Old Fuss and Feathers' drew irresistible attention. His reputation for quarrelling with his military rivals was also remarked upon, as were his 'blundering letters', proof that he was '*hasty* and extravagant' in his opinions. (A letter he had written to the secretary of war in 1846 as he sat down 'to take a hasty plate of soup' had caused some public amusement.) Such foolish indiscretions demonstrated that he was 'incapable of guiding or directing the vast machinery of our government'. And although the Democrats portrayed Scott's character as ridiculous rather than sinister, they could not resist reviving the Military Chieftain charge. 'From Caesar to Cromwell, and from Cromwell to Napoleon, ... history presents the same solemn warning', intoned James Buchanan, ' – beware of elevating to the highest civil trust the commander of your victorious armies.' Andrew Jackson, after all, had retired virtuously to his farm after his military engagements, but Scott was 'the actual commander of the army', and had defeated his own 'constitutional commander-in-chief' for the Whig nomination. As for his political views, the Democratic press simultaneously denounced Scott for inconsistency and non-committalism on the one hand and Federalist or American System sympathies on the other. 'Gen. Scott's views are unknown upon all the questions likely to affect the interests of our country', was one complaint. 'He advocates a loose interpretation of the constitution;' fumed another Democratic editor, '. . . is in favor of a United States Bank, the distribution of the proceeds of the sales of the public lands among the States, the prosecution of a gigantic system of internal improvements by the federal government, a high protective tariff, a large increase of the army, and a repeal of the naturalisation laws.' Scott was further contaminated with antimasonry and nativism. Finally, it was also suggested that Scott was the creature of the free soil Whigs of New York, particularly of William H. Seward, 'a man who is styled, by members of his own party, an "abolitionist, arch intriguer, demagogue, enemy to his country, not worthy to hold a seat in the U.S. Senate, and the worst man in America"'. This was the most potent charge levelled against the hapless Scott, and it probably did him considerable damage in the election.[12]

The sketches of Clay and Scott indicate some of the characteristics of the party anti-image of the Whig nominee – his fondness for the American System, secret or public, his sympathy with nativism, his undemocratic temperament. But there was no very clear definition of the Whig presidential personality. The Democratic critics did, of course, attempt to establish the essential conservatism of the Whig candidate. While the nominees of both parties were accustomed to being branded as Federalist, the charge seems to have been levelled more regularly by Democrats against Whigs, who were said to be Federalists still, while the Democratic offence had usually been no more than a youthful indiscretion. So Harrison was 'a Federal Politician of the Webster School', Clay was also in league with 'Daniel Webster and all the leading Hartford-convention Federalists', while Scott as late as 1852 was still 'an old-fashioned federalist'. The charge carried with it implications of a lack of patriotism, of a liking for a high-toned, authoritarian and consolidated government, and of a conservative and even reactionary temperament.[13]

But whatever his personality, there was little doubt about what the Whig candidate stood for. To be sure, the reluctance of military heroes to commit themselves on issues and the variety of political stances that Clay had adopted during his long career provoked Democratic charges of non-committalism and vacillation. 'For non-committalism', one exasperated Democrat said of Taylor's first Allison letter, 'that letter out-Herods Herod, in my judgment.' But such charges were levelled against all candidates and contributed to the shaping of the primary anti-image. In fact, insisted the Democrats, the essential Whig candidate did hold distinctive political principles, whether he avowed them or not. Old Tippecanoe was confidently condemned as 'a Tariff man, an Internal Improvements man, a Bank man, a Distributionist, a National Colonizationist . . .'. Among the reasons why Henry Clay should not be president were his support for the Bank, his uncertain course on the tariff, his advocacy of a random scheme of internal improvements, and his opposition to the Independent Treasury. Zachary Taylor might not have revealed his views, but he was the formal candidate of a party which favoured a 'latitudinous construction' of the Constitution, which would authorize 'the establishment of a bank of the United States – a distribution of the proceeds of the public lands amongst the States – assumption of State debts by the National Government – "protection for protection", without regard to revenue – and even the construction of roads and canals between points within States alone under the jurisdiction of State Governments'. Winfield Scott was also charged with being a supporter of the regular litany of Whig causes. The Democrats, then, had no hesitation about associating the Whig nominees with the traditional Whig measures, an association that they seemed confident could only mean a loss of votes for their opponents.[14]

Above all it was the banking and money questions which damned the Whig candidate. The Democrats were always eager to encumber the Whigs with the Monster Bank. Harrison, it was said, had 'declared himself an advocate of a National Bank and a paper system, which, at this moment, is grinding the face of the poor, harassing the laboring classes by alternate vicissitudes of delusive prosperity and long continued depression'. Winfield Scott was represented as favouring a Bank and other measures drawn up by 'speculators' for their own mercenary ends. But it was Henry Clay, of course, who was the real champion of the Bank and its sinister designs. His part in the Bank War of 1833–34 was described as a 'struggle, aided by the Purse of the Bank, to subvert the Republic'. Clay, indeed, had revealed himself an outright traitor to the cause of republican government: 'The very worst principles of Federalism are involved in this question – constructive powers, corrupting influences, subversion of popular will, encroachment on State rights, supremacy of the central power controlled by agencies not responsible to the people.' In Democratic eyes, the Bank represented the very negation of the

American mission, an aristocratic and unpatriotic power in league with British capitalists which threatened to deprive the American people of their liberty.[15]

The Democratic identification of the Whig candidate with the Bank was an attempt to exploit popular resentments and jealousies of the rich, and to suggest that an egalitarian republic could only be safe in Democratic hands. But in addition to appealing to class feelings, the Democrats also sought to turn ethnic friction to useful political account. The Whig nominees were regularly cast as hostile to foreigners and sometimes to Catholics. While they loved foreign aristocrats, Harrison and the Whigs felt only 'hatred' for naturalized citizens. Some indiscreet remarks of Henry Clay were represented as 'the outpouring of deep-seated malignity upon the whole body of emigrants who fly from the hand of tyranny and oppression'. A larger target was Winfield Scott, who had dabbled with Native Americanism in the past, as was shown by some of his public letters, which Democratic editors happily reprinted. '*General Scott's great idea of politics is, dread of the vote and influence of the adopted citizens*', insisted one publication. James Buchanan even contrived to find anti-Catholic sentiments in Scott's letter accepting the Whig nomination. Immigrants, particularly the Irish, were evidently being invited to vote against the Whig nominees.[16]

Finally, the Democrats were not happy about the Whig candidate's position on the question of the executive veto. Henry Clay, they claimed, should not be president because he was 'for so amending the Constitution as to deprive the President of the veto power'. This was also the one political issue on which Zachary Taylor did make a pronouncement, to the effect that the veto should be exercised only in exceptional cases, which doctrine was denounced as 'wrong to-day, and will be so forever'. Winfield Scott, too, was ridiculed for wanting to modify the veto, which had twice 'saved the country from the corrupt and corrupting influence of a Bank'. In Democratic rhetoric, the veto power became the weapon of last resort of the popular tribune, a democratic device to be used to protect the people's liberties from the incursions of the monied classes and other aristocratic interests. Opposition to the veto power betrayed an unrepublican design.[17]

The party anti-image that the Democrats assembled around the Whig nominees thus focussed on their principles rather than their personalities. Clay's character might be traduced, but for the most part the Democrats seemed to assume the men were less important than the measures. This in itself was perhaps a reflection of something in the Democratic party character. In their own campaigns, the Democrats readily identified their candidates with specific views and policies, and regularly invited the electorate to choose between the programmes of the two major parties. In part this presumably reflected an assumption that Democratic policies *were* more popular than Whig policies. In connecting the Whig candidate with the Bank, loose constructionism, the protective tariff, a profligate system of internal improvements, and nativism, the Democratic propagandists presumably hoped to detach batches of voters from the Whig cause, or at least to arouse their own sufficiently against the hated enemy as to get them to the polls. But the Democratic attention to policies may also in part have reflected an assumption that politics really were about measures rather than men, that in a democratic polity the majority of the people made the primary decision at the polls, and that their political servants in government then dutifully executed their will.

Certainly the Democratic anti-image of the Whig candidate suggested that he had little empathy with the people. His outdated Federalism, his association with the moneyed aristocracy, his distaste for foreign immigrants, all emphasized that he lacked the common touch. Even his lack of enthusiasm for the executive veto, which the Democrats had to defend because of their own history, could be represented as resulting from a conservative fear of a populist weapon. As in its use of the presidential image, the Democratic party was using the anti-image to claim that it alone possessed the ark of the democratic covenant. If the antithesis to the ideal Democratic candidate was a loose constructionist aristocrat, fearful of the popular will and intent on bending the government to the interests of a privileged commercial class, the Democrats were defining themselves as strict constructionist and levelling agrarians who were prepared to put their faith in the people.

The Whigs appear to have devoted more energy to the fashioning of anti-images than the Democrats. Andrew Jackson and Martin Van Buren in particular attracted an unusual number of lengthy *exposés*, and even their successors probably won more hostile attention than the Whig candidates. It may be that the unconventional nature of the early Democratic nominees, notably Jackson and Van Buren who were being promoted at a time when traditional statesmanlike qualities were still expected, provoked an unusual degree of wrath, fear and protest. It may be that the Whig party, as the minority and opposition party, felt that it had to try harder. Perhaps, too, the better-financed Whigs could afford more campaign publications (they had more newspaper outlets), while their reluctance to vouchsafe their own policies may have persuaded them that the best mode of defence was attack. At any rate, it is possible to give a somewhat fuller impression of the Whig conception of the Democratic candidate than of the Democratic conception of the Whig candidate, but before doing so it is instructive to examine the personal anti-images assembled around particular Democrats.

Probably no one aroused the ire of his political enemies in this period more than Martin Van Buren. Jackson's military prowess had at least commanded respect as well as fear, but Van Buren seemed the very personification of the degeneration of American public life. His entry into presidential politics provoked a full-scale biography (or anti-biography), tellingly entitled *The Life of Martin Van Buren, Heir-Apparent to the 'Government', and the Appointed Successor of General Andrew Jackson*, ostensibly by Davy Crockett, as well as several shorter hostile sketches. His personal character was evidently beneath contempt. One author, arguing by analogy with the fox, argued that a head which was broad at the top was a sign of slyness, and claimed that Van Buren's head was 'broader on the top than any person that I have ever saw or noticed'. Phrenological experts were summoned to confirm that he was a 'sly, cunning person'. Davy Crockett made much of Van Buren's 'secret, sly, selfish' nature and his penchant for intrigue and non-committalism. His lowly birth won him little credit, for 'He forgot all his old associates because they were poor folks.' He had acquired proud, aristocratic and effeminate ways, and as president sought to turn the White House into 'a PALACE *as splendid as that of the Caesars, and as richly adorned as the proudest Asiatic mansion'*. This disagreeable upstart owed his rise not to any worthy talents but to a self-serving ambition combined with a genius for intrigue. De Witt Clinton was one of those he had at first supported and then forsaken on his way up. But it was Andrew Jackson who had really raised him to the heights, by making him his 'Appointed Successor'. Thus, although in public stations for over thirty years, it was said of Van Buren in 1840, 'it is a fact as well known as it is astonishing that he cannot point to one solitary measure during his whole life, originated by him for the improvement of the condition of his fellow-men'. His career, indeed, had been that of an unprincipled office-seeker and his services had been of 'a mere *party* character'. Yet this party man represented a serious threat to the republic. He had abetted Jackson in his executive usurpation, and was himself '*the author and perfecter of the great spoils system'* which so enlarged presidential power. In addition, he had introduced the Independent Treasury in order to concentrate and monopolize the money power in his own hand, and had aimed, through Poinsett's army reforms, 'to place the citizens of this Republic *under a System as odious as the* SEDITION LAW of 1794' [sic]. Van Buren, in Whig eyes, was the quintessential party politician, an unprincipled demagogue and spoilsman whose lust for personal power threatened the very foundations of the republic.[18]

The Little Fox's successors as Democratic nominees were scarcely improvements. Franklin Pierce, the suspiciously dark horse of 1852, provides as dispiriting an example as any of them. His personality was evidently crabbed and mean, and his speech against a bill to provide a pension for President Harrison's widow was said to be 'a specimen of cold-hearted special pleading'. He had spent eight years in Congress, but like Van Buren 'HE MADE HIS MARK NO WHERE'. He had served in the Mexican War, but, it was said, without distinction, and there were occasional hints about his cowardliness on the field of battle and his fondness for drink. The 'Hero of many a well-fought *Bottle*', was a sly comment in the *New York Tribune*. His voting record in Congress was tiresomely negative, proving him hostile to a protective tariff and internal improvements of all kinds. 'His whole career . . . is made up of negatives of the most extraordinary character', agreed the Washington *Signal*, adding that Democratic praise for his 'negative strength' was like complimenting a woman for her 'negative beauty'. 'There is something uniform and remarkable in the political course of this gentleman', summed up another review. 'Signalized by nothing in Mexico, he attains a political station in New-Hampshire, he is deputed to represent nothing in the Senate, where, by a line of consistent opposition to harbors, roads, and widows, he attains the extreme point of the negative.' He was an obscure and unremarkable servant of the party of the office-seekers. 'Fifty years of masterly inactivity in the service of Democracy have qualified the New-Hampshire Senator.'[19]

Democratic candidates, indeed, were normally regarded with contempt by Whig propagandists. The standard Whig anti-image of the Democratic contender presented him as the lowest form of political life. The Democratic candidate, of course, shared all the vices of the primary or archetypal anti-image: inconsistency, a self-serving ambition, pretentiousness, aristocratic and unpatriotic impulses, a failure genuinely to represent the people. But the Whigs were able to delineate the Democratic contender with greater venomous precision than this. His character was flawed at the very centre, as shown by his questionable religious principles. He was sometimes identified with the Roman Catholic faith, Andrew Jackson on occasion being credited with an Irish Catholic lineage and Martin Van Buren being said to be a member of that church. Franklin Pierce could not be charged with the same error, for the New Hampshire constitution had not long since contained a clause barring Catholics from office, and so a different kind of bigotry was imputed to Pierce as an alleged upholder of that clause. Something was made of Jackson's callous indifference to the fates of the 'TWO MINISTERS OF RELIGION' who were held in prison by the state of Georgia in defiance of the ruling of the Supreme Court, and Polk was criticized for having voted against Henry Clay's resolution for a day of fasting and prayer in 1832. Van Buren had to be turned out of the White House, it was said, because an object of his party was 'the OVERTHROW OF THE CHURCH IN ALL ITS FORMS AND SECTS and the *destruction of the ministers of religion*'. The Whig aspersions on the religious views of the Democratic nominees were not altogether coherent, but the message seems to have been that they were not the God-fearing men that the republic needed in its highest office.[20]

The Democratic indifference or hostility towards the life of the spirit was also reflected in the candidate's pinched personality. Van Buren was 'cold, calculating, distrustful, treacherous', indeed 'infinitely the smallest man that has ever filled the presidential chair'. By contrast, 'in point of talents', James K. Polk was 'the *baldest* candidate ever presented to the American people for their Chief Magistrate'. Further, his opposition to a congressional proposal to give some wood to the poor of Georgetown one cold mid-winter revealed him to be 'insensible to the dictates of humanity' and 'deaf to the cry of distress and suffering'. Franklin Pierce, of course, could always be counted on to take a 'narrow, contracted, prejudiced, or illiberal view ... of any subject'. Democratic candidates, more than Whigs, also seemed to have a weakness for princely extravagances, such as Van Buren's 'English Coach', James K. Polk's splendid Speaker's chair, and Lewis Cass's revels in the 'splendors and luxuries' of 'voluptuous' Versailles. The image of the crabbed and cold-hearted killjoy wallowing in regal comforts is perhaps a somewhat discordant one, but both his lack of humanity and his princely pretensions demonstrated his distance from the people he was meant to represent. The Democrats' claim to be the party of the people was bogus, according to the Whigs, for their candidate conspicuously lacked the common touch and looked with disdain on his more humble fellows.[21]

The Democratic candidate, then, was not a man of the people. Rather he was a creature of party. One symptom of this was the lack of views of his own. Martin Van Buren, it could be shown, 'has been every thing in turns', Polk had changed his views 'on more subjects than one . . . without giving any substantial reasons for the change', and Cass had 'shrunk' from a confrontation with a Democratic president over the development of the West. A candidate without opinions made an admirable party servant. 'Hence the unanimity of the Convention', remarked the *American Whig Review* in 1852 after noting Pierce's failure to identify himself with any act, policy or measure. The Democratic nomination was a reward for contributions not to the public welfare but to the party cause. This the Whigs repeated time and again. Thus, 'pretending to no merit of any description as a public man', it was said of Van Buren, 'he bases his title to the support of his party'. Polk's principal achievement had been to be 'a *party* Speaker of the House of Representatives', and Cass was no more than 'a mere party politician'.[22]

Party men entered politics not in pursuit of the common good but in pursuit of office, it seemed, and it was their obsession with spoils rather than measures which marked them out from their fellows. 'The offices and salaries of the government are assumed to be the property of Mr. Van Buren', complained one Whig, 'to be used by him for the purpose of entrenching himself in power, and rendering himself secure against the remonstrances of public opinion'. The spoils system thus conveniently explained the success of the Democrats, who were sustained in power by their corps of officeholders rather than by the majority will. The image of the Democrats as spoilsmen was immeasurably strengthened during Van Buren's administration by the celebrated defalcations of Swartwout and then of one of his investigators, William Price. The allegation that Cass had improperly pocketed over $60,000 as Governor of Michigan Territory was cited as evidence of his hunger for the spoils of office and as a warning against entrusting him with a vastly larger public budget, one opponent invoking 'a duty I owe to my country, to save it if I can from falling into the hands of "the spoilers".' Franklin Pierce's lengthy 'do nothing' record was also proof of his view 'that government is constituted only to take money out of the pockets of the people, and to hand it over to the cormorants of office'.[23]

The party, then, was no more than a machine for transferring public office and public treasure to greedy parasites indifferent to the public good. Further, once in office Democratic chieftains tended to use the instruments of party, patronage and government to establish arbitrary control. President Jackson's usurpations, for example, constituted 'a heresy in our system more portentous than the bitterest denouncer of CONSOLIDATION had ever supposed possible'. The destruction of the Bank and the establishment of the Independent Treasury were said to be the consummation of the Democratic drive towards despotism, giving the president personal control over the financial resources of the government as well as its offices. Like another Walpole, Van Buren apparently aimed 'to grasp the liberties of the people, by getting the absolute control of their money'. When Tyler stubbornly vetoed Clay's Bank bills and Polk plunged the country into war with Mexico and re-established the Independent Treasury, the Whigs became more persuaded than ever that Democratic presidents rejoiced in arbitrary power. In their view the Democratic presidential candidate personified despotism rather than democracy.[24]

The Whig anti-image of the Democratic candidate, then, denied that he was the authentic agent of the people. He was an aloof, narrow-minded, cold-hearted creature, indifferent or even hostile to the principles of religion and humanity, with an aristocratic taste for the pomp and splendour of office. Uninterested in the public welfare and devoid of firm principle, what really moved him was a passion for spoils. To win them, he shamelessly abandoned himself to party, which he served with slavish and cynical devotion. Once he had gained his coveted goal, and fearful of the wrath of the people, he sustained himself in power by a mixture of force and corruption. The Democratic candidate had no respect for that liberty which the republic was meant to protect.

This perception of the Democratic nominee betrayed something of the nature of the Whig party. Many Americans regarded party with suspicion and politicians with distaste, attitudes which found political expression in Whig propaganda. To some extent the Whigs may have been consciously trying to exploit this public disfavour, but they were never at ease with party politics, even as they resorted to the weaponry of party themselves. The streak of evangelicalism in Whiggery served to encourage the belief that politics should be subordinate to religion and morality. The streak of old-fashioned conservatism encouraged the belief that the presidential office should somehow be above politics. In the Whig perspective party politicians like Van Buren were unprincipled upstarts who were elbowing aside the country's real statesmen.

This critique of the Democratic candidate gave relatively little attention to the policies he had avowed. The emphasis was on his personality and on the discreditable political techniques that he employed. Behind Whig perceptions of presidential politics seems to have been an assumption that measures were less important than men. The republic, the Whigs implied, could only be safe in the hands of public-spirited gentlemen of expansive humanity and firm principles, respected public figures in their own right, who would govern for the benefit of all. Such men were presumably found more often in their own patriotic party than in the disreputable corps of spoilsmen and political hacks that constituted their opponents. There was much that was traditional in this view of the presidency. The Whigs were betraying their innate and élitist conservatism in their attempts to disqualify the Democratic candidate because he was a mere party man.

The anti-image fashioned by the Whigs probably seemed the more compelling to them because it helped explain their own relative lack of success in national elections. Not only would they themselves disdain to stoop to the Democrats' demagogic tactics, but the Democratic administrations were employing the apparatus of party and the resources of government to maintain their power. Democratic candidates, even successful ones, were not *really* the choice of the people; rather it was by the use of illicit methods that they were flaunting the popular will. Their weakness for royal trappings further confirmed that they did not truly represent the ordinary people of America. The Whigs' analysis thus simultaneously denied the opposing candidate's pretensions to democracy, cast their own as a virtuous underdog, and offered a forceful reason for his election. Repeated Democratic success could only mean ruin for the republic.

The Whigs were also reaching for voters as well as expressing their own fears in the anti-images they assembled around the Democratic nominee. The doubts they cast on his religious principles, and their attempts to deny him benevolence, were presumably meant in part to activate the pious Protestants of the land against the Democratic ticket. Their emphasis on his lack of real stature and on his shameless partisanship was presumably meant to outrage conservatives of all ranks. But for the most part voters of these kinds were probably in the Whig camp already. The anti-image of the Democratic candidate acted more to send them to the polls by keeping alive their fears. But the anti-image constructed by the Whigs was also a vivid expression of a deep Whig conviction that the American mission was going badly awry.

In their anti-images, as in their images, the two major parties revealed the chasm between them. These were not the Tweedledum and Tweedledee parties of the Gilded Age, but rival groups of men, both pragmatic and principled, who looked on politics in profoundly differing ways. The Democrats betrayed something about themselves in their perceptions of the Whigs, not least in their concern with what the Whig presidential candidate stood for. Their unflattering portrait of the typical Whig contender anticipated a later style of politics by dwelling less on his personality than on the views he supposedly represented. The Democrats were attempting to mobilize voters against the measures of the American System, most conspicuously a national bank, but also those other devices that the federal government might use to promote industrial and commercial development. Offensive to their egalitarian creed, too, was the nativism associated with Whiggery. The Democrats launched an appeal to the people to reject the Whigs for their loose constructionist, commercial and plutocratic ways, and expressed their confidence in the people by asking them to make their judgment on policies rather than personalities. The Whigs revealed themselves a world apart from the Democrats by concerning themselves less with the creed of the Democratic candidate than with his character. What appalled them was his personal unfitness for high office. In their eyes what disqualified him was not so much the policies he espoused but his corrupt and avaricious nature. Indeed, the Democratic parvenu had no genuine views of his own on the issues of state, for he had entered politics in pursuit of gain and his only loyalties were to himself and to his party of like-minded men, bent on plundering the public domain. The Whigs were inviting the voters to reject not so much the measures of the Democrats as their means, to rebuff the professional politicians in favour of the statesman of the old school. The Whigs betrayed an assumption that a good political society would be one in which the people trusted in the judgment of their leaders. Yet this clash between conservative and radical temperaments also had economic and social dimensions. The Democrats' hostility to the role of the federal government in the distribution of economic resources implied a democratic agrarianism; the Whigs' opposition to the creatures of party implied that there was no intrinsic fault in government, which in the right hands could be trusted to promote private enterprise.

But the anti-images paradoxically united Americans as well as divided them. There was considerable agreement on the kind of man who should not be president. Personal ambition was censured as much as it had ever been. Democrats as well as Whigs conceded that a self-serving and voracious individual would endanger the republic once placed in the White House. Such a man would be prepared to use force or fraud in order to sustain himself. He would become the anti-president, the very reverse of the true representative of the people, one who owed his position not to the popular will but to corruption or military might. In all probability, since he was not the people's agent he was the agent of some sinister cabal. In any case the republic would eventually be lost, for master or servant the anti-president was the embodiment of the very antithesis of the republic's ideals, and was bent on restoring an aristocratic society and conceivably even subjecting America once more to English rule.

The anti-image of the president revealed a political world marked by insecurity. Behind the rhetorical assaults of the presidential contests of this period there lurked a measure of anxiety, a fear that the republic was not yet safe. Both major parties seemed at least to share that conviction, a conviction which both deepened their commitment to the republican experiment and enhanced their capacity to espy designs upon it. To them the republic was still young and fragile, could still be destroyed by a president who was temperamentally or ideologically flawed. The framers of the Constitution had tried to create a set of procedures which would serve to place the best men in the White House, for they had believed that the survival of freedom rested in part on the selflessness of those in government. The party battles of the *antebellum* years represented the attempt of a new generation to ensure that the president remained the embodiment of republican virtue.

CHAPTER TEN

# Conclusion: presidential campaigns and American political culture

The framers of the American Constitution had in some measure intended that the office of president should serve a conservative function in the American political system. They had given the president a degree of independent authority which might enable him to curb the whims of the legislature. They had arranged that he should be elected in such a way as to make it more likely that the office would fall on a man of distinction and renown than on a petty party politician. However sunk in mischief and faction the state governments might be, the republic would in part be secured by the patriotism, virtue and sagacity of its Chief Magistrate. These thoughtful electoral arrangements of themselves proved of little avail, but in the end a form of conservatism did triumph. The presidency was not always filled by distinguished statesmen, but the hullabaloo which came to surround presidential elections was in part the product of a resistance to the forces of radicalism and localism. The Democrats could complain with some legitimacy that the Whig campaigns of the 1840s, with their 'Jubilees, feasts and processions', were designed to distract the voter and thus 'to destroy,in its practical working, that plan of government which alone has been founded on just principles of human equality and individual right'. The Whigs themselves passed from the scene, but their extravagant rituals survived, eagerly aided and abetted by the increasingly less radical Democrats and by the people themselves. By the late nineteenth century presidential elections were performing a highly conservative function for the American polity.[1]

In the 1880s Lord Bryce found few differences between the Democrats and Republicans:'neither party has any clean-cut principles, any distinctive tenets. Both have traditions. Both claim to have

213

tendencies.... All has been lost, except office or the hope of it'. But the political culture of the mid-nineteenth century was a divided one. Democracy, in the form of virtual universal (white) manhood suffrage, had arrived in the United States before industrialization. In this largely agrarian society of farmers and small producers the democratic ethic had been carried to some very egalitarian conclusions, much to the alarm of conservatives of all ranks. It stood opposed to the hierarchy of money and merit which the gathering forces of commercialism were already ushering in. This confrontation occurred in a society which was not yet fully convinced of the stability and resilience of its political institutions. The presidential contests of this period were more than mere shadow-boxing. They seemed to their participants to involve the fate of the republic.[2]

The question of who was to be president had always greatly concerned Americans in public life, but popular interest in presidential politics was especially marked in the middle third of the nineteenth century. 'The election of President, being one affecting the whole country, the respective candidates for that office were made the butts at which all political shafts were aimed, and to which every other election was rendered subservient...', observed a British traveller in 1827-28. 'All things are gravitating to one grand centre', worried a respectable Philadelphia newspaper a few years later. 'The Presidency is becoming a potent maelstrom, ingulfing and breaking down to pieces all other powers'. The presidency itself was not that powerful an office, as its incumbents unhappily found, but the process of making a president did dominate American political life. By the 1840s the turnout in presidential elections was surpassing that for state elections and was reaching between 70 and 80 per cent of the electorate, an extraordinary proportion which has not been equalled in the twentieth century. 'The whole country was divided, as if in civil war, into hostile factions', Joseph G. Baldwin remarked of the campaign of 1840. 'Banners flouted the sky; the air rang with acclamations; the people met in armies; and an excitement careered over the land, which, in any other country would have drenched it in blood, and upheaved the government from its foundation stones.'[3]

One reason for the obsession with the presidency was the enduring conviction that it represented a frail point in the American political edifice. There seemed to be no clearer lesson in history than that a power-hungry executive was a deadly enemy of liberty, and the American Revolution itself had begun as a rejection of the overweening pretensions of the English king. Concern about the power of the executive for good or for ill had influenced the Constitution's makers, with their interest in filling the office with statesmen, and had done something to precipitate the first national two-party system, with Alexander Hamilton's conviction that the presidency was not powerful enough and Thomas Jefferson's that Hamilton aimed at a new form of monarchy. The early republic's pervasive anti-power beliefs contributed to the reduction of the presidency to little more than a figurehead, though even this did not banish the fear that an unprincipled and determined man in the White House might do irreparable harm to the republic. From out of that political world emerged the figure of the Mute Tribune, whose self-effacing diffidence was a testimony to the strength of the continuing distrust of ambition and corruption in public men. A philosophy of *noblesse oblige* would make possible an aristocracy of talent and preclude a destructive rule by ambitious demagogues. All the old fears about the subversive potential of the presidency and presidential elections were paraded repeatedly in the persisting discussions over the wisdom of amending that part of the Constitution which related to the executive and were given a new urgency with the anticipated revival of the contest for the presidency in the 1820s. The second American party system had its origins in part in the conviction that the presidential office was being turned against the heritage of liberty, as the Jacksonians accused the Adams administration of striking a 'corrupt bargain' and the Whigs in turn accused the Democrats of 'executive usurpation'.

The destructive potential of the presidency and of presidential elections seemed all the more apparent at a time when Americans were becoming highly conscious both of the heterogeneous nature of their society and of the growth of democracy. The president may have wielded little actual power, but in such a political culture he occupied a highly strategic position. By the 1820s men in public life were increasingly uneasy about the frayed state of the Union: the varied economic discontents arising from the Panic of 1819, the populistic resentments of political establishments, the menacing jealousies between the great geographical sections. American society seemed increasingly to be composed of a multitude of disparate elements, each vividly alert to its own interest, at a time when the political system was operating more than ever on the principle of majority rule. Any vulnerable minority interest, whether economic, sectional, class or ethnic, would feel safer with a friend in the White House. Even if a president could not enact a programme of his own, he could at least protect any endangered interest with his veto power and his control over patronage. Most such political factions wanted access to the president and the outcome of presidential elections was of deep concern to them. It was no coincidence that the revival of the contest for the presidency occurred at a time when American politicians were worried about the capacity of their institutions to withstand the ravages and strains of sectionalism, of economic and social change, and of political innovation.

The increased focus on the presidency was also a reflection of the growing interest of the people at large in presidential politics. State legislatures were finally abandoning their claim to appoint presidential electors and were vesting the right in the people, while the death of King Caucus and the advent of the convention system also tended to enhance the role of the grassroots. The Jacksonians deliberately sought to create a popular political party to elect their chief against the wishes of the Washington politicos, and their rivals, too, were obliged to mobilize support in the country at large. The strikingly high turnouts in presidential elections were in part the result of the relatively close competition between the two major parties in many states. The barbecues, rallies, parades and mass meetings of the period are also evidence of increased popular interest. Presidential elections came to assume a dominant role in American politics as the participation of the masses became more pronounced.

In this complex and popular political society the presidential election served to focus and to simplify political debate. Elections for state and local offices were often held at the same time as presidential elections and were keenly contested; the issues that concerned people at the grassroots varied from area to area. In this amorphous system of politics the presidency was a highly visible national symbol, elections to it were dramatic events, and they commanded popular attention in part because they served to condense and clarify political issues for the mass electorate, and because that electorate was being invited to participate in momentous affairs. If the president was the supreme personification of the American republic, the figure who above all presented an American identity to the world, then those who chose him were taking part in an attempt to define what America should be. 'What a sublime spectacle', marvelled one editor in 1844. 'Millions of men rushing to the polls under the full impression that the weal or woe of the nation was hanging as it were upon their individual act. ... Every voter in the broad expanse of the Union knows and feels that the PEOPLE are this day SOVEREIGNS; one of whom he is . . . .' Presidential elections became central to American political life partly because they provided an opportunity for all citizens to take a personal part in the nation's unique mission. Presidential candidates themselves were thus invested with a portentous responsibility.[4]

The burden of responsibility must have weighed heavily with those who calculated their own chances of reaching the White House. Even as presidents in effect became popularly elected the tradition of the Mute Tribune exerted its inhibiting presence. With the passing of the old party system candidates for a time were obliged to seek the presidency as the heads of personal factions and they explored ways of putting their cases before the somewhat restive electorate without abandoning too abruptly the diffidence of old. Their tentative gestures towards the people, however, were overshadowed by the intense propaganda campaigns conducted on their behalf by their partisans. These campaigns themselves suggested that little active participation by the candidates was to be expected, because they were based on the age-old assumption that a principal danger to the republic was betrayal by its leading men, whether Military Chieftains or corrupt office-holders. The second American party system had its origins in part in the belief that the well-being, even the survival, of the republic rested on the personal fitness of its Chief Magistrate. He was assumed to possess the capacity to undo the experiment in liberty. It was this conviction, indeed, which helped to put an end to the rule of the republic by experienced public servants, who were now said to have succumbed to the temptations of office, and which helped to make possible the election of a man (and later of other men) with little experience of statecraft.

The absolute necessity of placing the presidency in the right hands continued to condition the new two-party system. For both Democrats and Whigs, the candidate was to be the party's instrument for saving the republic from irreparable harm. *Every* presidential election was fervently described, as was 1832, as 'the most important which has been held in the United States'. A Pennsylvania Democrat argued in 1836 that 'the triumph of the opposition would be a death blow to Republican Institutions', while the *Richmond Whig* was equally certain that the election of 1840 would determine the survival of 'the free institutions of Republican America'. The hyperbolic utterances of editors in public were paralleled by the deep fears of politicians in private. 'One more Coonskin, Log Cabin, hard cider triumph upon the heels of the former one, would I fear put an end to the hopes of the friends of civil liberty throughout the world;' wrote a worried Democrat to James K. Polk in 1844, 'and if there ever was a time since the declaration of American independence when every democrat should put on his whole Armor & fight manfully the fight of faith; this is the time.' The Whig leader John J. Crittenden, in a letter marked '(Private)' could write to a colleague in 1848: 'The election of Genl. Taylor is to be *the* event – the great event – of our times – If we fail in that, our Government is but a wreck, and we are given over to proscription'. There were others who could shrug off defeat with equanimity, but the confidential correspondence of many of the politicians of the period shows clearly enough that the apocalyptic warnings in the party press were but graphic variations of fears expressed in private. Perhaps political activists needed to believe in their cause. At any rate, for many men in political life the security of republican liberty – as well as their own preferment – continued to depend on the winning of presidential elections.[5]

The inordinate fears and hopes with which every presidential election was greeted were reflections of the fact that American political culture was deeply divided. The Whig and Democratic parties could view elections with such alarm because each was the virtual antithesis of the other and because neither ever fully accepted the legitimacy of the other. It has been noted how, in the election of 1832, both Andrew Jackson and Henry Clay were each convinced that the success of the other would mean the destruction of America's political institutions. As the parties took firmer shape the personal dimension of the campaigns became less important, and fears about the opposition rested less on the person of the candidate and more on what he represented. They nonetheless remained strong. The extent to which the advent of the second party system dispelled fears of party competition has probably been exaggerated by recent scholars. There were certainly men in both parties who saw positive virtue in regular electoral competition. William H. Seward for the Whigs spoke of the way in which each major party controlled the government 'by turns', and when in opposition exercised 'a salutary restraint upon the controlling party'. In formally accepting the Democratic nomination in 1848 Lewis Cass noted the 'fundamental principles' dividing the parties, but also commented that the 'sublime spectacle of the election of a Chief Magistrate by twenty millions of people', conducted lawfully and peacefully and with mutual respect, would do 'more for the great cause of human freedom throughout the world, than by any other tribute we could render to its value'. But the virtues of party competition did not confer virtue on the opposition, as the worried comments of politicians of both parties testified. The minority party was useful only as long as it remained the minority party. Whig and

Democratic candidates did stand for contrasting visions of the republic, and to a committed partisan the success of his opponents could represent a savage blow to the kind of world he believed essential to liberty. This was not just a matter of self-indulgent ideological posturing, though that played its part. Each party accommodated an array of economic, sectional, class, ethnic, religious and other interests, and in broad terms there was a fair consistency between the world view of the party and the concerns of the particular groups of constituents it represented. The tendency for the more urban and commercial areas to vote Whig, for example, noted in a number of recent studies, was presumably related to that party's greater willingness to use the powers of government to promote economic enterprise. The United States of these years was still a relatively underdeveloped country, and it was still possible to hold differing views as to its political and economic future. Across the diversity of the American Union, of course, a great many views were held as to the ideal republican order, but to a large degree the two major parties did come to represent alternative courses for the republic. Certainly each regarded the political and economic attitudes associated with its opponents as representing the negation of republican ideals and of its own best interests.[6]

A party's selection of a presidential candidate, then, the image constructed around him, and his behaviour in the campaign, were matters of considerable moment. Together they went a long way to encapsulate the beliefs and character of the party. In presenting a presidential candidate to the people, and in damning that of its opponents, a party was saying something about itself and about its albeit rather blurred idea of the good republican order. The coalitional nature of the major parties ensured a measure of fuzziness in their ideals, but if anything helped to focus them it was the confrontation between the rival candidates for president.

The Democratic party in its campaigns for the White House revealed its own unique blend of radicalism and conservatism. The old distrust of personal ambition remained strong among Democrats, who sought to subordinate their candidate to the party. As such they kept alive the traditional conventions regarding the behaviour of candidates for president, and remonstrated against the personal campaigning of Whig candidates as evidence of egotism and greed. But the Democratic version of the Mute Tribune served an untraditional purpose; he was the personification of a movement which wanted to put into political effect the belief that all white men were equal.

This at least seemed to be the message of Democratic presidential campaigns. On occasion the Democrats nominated a dark horse for president, largely the result of an interaction of expediency with convention machinery, but also of a Democratic willingness to be represented by the obscure as well as by the great. It was Andrew Jackson himself, after all, who had said that the duties 'of all public officers' could be made 'so plain and simple that men of intelligence may readily qualify themselves for their performance', and Democratic intellectuals like George Bancroft had emphasized the universality of man's capacity for wisdom. The Democratic presidential nominee was to be a servant and not a master, and the more he was identified with plain folk the better. Once nominated, the Democratic nominee usually showed that he knew his place. Andrew Jackson, of course, had expected the party to follow him, but increasingly the candidate deferred to the party, adopting an ever lower profile with each election. He forthrightly committed himself to the platform drawn up by the convention and then retreated quietly to his home, for the most part avoiding public appearances, speeches and even the press. When a Democratic candidate did depart from his stance of passivity, notably Van Buren in his public letters, he made it clear that it was for the most democratic of reasons, acknowledging the electorate's right to question him and stressing the Democratic orthodoxy of his views. Publicly at least, the typical Democratic nominee offered little leadership, defined no issues, made few decisions. His campaign was left to his partisans, who in their depiction of their own candidate and in their hostile analysis of his opponent, again presented the Democratic party as the true vehicle of the people. They did not hesitate to portray their flagbearer as a faithful party servant who owed his position not to birth or even talent but to industry and perseverance, qualities which might be possessed by anyone. A strict constructionist, this earthy man of the people was cast as a loyal defender of agrarian simplicity against the designs of the monied, commercial and aristocratic cabals which were bent on subverting the republic. The Democratic candidate was usually made to embody the frugal, self-reliant and egalitarian virtues of a society of independent farmers and small producers, the Jeffersonian arcadia that Marvin Meyers and others have perceived in Democratic rhetoric.[7]

Ultimately it was the party rather than the candidate which the Democrats were offering in presidential elections. That their nominees were but the loyal and obedient servants of party was stressed repeatedly both by the nominees themselves and by their supporters. The Democrats disdained the campaign extravaganzas of the Whigs, but they made it clear what their candidate stood for – the Democratic party and its announced measures. In insisting that the electorate should accept or reject them on their platform, the Democrats were acting on the democratic conviction that the majority of the people should determine what governments should do. (The Democratic support for the doctrine of instructions, which argued the right of an electorate to instruct its representatives how to vote, although not normally an issue in presidential campaigns, rested on similar assumptions.) The Democrats were close to implementing a form of plebiscitary democracy, in which each citizen was given an equal voice in determining the measures by which he would be governed. Democratic politicians could afford their trust in the judgment of the people because they undoubtedly identified themselves with the body of the people. Their party they called 'the Democracy', barely distinguishable in their minds from 'the democratic people', that vast body of ordinary men who would naturally look with suspicion on privilege of any kind. Democrats tended to see the party battle, in the words of a *Globe* correspondent, as 'a mortal struggle for political supremacy between the Democracy of Numbers and the Aristocracy of Wealth'. The party was thus seen as a great brotherhood of equal men acting together to protect their liberties against the concentrated forces of aristocracy. Unpatriotic minorities were forever seeking power, pelf and privilege – in the Bank, in the Whig party, in Congress – for themselves, and could do so only at the expense of the (Democratic) people. The Democratic candidate, then, was but the dutiful agent of the people, and would embody their will. As their trusted servant, indeed, he need not be feared when he assumed presidential office. If the president was the loyal instrument of party and people, it was but right that he should enjoy a measure of independence from Congress and stand ready to strike down measures not mandated by the people, measures which were thus the work of those selfish minorities which forever preyed on the public domain. The values with which the Democrats associated themselves were both agrarian and unequivocally egalitarian. More perhaps than any other political movement in American history, they believed that only through the medium of party, that trade union of the people, could their goals be achieved. Implicit in their conduct of presidential campaigns was the assumption that the Democratic party itself, through its measures and its machinery, was the great levelling device in American life. The reversion of the Democratic candidate to the role of Mute Tribune was fitting for one who was barely first among equals.[8]

The Democratic view that the president could be made a safe custodian of the people's liberties if he were harnessed to their will did little to allay Whig fears of the destructive potential of the White House. The Whigs also believed that possession of the presidency was the key to saving the republic, which to them meant protecting it from the ruinous depredations of the Democrats. The Whigs made clear the gulf that existed between the two major parties by their own conduct of presidential campaigns. Their candidates amply embodied the ambiguous principles of Whiggery, not least by their own unabashed electioneering. The Whig candidates did more than their opponents to undermine the tradition of the Mute Tribune, but the rodomontade they substituted for reticence did more to obscure than to clarify. The Whigs possessed their own combination of conservatism and innovation, but their novel campaigning techniques seemed designed to sustain a traditional political order.

The Whig party preferred its presidential candidates to be men of stature, partly no doubt for electoral reasons but partly because Whigs seemed to be more comfortable with great men. A celebrated military man in particular, a figure of high visibility but low party and sectional identification, enabled Whigs both to indulge their respect for rank and to display themselves as the patriots they believed themselves to be. The candidates for their part were prepared to take their campaigns before the people themselves, and as their party ingeniously resorted to every variety of ballyhoo, the candidates toured the country, wrote letters for publication, and even on occasion delivered themselves of speeches. Their personal appearances, however, represented an attempt to play down their role as party candidates, for they affected to have been chosen 'spontaneously' by the people and they said little about specific policies, insisting on going untrammelled into public office. They were in effect inviting the people to judge them on their public characters and past services. This message was reinforced in the images constructed about them. Whig candidates were invariably depicted as exceptionally gifted men, but also as human and humane men, benevolent, pious and temperate Christians who set an exemplary standard for others. Through their candidates, the Whigs were suggesting that their own ranks were composed of men of talent, vision, humanity and virtue, capable of rising above partisan considerations in patriotic pursuit of the public good. Since the Whig candidates refused to make 'pledges', and since little was said about their political views, the implication was that like the statesmen of an earlier day the Whig leaders would determine their measures after due deliberation in office. To the Whigs, the republic would be better secured on the ideal of public service than on the plebiscitary democracy of the Democrats.

The Whig reluctance to make electoral commitments betrayed a willingness to use government to promote the common weal, for in the absence of strict constructionist pronouncements it had to be assumed that Whig administrations would enact positive measures. There was no secret that many leading Whigs were keen supporters of 'American System' measures, which Henry Clay and others would be expected to promote in Congress. Since the Whig distaste for the populistic style of presidency of the Democrats had led them to advocate the curbing of presidential power, a non-partisan president who would defer to the will of Congress presumably meant that Whig success at the polls (including congressional elections) would be followed by the kind of economic programme associated with Henry Clay. This would mean the promotion of commercial and industrial enterprise, but this vision of a new economic world did not belie the Whigs' political conservatism. The Whigs had made some accommodation to the egalitarianism of the day, and knew better than to tie privilege to birth or inheritance. In economics as in politics there was to be an equality of opportunity. Men were to be free to rise as high as their talents carried them. The Whig celebration of the 'genius' of their presidential candidates implied a hierarchy of talent, and it was because they believed that there were great differences between men's abilities that the Whigs were able to embrace democracy. In the ideal world of the Whigs, the distribution of rank, whether political, economic or social, would reflect the distribution of ability. It was this meritocratic ethic in Whiggery which made the Democratic Party anathema to many Whigs. It was above all opposition to the Democratic *party* which gave coherence to the Whig party. The Whig candidates said little about what Whig administration would do, but when they did speak out it was against Democratic Party discipline, the Democratic use of presidential power, and Democratic use of patronage. No doubt many Whigs genuinely believed that the Democratic party consisted of a machine of corrupt spoilsmen which threatened to win despotic control of the country. But they were also instinctively reacting against the Democrats' tendency to turn elections into referenda, against their populistic conception of the presidency, and against their view of their party as an instrument of the masses. The *Richmond Whig* captured one Whig sentiment when it sighed that America's institutions had been 'assailed by the levelling spirit which, in succession, has overthrown all Republics', an 'Agrarianism' which was 'far more dangerous than the hostility of Aristocrats, and the arms of Kings'. The Whig resort to highly visible but above-party presidential candidates, who energetically offered themselves for their characters rather than their views, represented a conservative instinct to leave the affairs of government to the 'best men'.[9]

The conservatism and contradictory nature of the Whig party ultimately contributed to its demise. The Whigs esteemed leadership but were reluctant to allow the president much authority. Many of them despised the operations of party but knew that they could not resist the Democrats without a party. They did possess a coherent economic philosophy, but they were reluctant to avow it at election time, perhaps because they were governed by the patrician instinct that men mattered more than measures. (Daniel Walker Howe has recently noted the Whigs' respect for the philosophical conservatism of Edmund Burke, as expressed in his phrase that 'Manners are of more importance than law'.) The Whigs were thus left without a cause, expect the thankless one of resisting the Democratic party and all its works, and this could only give credence to Democratic allegations about their aristocratic propensities. In the early 1850s the party found itself unable to withstand the sectional and nativist strains of the day, and the Whigs went the same way as earlier men of little faith. Only when the Republicans found in free labour, free soil, antislavery and anti-southernism, an emotive range of causes which both drew strength from the American libertarian tradition and showed confidence in the capacity of the ordinary citizen, was a party ideology forged dynamic enough to compete with that of the Democracy.[10]

The conduct of the presidential campaigns of the *antebellum* United States emphasizes the pre-modern nature of the age. The Revolution was not long past and it continued to condition the way men thought about politics. National independence may have been achieved, and reasserted by the War of 1812, but that did not of itself guarantee the success of the great experiment in republican liberty, and there was still intense dispute as to the character of the good American society. It was an ideological age, one in which Americans seemed driven both by great hopes and by great fears.

The fear that the experiment in republicanism could go badly awry arose in part from a persisting consciousness of its relative novelty. Permeating the presidential campaigning of the period were feelings of both pride and unease at the republic's recent birth and an assumption that it had not yet grown safely to maturity. The candidates themselves never quite shook themselves clear of the tradition of the Mute Tribune, even the energetic Whig hopefuls having to insist that they were not soliciting votes. There was still a need to disavow the personal ambition and the intrigue which the constitution-makers had been so concerned to guard against. The ideal president was delineated in the images so lavishly constructed around the nominee. He was to be the personification of his country, nurtured in patriotism and piety, close to the soil and the people, an agent of the providential mission to replace savagery with civilization, manly and homely and possessed of a rugged self-reliance which made him the master of his own destiny. The republic could feel secure with such a leader, as it could only be betrayed by his antithesis, the anti-president. The presidency was the supreme symbol of the American republic and in that office above all Americans wanted a living proof that their highest ideals could still be realized. The republic was still young and needed the reassurance of virtue in the White House.

The successive election campaigns served both as a force for consensus and for conflict. The values and attitudes encapsulated in the image of the archetypal president were held by most Americans, and the campaign rhetoric of all parties reminded Americans of their common allegiance to the political accomplishments of their revolutionary fathers. But in stressing the youth of the republic, the campaigners were also underlining its fragility. Simply because political activists felt a need to affirm their devotion to the republican ideal, the party contest became deeply divisive. The socioeconomic divisions consequent upon commercial growth were occurring at a time when Americans were still imbued with the sense of republican mission. As partisans insisted that they themselves were remaining true to the faith of the Founders, they could only see their opponents as betraying that faith. Each election campaign became a battle to save the republic by banishing the rascals who were subverting it. A correspondent of the Democratic presidential candidate in 1836 was worried about the 150 corporations which had been chartered by his state legislature in the last two sessions 'and are now entwining themselves around the interest of the people to such a degree that I tremble for our liberties'. Four years later the Whig vice-presidential candidate confided to a colleague that a 'last and final effort is to be made to beat back the tide of corruption which has been threatening to overflow the land for the last ten years'. But corruption was in the eye of the beholder. 'I do not despair of the Republic, but I assure you that I have felt . . . an anxiety on its account, which I have never before known', admitted the New York Democrat Silas Wright after the 1840 election. 'The state of things at home is dreadful, and in a political sense more than in a financial.' Political defeat could certainly sharpen the sense of the vulnerability of republican institutions. 'The storm is over, and we the people of the United States are shipwrecked, and I fear too much damaged ever to be repaired,' mourned a Whig in the aftermath of the 1844 election. In private as in public, partisan politicians were the guardians of the nation's heritage of liberty, fighting much the same battles as their fathers.[11]

The commitment to liberty, to the awesome heritage of the American Revolution, was woven deep into the fabric of American politics, but it moved men in different ways. In this diverse society, in which Americans were nurtured by a variety of sectional, economic, religious and other environments, all could feel equally dedicated to the libertarian tradition but each could perceive different threats to it. For many northerners, as William R. Brock has recently reminded us, the American declaration of war against Mexico in 1846, with its resort to violence, was incompatible with the model republic's avowed respect for human rights. To many Alabamians, their own devotion to liberty deepened by knowledge of slavery, as J. Mills Thornton III has demonstrated, both the Monster Bank and the northern antislavery men seemed intent on reducing southerners to dependency – that is to a form of slavery. Eric Foner has similarly emphasized the centrality of the notion of individual autonomy in the thinking of northern Republicans, who came to perceive the South as the very negation of free society. No one could seriously deny that prejudice, economic self-interest, personal ambition and a host of other motives, noble and ignoble, played their part in the political struggles of these years, but present, too, was the conviction that the unique bequest of liberty had forever to be protected from the encroachments of power. In a political culture formed in no small part by the revolutionary generation's conviction that freedom meant independence, that individual liberty meant individual autonomy, anything which could render men subservient, whether a monied aristocracy, party discipline, or an expansionary Slave Power, could seem like a betrayal of the American mission. Such despotic growths need not threaten national independence or social stability for them to appear to jeopardise republican liberty.[12]

The presidential contest, in which to its participants liberty continued to be pitted against power, could be said to have institutionalized the revolutionary conflict, and this in itself brought a measure of order to the republic. Presidential elections served as quadrennial purification ceremonies, their periodic return ensuring that hope did not entirely give way to despair. 'If I can aid in any way', wrote one

Whig to another in 1839, 'to rid the country of the plunderers, the knaves, the rascals, the blackguards & fools... with whom the administration is infested you may rely upon it'. The republic might be cleansed and a faith in republican virtue reborn. A Democrat privately took sustenance from the proceedings of his party's national convention in 1844: 'I see in them the hope renewed of the perpetuation of our institutions, as well as the diffusion of Republican principles beyond our borders.' Presidential campaigns, which linked the ordinary citizen with the first officer of the Union, both served as a vivid affirmation of self-government and held out the prospect not only of the restoration of virtue to the White House but to the whole body politic. The conservative William C. Rives on one occasion definitively described the conservative function of a presidential election: 'The election of Chief Magistrate of the nation is one of those vital processes provided by the Constitution of the country, for the periodical regeneration of our system by a fresh infusion into it of the elements of popular health and virtue, in which no good citizen ... can properly refuse to take a part....'[13]

It may be, as has been observed elsewhere, that government by majority rule works best when the issues dividing the parties are relatively superficial, that is, where the parties share many fundamental values. That the parties must accept the basic constitutional structure, so that they are prepared to abide by the results of lawful elections, is presumably beyond serious dispute. But it should not be overlooked that the American constitutional system, particularly the provision for frequent elections, can make it possible for two fundamentally different political movements to exist side by side. Both during the first and during the second American party systems there were profound social and ideological differences between the competing parties. While the value of party competition was coming to be recognized by the Jacksonian era, many politicians, particularly the party doctrinaires, were loathe to concede the legitimacy (as opposed to the inevitability) of the rival party, which seemed too much like a threat to republican forms. Yet the recurring elections, especially presidential elections, offered grounds for hope as well as fear. They made possible the consolatory thought that the republic might at least be rescued from the barbarians four years hence.[14]

Yet perhaps the intense battles between Democrat and Whig did ultimately serve to disrupt the American Union. The ferocity of the second party system may have contributed to that of the party system of the Civil War era. Americans had been told since Washington's administration that the fate of the republic rested on the outcome of the next presidential election. They had long been accustomed to a system of politics in which each major party considered its rival to be a hazard to free institutions. Thus far this ideological divide had not coincided with a sectional polarization, but when it did the effects were fatal. In the 1850s the new Republican party and the surviving Democratic party were the recipients of much of the conventional wisdom perpetuated by the old party contests, such as the set of convictions which held that the republic was still vulnerable, that the opposition menaced it, and that a principal safeguard was virtue in the White House. Presidential elections had long had to carry immense emotional and ideological weight; in 1860-61 an old prophesy was at last fulfilled.

In the course of time much of the fervour did disappear from presidential elections, if not the hullabaloo. In a more cynical and pragmatic age the apocalyptic nature of American campaign rhetoric would sound like hyperbole. No doubt a number of influences contributed to the rhetorical extravagance of the *antebellum* years: the endless social ferment which created insecurity and a tendency to imagine or magnify an enemy; the intrusion into politics of the moral imperatives of evangelical Protestantism; the belief that social order in a republic rested above all on the persuasive oratory of its public men. But the apocalyptic language was also the language of a society which was at once both extravagantly optimistic and deeply apprehensive about itself, of a political culture which was divided against itself. Americans were still highly conscious of both the singularity and the novelty of their mission to demonstrate the virtues of republican liberty to mankind, a mission which was as yet unfulfilled. 'We hold an immense stake for the weal or woe of mankind . . .' wrote Martin Van Buren in formally accepting the Democratic nomination for 1836. 'The interest manifested abroad in every movement here, that threatens the stability of our system, shews the deep conviction which pervades the world, that upon its fate depends the cause of republican government'. This historic trust could both exhilarate and unnerve, and it now appeared to many Americans that their novel experiment was at a crossroads. The United States had achieved a form of political democracy before it had undergone the process of industrialization, and the rise of commerce, industry and the city seemed to some citizens to threaten the full implementation of the declaration that all men are created equal. To others the growth of party forms threatened the individual judgment which was the basis of liberty. Of course, the two major parties were not as ideologically pure as they liked to portray themselves, they were certainly not monolithic bodies, and they each contained their share of cynics and organization men. Like politicians in most societies, the party activists of mid-nineteenth-century America were capable of combining principle with pragmatism, as their conduct of presidential campaigns demonstrated. Yet their commitment to principle, and the degree to which they were separated by principle, has sometimes been underestimated, perhaps because those principles fared badly in the longer perspective of history. After the ideological passions had faded and American political culture had taken on a more relaxed aspect, the highest ideals of both Whigs and Democrats could be seen to have come to naught. By the time of the Gilded Age both the radical egalitarianism of the Democrats and the public service ideals of the Whigs seemed like grotesque anachronisms. Ironically, not the best hopes but the worst fears of each party had come to pass. The Whig warning that the political practices of the Democrats were ushering-in government by spoilsmen seemed amply vindicated. The Democratic apprehension that the doctrines of Whiggery would give rise to economic and social inequality and a form of plutocracy seemed no less confirmed. Each party had been most successful in foretelling the future not in its own vision of the good republican order but in the sombre tendencies that each had espied in the other.[15]

The political culture of the Jacksonian years was less modern than the electoral hullabaloo might suggest. In the party battles of the 1830s and 1840s Americans were still acting out the drama begun in 1776. Certainly the role and behaviour of the presidential candidate were governed in no small measure by values and assumptions inherited from the eighteenth century. Yet candidates had begun to depart from the example of the Mute Tribune, as they sought to reconcile the self-denying ethic of republicanism with the demands of an active mass electorate. The Democrats contributed a recognition that the voters were entitled to know the views of the candidates and an emphasis on campaign organization and discipline, but guarded against personal ambition by subordinating the candidate to the party. The Whigs freed the candidate from the need to remain passive, though the energetic gyrations of their figureheads reflected a profound distaste for the party measures and machinery with which the Democrats hoped to democratize American life. The Whig contribution was an emphasis on rhetoric and ritual (rather than party discipline), as they attempted to invoke public sentiment on behalf of the traditional order. With the ending of the second party system presidential candidates were prompted to assume a more prominent role in campaigns. Stephen A. Douglas, the nominee of the northern Democrats in 1860, took to the stump knowing that he could not rely on the unquestioned support of his fragmenting party. In the post-Civil War years custom was more frequently defied when candidates took either to the stump, like James G. Blaine and a belated Grover Cleveland in 1884, or to a garrulous front-porch, like Benjamin Harrison in 1888. The presidency itself probably seemed a less fearful office in the wake of a series of ineffective incumbents, and corruption could conspicuously be seen elsewhere in the political system. As the ideological divide between the major parties diminished, and as the constraints of eighteenth-century values disappeared, both Democrats and Republicans and their ever more assertive candidates were to follow the Whig lead in subordinating issues to ritual in these quadrennial celebrations of the nation's greatness.

# References

## Chapter 1: The Mute Tribune

1. W. Lowndes to James Hamilton, 29 Dec. 1821, in Mrs St Julien Ravenal, *Life and Times of William Lowndes of South Carolina, 1782–1822*, Houghton Mifflin, 1901, p. 226; Leonard W. Labaree *et al.* (eds), *The Autobiography of Benjamin Franklin*, Yale U.P., 1964, p. 185.
2. Gouverneur Morris in Max Farrand (ed.), *The Records of the Federal Convention of 1787*, Yale U.P., (rev. edn), 1937, ii, p. 52.
3. George Washington to Benjamin Lincoln, 26 Oct. 1788, John C. Fitzpatrick (ed.), *The Writings of George Washington from the Original Manuscript Sources, 1745–1799*, U.S. Government Printing Office, 1939, xxx, p. 119; Washington to Charles Thomson, 14 April 1789, *ibid.*, xxx, p. 285; James Thomas Flexner, *George Washington and the New Nation, 1783–1793*, Little, Brown, 1970, pp. 171–2.
4. Jefferson to Madison, 27 April 1795, Andrew A. Lipscomb and Albert Ellery Bergh (eds), *The Writings of Thomas Jefferson*, Jefferson Memorial Association, 1907, ix, p. 303; John Adams, Diary, 12–21 July 1796, Adams Papers, Microfilm Reel 2, Massachusetts Historical Society; Page Smith, *John Adams*, Doubleday, 1962, ii, pp. 892–8; John Adams, Diary, 4 Aug. 1796; Madison to James Monroe, 29 Sept. 1796, in Irving Brant, *James Madison: Father of the Constitution*, Bobbs-Merrill, 1950, p. 444; Jefferson to Madison, 17 Dec. 1796, Lipscomb & Bergh (eds), *op. cit.*, ix, p. 351.
5. John Adams to his wife, Henry Cabot Lodge (ed.), *Life and Letters of George Cabot*, Little, Brown, 1878, p. 574; Monroe to Jefferson, 27 Feb. 1808, Stanislaus Murray Hamilton (ed.), *The Writings of James Monroe*, Putnam, 1898, v, p. 26.
6. Cleric quoted by Russel Blaine Nye, *The Cultural Life of the New Nation, 1776–1830*, Harper & Row, 1963, p. 51; Flexner, *Washington and New Nation*, p. 165.
7. For discussions of hope and anxiety see, e.g., Page Smith, 'Anxiety and Despair in American History', *William and Mary Quarterly*, xxvi (July 1969), pp. 416–24; Arthur Schlesinger, Jr, 'America: experiment

or Destiny?', *American Historical Review*, lxxxii (June 1977), pp. 505–22; on cyclical theory, see Stow Persons, 'The Cyclical Theory of History in Eighteenth Century America', *American Quarterly*, vi (1954), pp. 147–63; Washington quoted in Saul K. Padover (ed.), *The World of the Founding Fathers: Their Basic Ideas on Freedom and Self-Government*, Thomas Yoseloff, 1960, p. 560.

8. For themes touched on in this paragraph, see, e.g., J. G. A. Pocock, 'Machiavelli, Harrington, and English Political Ideologies in the Eighteenth Century', *William and Mary Quarterly*, xxii (Oct. 1965), pp. 549–83, and *The Machiavellian Moment: Florentine Political Thought and the Atlantic Republican Tradition*, Princeton U.P., 1975; Lance Banning, *The Jeffersonian Persuasion: Evolution of a Party Ideology*, Cornell U.P., 1978; Bernard Bailyn, *The Ideological Origins of the American Revolution*, Harvard U.P., 1967; Jack P. Greene, 'Search for Identity: An Interpretation of the Meaning of Selected Patterns of Social Response in Eighteenth-Century America', *Journal of Social History*, iii, (Spring 1970), pp. 189–220.

9. Padover, *op. cit.*, pp. 269–70; Gordon S. Wood, *The Creation of the American Republic, 1776–1787*, U. North Carolina P., 1969, p. 30; Jefferson to John Adams, 28 Feb. 1796, Charles Francis Adams (ed.), *The Works of John Adams, Second President of the United States*, Boston 1853, viii, p. 517.

10. *An Address to the People of the County of Hampshire by a Committee Appointed for that Purpose*, Northampton, Mass., 1809, p. 3.

11. Rev. Abraham Williams in Edmund S. Morgan (ed.), *Puritan Political Ideas, 1558–1794*, Bobbs-Merrill, 1965, p. 346; David Tappan, 1798, in Stow Persons, *op. cit.*, p. 153 (see also Wood, *op. cit.*, pp. 36–7); Samuel Langdon, 'Government Corrupted by Vice, and Recovered by Righteousness', 1775, in A. W. Plumstead (ed.), *The Wall and the Garden: selected Massachusetts election sermons 1670–1775*, U. Minnesota P., 1968, p. 361.

12. 'A Bill for the More General Diffusion of Knowledge', Julian P. Boyd (ed.), *The Papers of Thomas Jefferson*, Princeton U.P., 1950, ii, p. 526; Samuel Langdon in Plumstead, *op. cit.*, p. 365; Hamilton to Gouverneur Morris, 27 Feb. 1802, Henry Cabot Lodge (ed.), *The Works of Alexander Hamilton*, Putnam, 1904, vii, p. 591; Delaware revolutionary in Wood, *op. cit.*, p. 135.

13. Farrand (ed.), *Records of Federal Convention*, i, p. 376.

14. Azariah Mather, *Good Rulers a Choice Blessing. A Sermon Preached before the Great and General Assembly of the Colony of Connecticut, at Hartford in New England, May 13th, 1725*, New London, 1725, pp. 4, 14; Williams in Morgan (ed.), *op. cit.*, p. 349; Samuel Shepard, *A Sermon, Preached in the Audience of His Excellency Caleb Strong, Esq., Governor; His Honor Edward H. Robbins, Esq., Lieutenant-Governor; The Honorable the Council, Senate, and House of Representatives of the Commonwealth of Massachusetts, on the Anniversary Election, May 28, 1806*, Stockbridge, Mass., 1806, p. 29; Boyd (ed.), *Papers of Jefferson*, ii, p. 527; *Pennsylvania Mercury*, 8 July 1788, Merrill Jensen and Robert A. Becker (eds), *The Documentary History of the First Federal Elections, 1788–1790*, U. Wisconsin P., 1976, i, p. 245.

15. 'Notes on the Confederacy-April 1787', *Letters and Other Writings of James Madison*, Lippincott, 1865, i, p. 328.

16. Edmund Randolph in Farrand (ed.), *Records of Federal Convention*, ii, p. 89; Richard Henry Lee in Padover (ed.), *op. cit.*, p. 327; Morris in Farrand, ii, p. 29; Washington to Benjamin Fishbourn, 23 Dec. 1788, Fitzpatrick (ed.), *Writings of Washington*, xxx, p. 171.

17. Farrand (ed.), *Records of Federal Convention*, ii, pp. 56, 104; Alexander Hamilton, James Madison & John Jay, *The Federalist or, The New Constitution*, J. M. Dent, 1970, No. 68, pp. 347–48.

18. *Ibid.*, p. 349; Farrand (ed.), *op. cit.*, ii, pp. 56–7.

19. Pierce Butler quoted by Charles C. Thach, Jr, *The Creation of the Presidency, 1775–1789: A Study in Constitutional History*, Johns Hopkins U.P., 1922, p. 169.

20. Washington to John Armstrong, 25 April 1788; Washington to Charles Pettit, 16 Aug. 1788, Fitzpatrick (ed.), *Writings of Washington*, xxix, p. 464, xxx, p. 42; Jefferson to Madison , 27 April 1795, Lipscomb & Bergh (eds), *Writings of Jefferson*, ix, pp. 302–3; Adams to John Trumbull, 10 Sept. 1800, John Adams Letterbook, Adams Papers, Microfilm Reel 120.

21. Washington to Alexander Hamilton, 28 Aug. 1788, Fitzpatrick (ed.), *Writings of Washington*, xxx, pp. 66–7; Mason in Louise Burnham Dunbar, *A Study of 'Monarchical' Tendencies in the United States from 1776 to 1801*. U. Illinois P., 1922, p. 99; Washington's draft inaugural in Flexner, *Washington and New Nation*, p. 163; Adams to Henry Marchant, 3 March 1792, John Adams Letterbook, Adams Papers, Microfilm Reel 115; Page Smith, *John Adams*, ii, p. 1034.

22. Monroe to Jefferson, 12 July 1788, Hamilton (ed.), *Writings of Monroe*, i, p. 186; Jefferson to Philip Mazzei, 24 April 1796, Robert McColley (ed.), *Federalists, Republicans, and Foreign Entanglements, 1789–1815*, Prentice Hall, 1969, p. 82; *Mr. Tracy's Speech in the Senate of the United States, Friday, December 2, 1803, On the Passage of the Following Amendment to the Constitution*, [n.p., n.d.], p. 9; Augustus B. Woodward, *Considerations on the Executive Government of the United States*, Flatbush, N.Y., 1809, pp. 12–13; Hillhouse in [Thomas Hart Benton], *Abridgement of the Debate of Congress, from 1789 to 1856*, New York, 1857, iii, p. 610 (12 April 1808).

23. Jefferson to Madison, 17 Dec. 1796, 1 Jan. 1797, Lipscomb & Bergh (eds), *Writings of Jefferson*, ix, pp. 351, 359; Jefferson to Edmund Pendleton, 29 Jan. 1799, Jefferson to Archibald Stuart, 13 Feb. 1799, Jefferson to Monroe, 12 Jan. 1800, *ibid.*, x, pp. 86–8, 104, 136.

24. Jefferson to Gerry, 26 Jan. 1799, *ibid.*, x, pp. 74–86.

25. Jefferson to Mazzei, 24 April 1796, McColley (ed.), *op. cit.*, p. 82; Hamilton to Edward Carrington, 26 May 1792, Harold C. Syrett (ed.), *The Papers of Alexander Hamilton*, Columbia U.P., 1966, xi, p. 429. On the emergence of party see Banning, *The Jeffersonian Persuasion*, esp. Ch. 6, and M. J. Heale, *The Making of American Politics, 1750–1850*, Longman, 1977, esp. Chs 6 & 7.

26. Adams to Jefferson, 6 April 1796, Lester J. Cappon (ed.), *The Adams-Jefferson Letters: The Complete Correspondence Between Thomas Jefferson and Abigail and John Adams*, U. North Carolina p., 1959, i, pp. 261–2;

Charles Francis Adams (ed.), *Memoirs of John Quincy Adams, comprising portions of His Diary from 1795 to 1848*, Philadelphia 1874–7, i, p. 514 (13 Feb. 1808); Monroe to John Randolph, 23 March 1808, Hamilton (ed.), *Writings of Monroe*, v, p. 35 (see also Harry Ammon, *James Monroe: The Quest for National Identity*, McGraw-Hill, 1971, pp. 255–6, 269–77, and Irving Brant, *James Madison, Secretary of State, 1800–1809*, Bobbs-Merrill, 1953, pp. 419–67); *Niles' Register*, 5 March 1817, p. 20; Adams (ed.), *Memoirs of J. Q. Adams*, v, p. 90 (2 May 1820).

27. Monroe to Madison, 9 Oct. 1792, Hamilton (ed.), *Writings of Monroe*, i, pp. 242–3; Harold C. Syrett (ed.), *The Papers of Alexander Hamilton*, Columbia U.P., 1967, xii, p. 480; Adams to Elbridge Gerry, 30 Dec. 1800, John Adams Letterbook, Adams Papers, Microfilm Reel 120; Adams to Jefferson, 15 Nov. 1813, Cappon (ed.), *Adams-Jefferson Letters*, ii, p. 401.

28. John Tyler to Jefferson quoted in Charles S. Sydnor, *Political Leadership in Eighteenth-Century Virginia*, Clarendon Press, 1951, p. 14; Jefferson to Rutledge, 27 Dec. 1796, Lipscomb & Bergh (eds), *Writings of Jefferson*, ix, p. 354; 'Senex', *New Hampshire Spy*, 19 May 1789, John Wendell to Elbridge Gerry, 23 July 1789, Jensen & Becker (eds), *First Federal Elections*, i, pp. 842, 851.

29. *Mr. Tracy's Speech in the Senate*, p. 2. For recent works dealing with political values in the early republic, other than those cited previously, see Gerald Stourzh, *Alexander Hamilton and the Idea of Republican Government*, Stanford U.P. 1970; Richard Buel, Jr, *Securing the Revolution: Ideology in American Politics, 1789–1815*, Cornell U.P., 1972; Richard E. Ellis, *The Jeffersonian Crisis: Courts and Politics in the Young Republic*, Oxford U.P., 1971; David Hackett Fischer, *The Revolution of American Conservatism*, Harper Torchbooks, 1969; James Sterling Young, *The Washington Community, 1800–1828*, Columbia U.P., 1966; Robert M. Johnstone, Jr, *Jefferson and the Presidency: Leadership in the Young Republic*, Cornell U.P., 1978; Robert Dawidoff, *The Education of John Randolph*, W. W. Norton, 1979.

## Chapter 2: Changing the rules

1. *Propositions for Amending the Constitution of the United States; Submitted by Mr. Hillhouse to the Senate, on the Twelfth Day of April, 1808, with his Explanatory Remarks*, New Haven, 1808, p. 18; *Annals of Congress*, 15th Cong., 2nd session, p. 141 (13 Jan. 1819); 'Publius', *Richmond Enquirer*, 23 Dec. 1823; *Columbian Centinel* (Boston), 22 Oct. 1828.

2. *Register of Debates in Congress*, 19th Cong., 1st session, p. 1393 (16 Feb. 1826). For unease over the possible loss of republican virtue after 1815, see Fred Somkin, *Unquiet Eagle: Memory and Desire in the Idea of American Freedom, 1815–1860*, Cornell U.P., 1967.

3. *Annals of Congress*, 14th Cong., 2nd session, 333 (18 Dec. 1816). On attempts to amend the Constitution see Lucius Wilmerding, Jr, *The Electoral College*, Rutgers U.P., 1958, Ch. 3.

4. Herman V. Ames, 'The Proposed Amendments to the Constitution of the United States during the First Century of its History', *Annual Report of the American Historical Association for the Year 1896*, Washington, 1897, ii, provides a list of proposed amendments.

5. George McDuffie quoted in Wilmerding, *op. cit.*, p. 47.

6. *Annals of Congress,* 15th Cong., 2nd session, p. 149 (M. Dickerson, 13 Jan. 1819); 17th Cong., 2nd session, p. 222 (11 Feb. 1823).

7. Adams to Jefferson, 15 Nov. 1813, Cappon (ed.), *Adams-Jefferson Letters,* ii, 401; *Register of Debates,* 19th Cong., 1st session, p. 1393 (16 Feb. 1826), p. 1888 (29 March 1826), p. 1380 (16 Feb. 1826).

8. *Albany Argus,* 27 Feb. 1824; [T.H. Benton], *Abridgement of Debates,* v, p. 677 (17 Dec. 1816); 'A FARMER', *Washington Gazette,* 9 Feb. 1822; *Annals of Congress,* 17th Cong., 1st session, ii, 1700–1701 (27 April 1822); *Suggestions on Presidential Elections, with Particular Reference to a Letter of William C. Somerville, Esq.,* Boston, 1825, p. 24.

9. *Register of Debates,* 19th Cong., 1st session, ii, p. 1582 (9 March 1826); Richard Hofstadter, *The Idea of a Party System: The Rise of Legitimate Opposition in the United States, 1780–1840,* California U.P., 1970, p. 196; *Annals of Congress,* 18th Cong., 1st session, pp. 169–170, 173–6 (3 Feb. 1824); *Register of Debates,* 19th Cong., 1st session, pp. 369–70 (18 March 1824).

10. *Register of Debates,* 19th Cong., 1st session, p. 1678 (Silas Wood, 14 March 1826).

11. *Annals of Congress,* 18th Cong., 1st session, p. 184 (3 Feb. 1824); Hillhouse, *Propositions,* p. 14 and *Annals of Congress,* 15th Cong., 2nd session, pp. 147–9 (Dickerson, 13 Jan. 1819), 17th Cong., 2nd session, p. 222 (11 Feb. 1823), on monarchical fears; *Register of Debates,* 19th Cong., 1st session, p. 1951 (McDuffie, 31 March 1826). For a 'Bolingbrokean' critique see *ibid.*, pp. 1910–11 (John S. Barbour, 29 March 1826).

12. 'Z' in *Ohio State Journal,* reprinted in *National Intelligencer* (Washington), 8 Feb. 1826; Clinton quoted by Marchette Chute, *The First Liberty: A History of the Right to Vote in America, 1619–1850,* E. P. Dutton, 1969, p. 298. See also Chilton Williamson, *American Suffrage from Property to Democracy, 1760–1860,* Princeton U.P., 1960, Chs 8–12.

13. In 1800 ten states used the legislative method, three the district system, two the general ticket, while in Tennessee the election was vested in thirty-three designated individuals; see *Historical Statistics of the United States, Colonial Times to 1957,* U.S. Bureau of the Census, 1961, p. 681; Wilmerding, *op. cit.*, pp. 45–6. The people were not excluded entirely by the legislative system, because they elected the legislature, and the presidential question often did affect the conduct of legislative campaigns.

14. Richard P. McCormick, *The Second American Party System: Party Formation in the Jacksonian Era,* U. North Carolina P., 1966.

15. Quotation in Frederick W. Dallinger, *Nominations for Elective Office in the United States,* Longman, Green, 1897, p. 17. On the decline of the caucus see also James S. Chase, *Emergence of the Presidential Nominating Convention, 1789–1832,* U. Illinois P., 1973, esp. Ch. 2.

## Chapter 3: Towards the popular campaign: 1824

1. Gallatin to Walter Lowrie, 22 May 1824, Henry Adams (ed.), *The Writings of Albert Gallatin,* Antiquarian Press Reprint, 1960, ii, p. 290.

2. Chase C. Mooney, *William H. Crawford, 1772–1834*, U. Kentucky P., 1974, pp. 165–6; 'A Southron', *To the People of South-Carolina. An Address on the Subject of the Approaching Presidential Election, in which the claims of William H. Crawford, are impartially canvassed*, n.p., 1824, p. 62; *Eastern Argus* quoted in Chase, *op. cit.*, p. 45; *Albany Regency*, 27 Feb. 1824; see also *Richmond Enquirer*, 23 Dec. 1823, *National Intelligencer*, 5 Nov. 1823.

3. John Quincy Adams was convinced that Crawford used his extensive patronage opportunities to build a personal following: Adams (ed.), *Memoirs of J. Q. Adams*, v, pp. 89–90, 304, 482–3; *Washington Gazette*, 9 Nov. 1822.

4. Adams (ed.), *Memoirs of J. Q. Adams*, vi, p. 136 (23 Jan. 1823); Marie B. Hecht, *John Quincy Adams: A Personal History of an Independent Man*, Macmillan, 1972, p. 372; Adams (ed.), *Memoirs*, v, p. 478 (3 Jan. 1822); Wm Plumer, Jr, to Wm Plumer, 3 Jan. 1822, Everett Somerville Brown (ed.), *The Missouri Compromises and Presidential Politics, 1820–1825: From the Letters of William Plumer, Junior*, Missouri Historical Society, 1926, pp. 74–5; for Adams's electioneering moves see *Memoirs*, vi, pp. 343, 353, vii, pp. 269, 279, 289, 291 and Samuel Flagg Bemis, *John Quincy Adams and the Union*, Knopf, 1956, p. 29; Macbeth policy, Adams (ed.), *Memoirs*, vi, pp. 130–7 (23 Jan. 1823).

5. *Ibid.*, v, p. 299 (25 Feb. 1821), vi, pp. 17–18 (11 June 1822).

6. Adams quoted in Ernest R. May, *The Making of the Monroe Doctrine*, Belknap Press of Harvard U.P., 1975, p. 31; James F. Hopkins (ed.), *The Papers of Henry Clay*, U. Kentucky P., 1963, iii, p. 107n.; May, *op. cit.*, *passim*; Hecht, *op. cit.*, p. 387; Adams (ed.), *Memoirs*, vi, p. 120 (5, 6 Jan. 1823), vi, p. 135 (23 Jan. 1823).

7. Webster to Jeremiah Mason, 20 Nov. 1823, C. M. Wiltse (ed.), *The Papers of Daniel Webster*, U.P. New England, 1976, i, p. 333; Bemis, *JQA and Union*, pp. 25–6; Adams (ed.), *Memoirs*, vi, pp. 353–4 (24 May 1824). Southerners often queried Adams's stand on the Missouri Question, e.g., 'CATO', *Richmond Enquirer*, 31 Aug. 1824 and 'A Southron', *op. cit.*, pp. 8–10.

8. Charles M. Wiltse, *John C. Calhoun: Nationalist, 1782–1828*, Bobbs-Merrill, 1944, pp. 151–2, 164–74, 121; Adams (ed.), *Memoirs*, v, p. 361.

9. For Calhoun's electioneering activities see W. Edwin Hemphill (ed.), *The Papers of John C. Calhoun*, U. South Carolina P., 1971, v, vi, *passim*; J. Franklin Jameson (ed.), 'Correspondence of John C. Calhoun', *Annual Report of the American Historical Association for the Year 1899*, 1900, ii; The Galloway – Maxcy – Markoe Papers, Library of Congress; Thomas Robson Hay, 'John C. Calhoun and the Presidential Campaign of 1824', *North Carolina Historical Review*, xii (Jan. 1935), pp. 20–44. Quotation in C. Vandeventer to Virgil Maxcy, 10 July 1823, Galloway – Maxcy – Markoe Papers.

10. Adams (ed.), *Memoirs*, v, pp. 52–3 (31 March 1820); Glyndon G. Van Deusen, *The Life of Henry Clay*, Little, Brown, 1937, pp. 116–33, 163.

11. 'Speech on Tariff', 30–31 March 1824, Hopkins (ed.), *Papers of Clay*, iii, pp. 701, 727.

12. For Clay's activities, see Hopkins, *Papers of Clay,* iii, pp. 727n, 736–7, 737–8, 740–3, 743–4, 758; quotations from Clay to Peter B. Porter, 3 April 1824, Clay to Josiah H. Johnston, 3 Sept. 1824, 'Toasts and Speech at Public Dinner', 17 June 1824, *ibid;* iii, pp. 731, 827, 778–80.

13. Quotations from Cyrus T. Brady, *The True Andrew Jackson,* Lippincott, 1906, p. 288 and Jackson to A. J. Donelson, 6 Aug. 1822, John. S. Bassett (ed.), *The Correspondence of Andrew Jackson,* Carnegie Institution, 1926–35, iii, pp. 173–4. Clay was informed that the probable reason for Jackson's nomination was to use his influence to prevent the re-election of Senator John Williams, who was disliked by several prominent Tennesseans: Andrew Hynes to Clay, 31 July 1822, Hopkins (ed.), *Papers of Clay,* iii, p. 265. See Charles G. Sellers, 'Jackson Men with Feet of Clay', *American Historical Review,* lxii (April 1957), pp. 537–51.

14. Jackson to H. W. Peterson, 23 Feb. 1823, Bassett (ed.), *Corr. of Jackson,* iii, pp. 189–90; Jackson to John Coffee, 5 Oct. 1823, *ibid.,* iii, p. 210.

15. Charles P. Tutt to Jackson, 24 June 1823, *ibid.,* iii, p. 199; John H. Eaton to Mrs Jackson, 18 Dec. 1823, *ibid.,* iii, p. 217 (see also Wm Plumer, Jr to Wm Plumer, 22 Dec. 1823, Brown (ed.), *op. cit.,* p. 91); Jackson to George W. Martin, 2 Jan. 1824, *ibid.,* iii, p. 222 (see also Clay to B. W. Leigh, 20 Oct. 1823, Hopkins (ed.), *Papers of Clay,* iii, p. 501); Buchanan to Jackson, 29 May 1825, John Bassett Moore (ed.), *The Works of James Buchanan, Comprising his Speeches, State Papers, and Private Correspondence,* Lippincott, 1908, i, p. 139.

16. Jackson to Dr L. H. Coleman, 26 April 1824, Bassett (ed.), *Corr. of Jackson,* iii, pp. 249–51; *New York Evening Post,* 3 June 1824. In fact at least one Adams letter (favouring internal improvements) was published, but little notice was taken of it: Bemis, *J. Q. A. and Union,* p. 25. Jackson also wrote a similar letter to his Coleman letter to another interlocutor, but it does not appear to have been published: Jackson to James W. Lanier, 15 May [?] 1824, Bassett (ed.), *Corr. of Jackson,* iii, p. 253.

17. On campaign medalets see J. Doyle DeWitt, *A Century of Campaign Buttons,* Travelers Press, 1959, pp. 10–12.

18. *Franklin Gazette,* 14, 28 March, 11 April, 16, 30 May, 11, 27 June, 11 July 1822; Wiltse, *Calhoun,* p. 254, suggests Dallas wrote the Calhoun memoir; *The Letters of Wyoming, to the People of the United States, on the Presidential Election, and in Favor of Andrew Jackson. Originally Published in the Columbian Observer,* Philadelphia, 1824; see also Jackson to A. J. Donelson, 4 April 1824, Bassett (ed.), *Corr. of Jackson,* iii, p. 244 and Robert P. Hay, 'The Case for Andrew Jackson in 1824: Eaton's "Wyoming Letters"', *Tennessee Historical Quarterly,* xxix (Summer 1970), pp. 139–51. On the very eve of the election some rather uninspired sketches of Crawford appeared in the *Albany Argus,* 3,14, 28 Sept., 5, 19, 22 Oct. 1824.

19. *Sketch of the Life of John Quincy Adams . . . ,* n.p. 1824, pp. 6, 17, 52. Bemis, *J. Q. A. and Union,* p. 19, says that Adams originally prepared the sketch himself in 1809 – but at that time he could hardly have been looking to the presidency.

20. *Franklin Gazette,* 11 July, 11 April, 16 May, 11 July 1822; *An Examination of Mr. Calhoun's Economy and An Apology for those Members of Congress who have been Denounced as Radicals,* n.p. Dec. 1823, p. 1.

21. Sellers, 'Jackson Men with Feet of Clay', pp. 537–51; Clay to Peter B. Porter, 10 Aug. 1822, Hopkins (ed.), *Papers of Clay,* iii, p. 274; Crawford to Charles Tait, 17 Sept. 1822, J. E. D. Shipp, *Giant Days or The Life and Times of William H. Crawford,* Southern Printers, 1909, p. 234; Van Buren to Johnston Verplanck, 22 Dec. 1822, Van Buren Papers, Library of Congress; David Woods to Clay, 27 Aug. 1823, Benton to Clay, 23 July 1823, Hopkins (ed.), *Papers of Clay,* iii, pp.476, 460 (see also Langdon Cheves to Clay, 9 Nov. 1822, *ibid.,* iii, p. 315); Willie P. Mangum to Duncan Cameron, 10 Dec. 1823, Henry Thomas Shanks (ed.), *The Papers of Willie Person Mangum,* Raleigh, 1950–6, i, p. 83 (see also Wm Plumer, Jr, to Wm Plumer, 9 Feb. 1824, Brown (ed.), *Missouri Compromises,* p. 98).

22. Return Jonathan Meigs to Clay, 3 Sept. 1822, Hopkins (ed.), *Papers of Clay,* iii, p. 282; Wm Plumer, Jr, to Wm Plumer, 29 Feb. 1824, Brown (ed.), *Missouri Compromises,* pp. 102–103; Gallatin to Walter Lowrie, 22 May 1824, Adams (ed.), *Writings of Gallatin,* ii, pp. 291–2; 'Notes of Mr. Jefferson's Conversation 1824 at Monticello', Wiltse (ed.), *Papers of Webster,* i, pp. 375–6.

23. Clay cited in Marquis James, *The Life of Andrew Jackson, complete in one Volume,* Bobbs-Merrill, 1938, p. 299; *Washington Gazette,* 29 Oct. 1823, 26 Jan. 1824; *Indianapolis Gazette,* 26 Oct. 1824, in Thomas W. Howard, 'Indiana Newspapers and the Presidential Election of 1824', *Indiana Magazine of History,* lxiii (Sept. 1967), p. 192; Jesse Benton, *An Address to the People of the United States, on the Presidential Election,* Nashville, 1824, p. 34. For typical attacks see *Richmond Enquirer,* 20 Jan., 2, 6 March, 6 April, 19 Oct. 1824; *Washington Gazette,* 9 July 1823, 26 Jan. 1824; 'A Southron', *op. cit.,* pp. 11–20.

24. *Richmond Enquirer,* 30 July 1822.

25. John H. Eaton, *The Life of Andrew Jackson, Major-General in the Service of the United States,* Philadelphia, 1824, p. 66; *Biographical Sketch of the Life of Andrew Jackson, Major-General of the Armies of the United States, the Hero of New-Orleans,* Hudson, N.Y., 1823, p. 62; *Address of the Committee Appointed by a Republican Meeting in the County of Hunterdon, Recommending Gen. Andrew Jackson, of Tennessee, to the People of New-Jersey, as President of the United States,* Trenton, N.J., Sept. 1824, p. 19.

26. *Wyoming Letters,* pp. 10, p. 38.

27. *Ibid.,* pp. 4, 11.

28. *Ibid.,* p. 23.

29. *Ibid.,* pp. 51–2, 89.

30. Kim T. Phillips, 'The Pennsylvania Origins of the Jackson Movement', *Political Science Quarterly,* 91 (Autumn 1976), pp. 489–508; Wm Plumer, Jr, to Wm Plumer, 20 Feb. 1824, Brown (ed.), *Missouri Compromises,* p. 102; George M. Bibb to J. J. Crittenden, 8 March 1824, Mrs Chapman Coleman, *The Life of John J. Crittenden, with Selections from his Correspondence and Speeches,* Lippincott, 1871, i, p. 61; J. P. Kennedy to Maxcy, 11 Oct. 1823, Galloway – Maxcy – Markoe Papers; *Niles' Register,* 10 Jan. 1824, p. 291; Michael Holt to Willie P.

Mangum, 23 March 1824, Priestley H. Mangum to Mangum, 15 April 1824, Shanks (ed.), *Papers of Mangum,* i, p. 129, 134; Webster to Ezekial Webster, 14 March 1824, Wiltse (ed.), *Papers of Webster,* i, p. 346.

31. *Lancaster Journal,* 6 Dec. 1822, in Phillips, 'Pennsylvania Origins', p. 502; Harrisburg Address reprinted in *Address of the Committee . . . Hunterdon,* p. 21; Isaac Watts Crane, *Address delivered before the Jackson Convention of Delegates, from the different Townships of the County of Cumberland assembled at Bridgeton, July 27, 1824,* Philadelphia, 1824, p. 5; *Address of the Committee . . . Hunterdon,* p. 8; *Proceedings of the New-Jersey Convention, Held at Trenton, September 1st, 1824,* Bridgeton, N.J., 1824, p. 5; *An Address to the People of Ohio, on the important subject of the Next Presidency; by the Committee appointed for that purpose . . . ,* Cincinnati, 1824, p. 9 (see also Donald J. Ratcliffe, 'The Role of Voters and Issues in Party Formation: Ohio, 1824', *Journal of American History,* lix, March 1973, p. 861); Detroit *Gazette* in Hay, 'Eaton's Wyoming Letters', p. 149; *Western Volunteer* (Frankfort, Ky) 20 Oct. 1824. On Jacksonian sentiment among 'outsiders', see, e.g., Phillips, 'Pennsylvania Origins', pp. 489–508; Sellers, 'Jackson Men with Feet of Clay', pp. 537–51; Ratcliffe, *op.cit.,* pp. 860–2, Lynn L. Marshall 'The Genesis of Grass-Roots Democracy in Kentucky', *Mid-America,* 47 ( Oct. 1965), pp. 269–87.

## Chapter 4: The conservative origins of the new party system: 1828

1. Calhoun to Andrew Jackson, 4 June 1826, Clyde N. Wilson and W. Edwin Hemphill (eds.), *The Papers of John C. Calhoun,* U. South Carolina P., 1977, x, pp. 110–111; Van Buren to Azariah Flagg, 22 Dec. 1826, Flagg Papers, Columbia University Library; Col. Arthur P. Hayne to Jackson, 20 July 1826, Bassett (ed.), *Corr. of Jackson,* iii, p. 306.

2. Adams (ed.), *Memoirs of J. Q. Adams,* vii, pp. 346–7 (29 Oct. 1827), 469 (8 March 1828), and *passim;* Adams to George Sullivan, 22 Sept. 1827, in Bemis, *JQA and Union,* p. 139.

3. *Ibid.,* pp. 65–70, 102; Calhoun to J. G. Swift, 11 Dec. 1825, Wilson & Hemphill, *Papers of Calhoun,* x, p. 56; Adams (ed.), *Memoirs,* vii, p. 297 (29 June 1827), viii, p. 48 (3 July 1828).

4. E. Pentland to Clay, 18 Feb. 1827, Thomas H. Baird to Clay, 24 May 1827, P. B. Porter to Clay, 11 July 1827, Clay Papers, Library of Congress; *Springfield Republican,* 21 May 1828; *Niles' Register,* 13 Sept. 1828, p. 45; *An Address of Henry Clay, To the Public, containing certain testimonials in refutation of the charges against him, made by general Andrew Jackson, touching the last presidential elections,* reprinted in *Niles' Register,* 5 Jan. 1828, pp. 296–304; Address, 5 June 1828, *The Works of Daniel Webster,* 15th edn, Little, Brown, 1869, i, pp. 163–71; *N.Y. Enquirer* quoted in *Albany Argus,* 11 July 1828.

5. Jackson to the Tennessee Legislature, 12 Oct. 1825, Bassett (ed.), *Corr. of Jackson,* iii, pp. 293–6.

6. Eaton to Jackson, 27 Jan. 1827, in James, *Andrew Jackson,* p. 464; Van Buren to Jackson, 14 Sept. 1827, Van Buren Papers; Jackson to a Committee of the Davidson County Bible Society, 30 Sept. 1826, Bas-

sett (ed.), *Corr. of Jackson,* iii, p. 315; Jackson to George W. Campbell, 14 Feb. 1828, *ibid.,* iii, pp. 390–1; Eaton to Jackson, 28 March 1828, in James, *Andrew Jackson,* p. 471; Jackson to Gov. Ray, 28 Feb. 1828, *Niles' Register,* 3 May 1828, p. 158; for Jackson's disclaimers, see *Niles' Register,* 8 Sept. 1827, p. 20, *Richmond Enquirer,* 8 Dec. 1827.

7. Robert Y. Hayne to Jackson, 5 June 1827, Bassett (ed.), *Corr. of Jackson,* iii, p. 358; Robert V. Remini, *The Election of Andrew Jackson,* Lippincott, 1963, p. 63; Jackson to William B. Lewis, 19 Aug. 1828, Bassett (ed.), iii, pp. 427–8; 'TO THE PUBLIC', *United States Telegraph Extra,* 11 Oct. 1828, pp. 481–95 (see also *ibid.,* 28 March 1828); Jackson to William B. Lewis, 5 May 1827, Bassett (ed.), iii, p. 355.

8. Jackson to Carter Beverley, 5 June 1827, *ibid.,* p. 357; *Louisiana Advertiser,* 14 Jan. 1828, in *Niles' Register,* 9 Feb. 1828, pp. 392–3; *Reminiscences of James A. Hamilton; or, Men and Events, at Home and Abroad, During These Three-Quarters of a Century,* New York, 1869, p. 69; *Niles' Register,* 9 Aug. 1828, p. 378.

9. Adams (ed.), *Memoirs,* viii, p. 76 (5 Aug. 1828); *Niles' Register,* 19 Jan. 1828, p. 334, 12 July 1828, p. 314; *Albany Argus,* 9, 16 Jan. 1828; *Richmond Enquirer,* 11 July 1828; DeWitt, *Campaign Buttons,* pp. 13–18. Examples of Jackson memorabilia may be seen in the Smithsonian Institution.

10. *The Political Primer,* 12 April 1828; *U.S. Telegraph Extra,* 1 March, 19 April 1828; *The Nose,* 24 July 1828. On the press, see Remini, *Election of Jackson,* pp. 76–80, 128–9.

11. *Columbian Centinel* (Boston), 1 Nov. 1828; 'Address of the Jackson Central Committee To the People of Virginia', *Richmond Enquirer,* 7 Oct. 1828; *Address of the Jackson State Convention to the People of Maryland, on the Late and Approaching Election of President,* Baltimore, 1827, p. 14.

12. S. Southwick to Clay, 3 Dec. 1827, Clay Papers; Clay to Webster, 24 Oct. 1828, Wiltse (ed.), *Papers of Webster,* ii, p. 371; Webster to John Evelyn Denison, 28 July 1827, Webster to Ezekiel Webster, 17 Jan. 1829, *ibid.,* ii, pp. 235, 388; Adams (ed.), *Memoirs,* vii, p. 383 (17 Dec. 1827); Jabez D. Hammond to Henry S. Randall, 28 June 1849, in Remini, *Election of Jackson,* p. 121.

13. Lewis to Van Buren, 8 Aug. 1828, Van Buren Papers; Caleb Atwater to Jackson, 30 Nov. 1827, Jackson-Lewis Papers, New York Public Library; Calhoun to Jackson , 4 June 1826, Wilson & Hemphill (eds), *Papers of Calhoun,* x, p. 110 and *passim;* Jonathan Webster to Polk, 10 Feb. 1828, Herbert Weaver and Paul H. Bergeron (ed.), *Correspondence of James K. Polk,* Vanderbilt U.P., 1969, i, p. 143; White to Jackson, 7 April 1827, Bassett (ed.), *Corr. of Jackson,* iii, p. 353. See also *ibid.,* iii, pp. 276, 286–8, 329, 332, 344, 357–60, 385, 394, 403.

14. For the quotations see *The Political Primer,* 2 June 1828; *Proceedings of the Delegates of the Friends of the Administration of John Quincy Adams, Assembled in Convention at Baton Rouge, New Orleans, 1827,* p. 21; *Our Country,* 20 Sept., 1 Nov. 1828; *The Political Primer,* 14 July 1828; *Truth's Advocate and Monthly Anti-Jackson Expositor,* Cincinnati, April, May, Aug. 1828, pp. 121, 161, 306; *A Brief Inquiry into Some of the Objections Urged Against the Election of Andrew Jackson to the Office of President of the United State* [n.p., 1828], p. 4. This paragraph is based

on an extensive reading of anti-Jackson propaganda. For example, see *Proceedings of the Maryland Administration Convention, Delegated by the People, and Held in Baltimore, on Monday and Tuesday, July 23d. and 24th. 1827*, Baltimore, 1827; *Proceedings of the Delegates of the Friends of the Administration of John Quincy Adams, Assembled in Convention at Baton Rouge*, New Orleans, 1827; *Proceedings of the Administration Convention, held at Frankfort, Kentucky, on Monday, December 17, 1827* [Frankfort? 1827?]; *Address of the Administration Convention, Held in the Capitol At Raleigh, Dec. 20th, 1827. To the Freemen of North-Carolina*, Raleigh, 1827; *Proceedings, and Address of the Convention of Delegates, That met at Columbus, Ohio, Dec. 28, 1827, To Nominate a Ticket of Electors Favorable to the Reelection of John Quincy Adams, President of the United States, to be Supported at the Electoral Election of 1828*, n.p. 1827; *Democratic Convention* [Harrisburg, 1828]; *An Address to the Freemen of Kentucky. From a Convention . . . held in the town of Frankfort, on the 17th, 18th, and 19th days of December, 1827* [Frankfort 1828?]; *Proceedings of the Administration Convention, Held at Indianapolis, January 12, 1828* [Indianapolis 1828]; *The Light of Truth; An Account of Some of the Deeds of Andrew Jackson* [Washington 1828]; *The Principles and Acts of Mr. Adams' Administration, Vindicated Against the Aspersions Contained in the Address of the Jackson Convention, Assembled at Concord, On the 11th and 12th of June, 1828*, 'By a Freeman', Concord, 1828; *Address of the Central Committee Appointed by a Convention of both branches of the Legislature friendly to the election of John Q. Adams . . . held at the State-House in Boston, June 10, 1828, to their fellow-citizens* [n.p. 1828]; *Proceedings of a Convention of the People of Maine, Friendly to the present Administration . . .*, n.p., 1828; *The Virginia Address*, n.p., 1828. See also the 1827–8 files of such administration newspapers as *The Ohio State Journal, and Columbus Gazette, Daily National Journal* (Washington), *The Springfield Republican, Daily National Intelligencer, Boston Patriot & Mercantile Advertiser, Columbian Centinel* (Boston), and the special campaign papers cited above.

15. For quotations see 'A Bargain, Proved and Confessed', *Argus of Western America* (Frankfort), 21 May 1828; *Address to the People of Connecticut, adopted at the State Convention, held at Middletown, August 7, 1828*, Hartford, 1828, p. 16; *Albany Argus*, 9, 12, 17, 19 Jan. 1828; *Address of the People of Connecticut . . .* , p. 22. For characteristic Jacksonian propaganda see, e.g., *Address of the Jackson State Convention to the People of Maryland, on the Late and Approaching Election of President*, Baltimore, 1827; *Address to the People of Connecticut, adopted at the State Convention, held at Middletown August 7, 1828* Hartford, 1828; *Address of the Republican Committee of Correspondence of Philadelphia, to the People of the United States*, Philadelphia, 1828; *Proceedings and Address of the New-Jersey State Convention, assembled at Trenton, on the Eighth Day of January, 1828, which nominated Andrew Jackson for President, John C. Calhoun for Vice-President, of the United States*, Trenton, 1828; 'Address of the Jackson Central Committee To the People of Virginia', *Richmond Enquirer*, 7 Oct. 1828; *Letters addressed to John Sergeant, Manuel Eyre, Lawrence Lewis, Clement C. Biddle, and Joseph P. Norris, Esqs. Authors of An Address to the People of Pennsylvania, Adopted at a Meeting of the Friends*

to the Election of John Quincy Adams, held in Philadelphia, July 7, 1828: containing Strictures on their Address, Philadelphia, 1828; To The People. The Bargain Proved, By the Testimony of Mr. Clay's Friends and from his own Letters [Philadelphia 1828]; Proceedings and Address of the New-Hampshire Republican State Convention of Delegates Friendly to the Election of Andrew Jackson to the next Presidency of the United States, assembled at Concord, June 11 and 12, 1828, Concord, 1828; Essex Jackson Meeting [Haverhill? Mass. 1828]; The Striking Similitude between the Reign of Terror, of the Elder Adams, and the Reign of Corruption, of the Younger Adams. An Address adopted by the Albany Republican County Convention . . ., Albany, 1828. See also the files for 1827–8 of such Jacksonian newspapers as the Richmond Enquirer, Albany Argus, Argus of Western America, New-York Evening Post, United States' Telegraph, and such special campaign papers as the United States' Telegraph . . . Extra and The Nose: Or Political Satirist (Jersey Shore, Pa).

16. Speech at Fanueil Hall, 5 June 1828, Works of Webster, i, p. 170.

## Chapter 5: The quest for the White House: Democratic style

1. On Jackson and internal improvements, see Jackson to James W. Lanier, 15 May [?] 1824, Bassett (ed.), Corr. of Jackson, iii, p. 253; 'Notes for the Maysville Road Veto', ibid., iv, pp. 137–9; John C. Fitzpatrick (ed.), The Autobiography of Martin Van Buren, Da Capo Press, 1973, i, pp. 320, 322. On the renomination of Jackson see Chase, Nominating Convention, pp. 233–4. For the 1832 campaign see Samuel Rhea Gammon, The Presidential Campaign of 1832, Johns Hopkins U.P., 1922.

2. Jackson to Van Buren, 8 Aug. 1831, Bassett (ed.), Corr. of Jackson, iv, p. 329.

3. Jackson to Anthony Butler, 6 March 1832, ibid., iv, p. 415.

4. Jackson to Lewis, 18 Aug. 1832, ibid., iv, p. 467.

5. Jackson to John Coffee, 21 Jan. 1822, Jackson to Van Buren, 18 Nov. 1832, ibid., iv, pp. 401, 489; on Jackson's belief in eternal vigilance, see Farewell Address, Joseph L. Blau (ed.), Social Theories of Jacksonian Democracy: Representative Writings of the Period 1825–1850, Bobbs-Merrill, 1954, p. 18.

6. Van Buren to the Shocco Springs Committee, 4 Oct. 1832, in Gammon, Campaign of 1832, p. 163; Van Buren to Prosper M. Wetmore et al., 17 Oct. 1832, Niles' Register, 27 Oct. 1832, p. 139.

7. Van Buren to A. Stevenson et al., 29 May 1835, ibid., 13 June 1835, p. 257; Van Buren to Junius Ames et al., 6 March 1836, ibid., 16 April 1836, p. 127.

8. Williams to Van Buren, 7 April 1836, Van Buren to Williams, 20 April 1836, Williams to Van Buren, 9 June 1836, Mr. Van Buren's Opinions. Correspondence, [1836], p. 1.

9. Van Buren to Williams, 8 Aug. 1836, Van Buren Papers; Sister Mary Raimonde Bartus, 'The Presidential Election of 1836', Ph.D. dissertation, Fordham Univ., 1967, p. 303; Van Buren's Opinions, pp. 3, 9, 4.

10. Bartus, 'Election of 1836', pp. 305–306; R. Riker to Van Buren, 29

Aug. 1836, Van Buren Papers (and see other letters from friends); *Richmond Enquirer*, 23 Aug. 1836.

11. For the early part of the tour see *New York Herald*, 1, 3 July 1839; a detailed description of the tour is in Denis Tilden Lynch, *An Epoch and a Man: Martin Van Buren and His Times*, Horace Liveright, 1929, pp. 428–38; quotations in *National Intelligencer*, 8 July 1839, and Lynch, p. 429.

12. For Van Buren letters see *Niles' Register*, 8 Aug. 1840, pp. 364–5, 29 Aug. 1840, pp. 408–9, 5 Sept. 1840, p. 6, 19 Sept. 1840, pp. 40–1, 26 Sept. 1840, p. 59, 24 Oct. 1840, pp. 122–4, 31 Oct. 1840, pp. 138–40. For quotations see Van Buren to John M. McCalla *et al.*, 4 July 1840, *Niles' Register*, 8 Aug. 1840, pp. 364–5; Van Buren to John B. Cary *et al.*, 31 July 1840, *ibid.*, 22 Aug. 1840, pp. 393–6; *Richmond Whig*, 11 Aug. 1840.

13. Silas Wright to Van Buren, 20 Aug. 1840, Van Buren Papers; John Forsyth, *Address to the People of Georgia*, 1840; *National Intelligencer*, 26 Sept. 1840.

14. Butler to Harmanus Bleecker, 20 Nov. 1841, Harriet Langdon Pruyn Rice, *Harmanus Bleecker: An Albany Dutchman, 1779–1849*, Albany, 1924, p. 228; James E. Pollard, *The Presidents and the Press*, Macmillan, 1947, p. 194; William N. Chambers, *Old Bullion Benton, Senator from the New West*, Little, Brown, 1956, p. 259; Lynch, *Van Buren*, p. 479; D. R. Floyd Jones to Van Buren, 8 May 1843, Van Buren Papers; Glyndon G. Van Deusen, *The Jacksonian Era, 1828–1848*, Hamish Hamilton, 1959, p. 179; Robert S. Lambert, 'The Democratic National Convention of 1844'. *Tennessee Historical Quarterly*, (March 1955), pp. 4–5; Charles Sellers, 'Election of 1844', Arthur M. Schlesinger, Jr and Fred L. Israel (eds), *History of American Presidential Elections, 1789–1968*, Chelsea House, 1971, i, pp. 755–7.

15. Polk to Henry Hubbard *et al.*, 12 June 1844, *ibid.*, i, p. 854. On Polk's candidacy see also Charles Sellers, *James K. Polk, Constitutionalist, 1843–1846*, Princeton U.P., 1966, Chs 2–4.

16. Cave Johnson to Polk, 10 June 1844, Polk Papers, Library of Congress.

17. Muhlenberg to Polk, 3 June 1844, Walker to Polk, 30 May 1844, Polk to Kane, 'Confidential', 19 June 1844, Gideon J. Pillow to Kane and Horn, 2 July 1844, Polk Papers; Polk to Kane, 19 June 1844, *Niles' Register*, 6 July 1844, p. 295; *Richmond Whig*, 2 Aug. 1844.

18. S. H. Laughlin to Polk, 5 July 1844, Edwin Polk to Polk, 12 Sept. 1844, Laughlin to Polk, 19 Sept. 1844, Polk Papers. Quotations in Wm E. Cramer to Polk, 17 Sept. 1844, Rush to Polk, 7 June 1844, Polk Papers.

19. Quotation in Sellers, *Polk, Continentalist*, p. 101.

20. Cass to A. Stevenson *et al.*, 30 May 1848, *Niles' Register*, 5 July 1848, p. 7; Pierce to J. S. Barbour *et al.*, 17 June 1852, *Proceedings of the Democratic National Convention at Baltimore, June 1st, 1852*, 1852, p. 76.

21. For the Nicholson letter and Democratic manoeuvrings, see *Richmond Enquirer*, 4 Jan. 1848; Joseph G. Rayback, *Free Soil: The Election of 1848*, Kentucky U.P., 1970, pp. 115–20, 136–8. For Pierce see Roy Franklin Nichols, *Franklin Pierce: Young Hickory of the Granite Hills*, U.

Pennsylvania P., 2nd edn, 1958, pp. 189–206; Roy and Jeannette Nichols, 'Election of 1852', Schlesinger & Israel (eds), *Presidential Elections*, pp. 921–50.

22. Chambers, *Benton*, p. 334; Walter W. Stevens, 'Lewis Cass and the Presidency', *Michigan History*, 49 (June 1965) p. 129; Frank B. Woodford, *Lewis Cass: The Last Jeffersonian*, Rutgers U.P., 1950; *Richmond Enquirer*, 7 Sept. 1852; *Albany Argus*, 9 Oct. 1852; *New York Tribune*, 1 Nov. 1852; Nichols, *Pierce*, pp. 206–14; Pollard, *Presidents and Press*, p. 283.

23. On the 'rise of party', and the Democratic commitment to party, see Michael Wallace, 'Changing Concepts of Party in the United States: New York, 1815–1828', *American Historical Review*, lxxiv (1968) 453–91; Richard Hofstadter, *The Idea of a Party System: The Rise of Legitimate Opposition in the United States, 1780–1840*, Columbia U.P., 1970; M. J. Heale, *The Making of American Politics, 1750–1850*, Longman, 1977. The creation of the new party system is well described in Richard P. McCormick, *The Second American Party System: Party Formation in the Jacksonian Era*, U. North Carolina P., 1966.

## Chapter 6: *The quest for the White House: Whig style*

1. DeWitt, *Campaign Buttons*, pp. 37–63, 65–87; 'Democratic Platform of 1844', Kirk H. Porter and Donald Bruce Johnson, compilers, *National Party Platforms, 1840–1964*, U. Illinois P., 1966, p. 3.
2. Clay to Francis Brooke, 10 Jan. 1829, Calvin Colton (ed.), *The Private Correspondence of Henry Clay*, Boston, 1856, p. 218; Clay to citizens of Vincennes, 18 Oct. 1831, *Niles' Register*, 19 Nov. 1831, p. 226.
3. For pressure on Clay, see, e.g., Joseph Gales, Jr, to Clay, 27 Aug. 1831, Clay Papers.
4. Webster to Clay, 5 Oct. 1831, Colton (ed.), *Clay Corr.*, pp. 317–18; J. Sloane to Clay, 15 Oct. 1831, Clay Papers; Dearborn to Clay, 3 Sept. 1831, Colton (ed.), p. 310.
5. Cincinnati *National Republican* in *N.Y. Evening Post*, 16 Jan. 1832.
6. *Ohio State Journal*, 24 March 1832; Clay to Francis Brooke, 21 Feb. 1832, James Barbour to Clay, 7 March 1832, H. G. Otis to Clay, 8 March 1832, James Madison to Clay, 13 March 1832, Colton (ed.), *Clay Corr.*, pp. 326, 328, 329; *Albany Argus*, 3 July 1832; Van Deusen, *Life of Clay*, pp. 256–7.
7. The main task of both national conventions that year had been to select running-mates.
8. *Proceedings of the National Republican Convention of Young Men, Which Assembled in the City of Washington May 7, 1832*, Washington, 1832, pp. 8–9.
9. Joel H. Silbey, 'Election of 1836', Schlesinger & Israel (eds), *Presidential Elections*, i, p. 584; White to John B. Smith, 17 March 1836, *Niles' Register*, 16 April 1836, p. 128; White to Williams, 2 July 1836, *ibid.*, 17 Sept. 1836, p. 44; *ibid.*, 24 Sept. 1836, pp. 59–60.
10. Bartus, 'Election of 1836', pp. 177–8, 181; James A. Green, *William Henry Harrison: His Life and Times*, Garrett & Massie, 1941, pp. 296–

References

7; *National Intelligencer,* 18 Aug. 1835; Bartus, pp. 182, 185–8; Silbey, *op. cit.,* p. 584.

11. Quotation in Green, *Harrison,* p. 295.

12. For Harrison letters see *Niles' Register,* 8 Oct. 1836, pp. 94–95, 5 Nov. 1836, pp. 150–1, 19 Nov. 1836, pp. 188–9. Quotations in Harrison to Williams, 1 May 1836, *ibid.,* 10 Sept. 1836, pp. 24–5; Harrison to William Bradley Tyler *et al.,* 9 Feb. 1836, *National Intelligencer,* 25 Feb. 1836; Bartus, 'Election of 1836', p. 192.

13. *New York Herald,* 2 Aug., 30 Sept. 1836; *National Intelligencer,* 26 Aug., 28, 30 Sept. 1836; *Niles' Register,* 24 Sept. 1836, p. 49; Green, *Harrison,* pp. 305, 307; *Frankfort Argus,* 28 Sept., 26 Oct. 1836; Rives to Van Buren, 13 Oct. 1836, Van Buren Papers.

14. Green, *Harrison,* p. 314; Harrison to Harmer Denny, 2 Dec. 1838, in Dorothy Burne Goebel, *William Henry Harrison, A Political Biography,* Indiana Historical Collections, 1926, p. 332; on tour see Green, pp. 320–1 and Goebel, p. 333. On the 1840 campaign see Robert Gray Gunderson, *The Log-Cabin Campaign,* U. Kentucky P., 1957.

15. Harrison to Clay, 25 Feb. 1840, Clay Papers; David Gwynne *et al.* to Miles Hotchkiss, 25 Feb. 1840, *The Rough-Hewer* (Albany), 16 April 1840, p. 71; *The Pennsylvanian* (Philadelphia), 17 April 1840; Harrison letters in *Niles' Register,* 20 June 1840, p. 247, 4 July 1840, p. 281, 22 Aug. 1840, p. 397; Harrison to Verplanck *et al.,* 23 May 1840, Anthony Banning Norton, *The Great Revolution of 1840,* Mount Vernon (O.), 1888, pp. 40–1.

16. *National Intelligencer,* 23 June 1840; *Gen. Harrison's Speech at Fort Meigs,* n.p., 1840, pp. 1–6; *Springfield Republican,* 4 July 1840; *Niles' Register,* 22 Aug. 1840, p. 396, 19 Sept. 1840, pp. 42–3, 26 Sept. 1840, p. 56; Norton, *Great Revolution,* pp. 166–78, 245–53, 342–4; *Niles' Register,* 3 Oct. 1840, p. 70.

17. *National Intelligencer,* 23 June 1840.

18. Crittenden to Robert P. Letcher, 1 May 1842, Coleman, *Crittenden,* i, p. 178; Clay to J. M. Clayton, 8 Aug. 1842, Clay to Clayton, 27 May 1843, Clayton Papers, Library of Congress; Crittenden to Letcher, 9 Dec. 1842, Coleman, i, p. 170.

19. Van Deusen, *Life of Clay,* pp. 360–1; Clay at Charleston, *Niles' Register,* 13 April 1844, p. 106; *ibid,* 6 July 1844, pp. 295–300.

20. *Niles' Register,* 13 April 1844, p. 105; Clay to editors of the *National Intelligencer,* 3 May 1844, in *Niles' Register,* 11 May 1844, p. 161; Clay to J. M. Berrien *et al.,* 2 May 1844, *ibid.,* 18 May 1844, p. 186.

21. Several Clay letters were republished in *Niles' Register* during the summer of 1844. Clay to editors of the *National Intelligencer,* 17 April 1844, *Niles' Register,* 4 May 1844, p. 152; Van Deusen, *Life of Clay,* p. 366; Betty Fladeland, *James Gillespie Birney: Slaveholder to Abolitionist,* Cornell U.P., 1955, pp. 235–6; 'Democratic Platform of 1844', Porter and Johnson, *Party Platforms,* p. 4; Clay to Stephen F. Miller, 1 July 1844, *Niles' Register,* 3 Aug. 1844, p. 372; Clay to T. M. Peters and J. M. Jackson, 27 July 1844, *ibid.,* 31 Aug. 1844, p. 439; Weed quoted in Albert D. Kirwan, *John J. Crittenden: The Struggle for the Union,* U. Kentucky P., 1962, p. 180.

22. *The Globe* (Washington), 10 Sept. 1844; Clay to editors of *National In-*

*telligencer,* 23 Sept. 1844, *Niles' Register,* 5 Oct. 1844, p. 74; Charles Augustus Davis to John J. Crittenden, 2 Oct. 1844, Crittenden Papers, Library of Congress.

23 Rayback, *Free Soil,* pp. 50–5; Taylor to Joseph R. Ingersoll, 3 Aug. 1847, *Niles' Register,* 26 Feb. 1848, p. 407; Calhoun to Thomas G. Clemson, 6 Sept. 1847, J. F. Jameson (ed.), 'Correspondence of John C. Calhoun', *Annual Report of the American Historical Association for 1899,* ii, p. 737.

24. Taylor to Capt. J. S. Allison, 22 April 1848, in Joseph Gales, *A Sketch of the Personal Character and Qualities of General Zachary Taylor,* [Washington, 1848], p. 7.

25. Rayback, *Free Soil,* pp. 156, 196, 242, 270–3; Taylor to George Lippard, 24 July 1848, *Niles' Register,* 13 Sept. 1848, p. 165; Clayton to Crittenden, 11 Aug. 1848, John Pendleton to Crittenden, 14 Sept. 1848, Crittenden Papers; Taylor to J. M. Morehead, 15 July 1848, *Niles' Register,* 2 Aug. 1848, p. 69; Taylor to Allison, 4 Sept. 1848, *ibid.,* 27 Sept. 1848, p. 201.

26. James R. Morrill, 'The Presidential Election of 1852: Death Knell of the Whig Party of North Carolina', *The North Carolina Historical Review,* xliv (Oct. 1967), pp. 342–59; Robert F. Dalzell, Jr, *Daniel Webster and the Trial of American Nationalism, 1843–1852,* Houghton Mifflin, 1973, pp. 259–77.

27. *The Signal* (Washington), 2, 16 Oct. 1852; *Ohio State Journal,* 23 Sept. 1852; *Springfield Republican,* 28 Sept., 14 Oct. 1852.

28. *The Union* (Washington), 28 Sept. 1852; *New York Herald,* 27, 30 Sept. 1852; *The Campaign,* 16 Oct. 1852, p. 304; *Public Ledger* (Philadelphia), 21 Oct. 1852.

29. On 'antipartyism' in this period, and in particular its connection with Whiggery, see Ronald P. Formisano, 'Political Character, Antipartyism, and the Second Party System', *American Quarterly,* xxi (Winter 1969), pp. 683–709, and *The Birth of Mass Political Parties: Michigan, 1827–1861,* Princeton U.P., 1971; Michael Wallace, 'The Ideology of Party in the Age of Jackson', Ph.D. dissertation, Columbia Univ., 1973, Chs 5 & 6.

## Chapter 7: Military heroes, dark horses and single terms

1. For discussions of the perceptions of British travellers, see Jane Louise Mesick, *The English Traveller in America, 1785–1835,* Columbia U.P., 1922, and Max Berger, *The British Traveller in America, 1836–1860,* Columbia U.P., 1943.

2. James Hall, *A Memoir of the Public Services of William Henry Harrison, of Ohio,* Philadelphia, 1836, pp. 321–3; John G. Miller, *The Great Convention. Description of the Convention of the People of Ohio, held at Columbus, On the 21st and 22d February, 1840,* Columbus, 1840, p. 4; *A Sketch of the Life and Public Services of General Zachary Taylor, the People's Candidate for the Presidency, with Considerations in Favor of His Election,* Washington, 1848, p. 32; *The Presidency – Winfield Scott – Franklin Pierce; Qualifications and Fitness for that High Office,* [1852], pp. 14, 1; Greeley to Henry Clay, 30 Nov. 1847, Clay Papers. See also Albert

Somit, 'The Military Hero as Presidential Candidate', *Public Opinion Quarterly*, 12 (Summer 1948), pp. 192–200.

3. Nashville Gazette in *Richmond Enquirer*, 30 July 1822; *Niles' Register* 19 Feb. 1848, p. 393.

4. *New York Tribune*, 16 June 1852.

5. 'THE CONTRACT', *Albany Argus*, 9 Jan. 1828; Josiah Quincy, Jr, *Eulogy on the Life and Character of the Late Zachary Taylor, Twelfth President of the United States*, Boston, 1850, p. 17.

6. Another Democrat with military experience was Lewis Cass, who had volunteered for the War of 1812 and reached the rank of brigadier-general, but from 1813, when he became Governor of Michigan Territory, his career was essentially civil and political. Other references: Cambreleng to Abraham Van Buren, 28 May 1840, Van Buren Papers; Thos. Jefferson Sutherland, *Three Political Letters, Addressed to Dr. Wolfred Nelson, Late of Lower Canada, Now of Plattsburgh, N.Y.*, New York, 1840, p. 32; *Ohio State Journal*, 13 Sept. 1852; *Great Speech of the Honourable James Buchanan, delivered at the Mass Meeting of the Democracy of Western Pennsylvania, at Greenburg, on Thursday, Oct. 7, 1852*, Philadelphia, 1852, pp. 4–6.

7. Baltimore *Republican*, 9 July 1847, New York *Courier*, 9 July 1847, in Rayback, *Free Soil*, p. 53.

8. *American Review*, ii (Oct. 1848), p. 337; (Sept. 1848), pp. 221–34; 'Republicanus', *The Restoration of the Constitution*, New York, 1848, p. 19; see also Gales, *Sketch of Taylor*, p. 6.

9. The statistics are from Walter Dean Burnham, 'Party Systems and the Political Process', William Nisbet Chambers and W. D. Burnham (eds), *The American Party Systems: Stages of Political Development*, Oxford U.P., 1967, p. 295. Quotations from: *Philadelphia Herald* in *Springfield Republican*, 4 Jan. 1840; *Considerations in Favor of the Nomination of Zachary Taylor by the Whig National Convention*, 'By a Conservative Whig', [Washington 1848], pp. 4–5; see also *Sun* (Baltimore), 19 April 1848.

10. Charles Sumner's comment on the eagle and the content of history textbooks are cited in Marcus Cunliffe, *Soldiers & Civilians: The Martial Spirit in America, 1775–1865*, Free Press, 1973, pp. 67, 69; *Davy Crockett in Davy Crockett's Own Story, as Written by Himself: The Autobiography of America's Great Folk Hero*, Citadel, 1955, p. 242.

11. On Lafayette's visit see Somkin, *Unquiet Eagle*, Ch. 4; the quotation is in Miller, *The Great Convention*, p. 11.

12. 'Hamilton', *An Address to the People of Rhode-Island, Published in the Providence Journal, In a Series of Articles During the Months of September and October, 1844*, Providence, 1844, p. 40; Sellers, *Polk, Continentalist*, p. 101.

13. *Signal* (Washington), 17 July 1852.

14. *New York Tribune*, 7 June 1852; Sellers, *Polk, Continentalist*, p. 91; 'Proceedings of the Democratic National Convention, Baltimore, June 1, 1852', Schlesinger & Israel (eds), *Presidential Elections*, ii, p. 962.

15. *Springfield Republican*, 8 June 1852.

16. *American Whig Review*, 92 (Aug. 1852), p. 133.

17. *New York Tribune*, 7 June 1852; *American Whig Review*, 92 (Aug. 1852) p. 127.

18. Cambreleng to Abraham Van Buren, 28 May 1840, Van Buren Papers. On Democrats' belief that they were the majority party see also Michael Wallace 'The Ideology of Party in the Age of Jackson', Ph. D. dissertation, Columbia U., 1973, esp. Ch. ix.
19. *New York Tribune*, 7 June 1852; Mackay in Berger, *British Traveller*, p. 91; Hone to Clay, 28 Nov. 1844, Colton (ed.), *Clay Corr.*, p. 508.
20. *Richmond Whig*, 22 June 1852.
21. On Tyler's failure to build a party, see Wallace, 'Ideology of Party', pp. 313–21, and William R. Brock, *Parties and Political Conscience: American Dilemmas, 1840–1850*, KTO Press, 1979, p. 107.
22. Green, *Harrison*, p. 314; 'Acceptance Letter of James K. Polk', 12 June 1844, Schlesinger & Israel (eds), *Presidential Elections*, i, p. 854; Lewis Cass to A. Stevenson, 30 May 1848, *Niles' Register*, 5 July 1848, p. 7; 'Whig Platform of 1844', Parker & Johnson, *Party Platforms*, p. 9; *New York Tribune*, 9 April 1852.
23. Francis Johnson to John J. Crittenden, 9 March 1838, Crittenden Papers; *Richmond Enquirer*, 20 Feb. 1840; A. V. Brown to Polk, 30 May 1844, A. Cullom to Polk, 30 May 1844, Polk Papers.
24. Chambers, *Benton*, p. 284; B. F. Butler to Jackson, 13 July 1844, Blair – Lee Papers, Princeton University Library. For a scheme for selecting a president by a mixture of election and lottery see [S. S. Nicholas], *Letters on the Presidency, by a Kentucky Democrat*, [1840].
25. 'Address of Jackson General Committee, N. Y.', *Speech of Mr. Bartlett, at a Meeting of Citizens Opposed to the Re-election of Andrew Jackson, holden at Portsmouth, N. H. Oct. 15, 1832*, p. 15; Miller, *The Great Convention*, pp. 34, 17; *The Whig Standard* (Washington), 25 April 1844; 'Hamilton', *Address to the People of Rhode-Island*, p. 37; *New York Tribune*, 9 April 1852.
26. 'A Voice From a Friend', *Richmond Enquirer*, in *Niles' Register*, 9 Sept. 1843, p. 23; *Philadelphia Herald* in *Springfield Republican*, 4 Jan. 1840; *New York Tribune*, 26 June 1852; *Richmond Whig*, 22 June 1852.

## Chapter 8: The presidential image

1. Daniel J. Boorstin, *The Image or What Happened to the American Dream*, Penguin Books, 1963, p. 208.
2. *The Life and Public Services of the Hon. James Knox Polk, with a compendium of his speeches on various public measures*, Baltimore, 1844; Cave Johnson to Polk, 10 June 1844; J. Geo. Harris to Polk, 19 July 1844, Polk Papers; Hawthorne quoted in Nichols, *Pierce*, p. 209. For a general study of campaign biographies see W. Burlie Brown, *The People's Choice: The Presidential Image in the Campaign Biography*, Louisiana State U.P., 1960.
3. 'Philo-Jackson', *The Presidential Election, written for the benefit of the People of the U. States, but particularly for those of the State of Kentucky; relating to the Seminole War, and the Vindication of General Jackson*, Frankfort, May 1824; *Maysville Eagle* (Ky) 5 Sept. 1848; *The Campaign* (Washington), 27 Sept. 1848, p. 274.
4. The anecdotes and phrases mentioned occur repeatedly in the several biographical sketches of their subjects. The principal sketches are cited

in the references for this chapter, although they represent only a small portion of such publications. The best collection of campaign material is in the Library of Congress.

5. *Franklin Gazette* (Philadelphia), 14 March 1822.
6. *Biographical Sketch of the Life of Andrew Jackson, Major-General of the Armies of the United States, the Hero of New-Orleans*, Hudson, N.Y., 1823, p. 7; William M. Holland, *The Life and Political Opinions of Martin Van Buren, Vice President of the Untied States*, Hartford, Conn., 1835, p. 28; Ben: Perley Poore, *Life of Gen. Zachary Taylor, the Whig Candidate for the Presidency*, n.p., n.d., p.l; *The Life and Public Services of Gen. Lewis Cass*, Hartford, 1848, p. 7; Nathaniel Hawthorne, *Life of Franklin Pierce*, Boston, 1852, p. 8; *Life of General Scott*, [New York, 1852], p. 1.
7. Eaton, *Life of Jackson*, p. 10; *The Life of Major-General William Henry Harrison: . . .* , Philadelphia, 1840, pp. 4–6; 'Hamilton', *An Address to the People of Rhode-Island*, p. 38; Poore, *Life of Taylor, p. 2;* Hawthorne, *Life of Pierce*, p. 11. On religion as a female domain see Barbara Welter, *Dimity Convictions: The American Woman in the Nineteenth Century*, Ohio U.P., esp. Chs 2 and 6.
8. *The Life of Major-General William Henry Harrison . . .* , p. 7; 'A Brief Biography of . . . Polk', *Young Hickory Banner*, 17 Aug. 1844, p. 17; Poore, *Life of Taylor*, p. 2; *Sketch of the Life of Major General William Henry Harrison. Comprising a Brief Account of his Important Civil and Military Services; . . .* , 1836, pp. 10–11; *Biographical Sketches of the Democratic Candidates for the Presidency and Vice Presidency*, [1844], p. 1; *Fifty Reasons Why the Hon. Henry Clay Should Be Elected President of the United States*, 'By an Adopted Citizen', Baltimore, 1844, p. 28; Poore, *Life of Taylor*, p. 1; *Life and Services of Cass*, p. 8; *The Life and Public Services of Gen. Franklin Pierce, the Democratic Candidate for the Presidency of 1852*, Boston, 1852, p. 4; Hawthorne, *Life of Pierce*, p. 7. On the political virtue of an identification with Nature, see John William Ward, *Andrew Jackson: Symbol for an Age*, Oxford U.P., 1962.
9. *A Brief History of the Public Services of Gen. William Henry Harrison . . .* , Harrisburg, 1835, p. 14; *Life and Services of Polk*, p. 4; *Clay and Frelinghuysen Songster*, New York and Philadelphia, 1844, pp. 10, 50; J. Reese Fry, *A Life of Gen. Zachary Taylor; comprising a Narrative of Events . . .* , Philadelphia, 1847, p. 17.
10. *Biographical Sketch of Jackson*, p. 64; James Hall, *A Memoir of the Public Services of William Henry Harrison, of Ohio*, Philadelphia, 1836, p. 57; *Biographical Sketches of the Democratic Candidates*, p. 1; Fry, *Life of Taylor*, p. 17; *A Sketch of the Life and Public Services of General Zachary Taylor, the People's Candidate for the Presidency, with Considerations in Favor of His Election*, Washington, 1848, p. 2; 'Oliver Oldschool', *Brief Outline of the Life of Henry Clay*, [Washington, 1844], p. 16.
11. *'Hero of Tippecanoe'; or the Story of the Life of William Henry Harrison*, 'Related by Captain Miller to his Boys', New York, 1840, p. 72; Fry, *Life of Taylor*, p. 328 *Life and Services of Cass*, p. 34; *Life and Public Services of Pierce*, p. 16.
12. Philo A. Goodwin, *Biography of Andrew Jackson*, Hartford, 1832, p. 6; *Life of Martin Van Buren*, Philadelphia [1844], pp. 1–2; James Hall,

*Memoir of Harrison*, pp. 11–12; *Political Biography: Polk, Dallas, & Shunk*, Philadelphia, 1844, p. 4; John S. Littell, *The Clay Minstrel; or, National Songster to which is prefixed A Sketch of the Life, Public Services, and Character of Henry Clay*, New York and Philadelphia, 1844, p. 15; *Life of General Scott*, p. 1.

13. *Biographical Sketch of Jackson*, p. 7; *Sketch of Life and Services of Taylor*, p. 2; *Life of General Scott*, p. 2; *Life and Public Services of Pierce*, p. 15; Holland, *Life of Van Buren*, pp. 94–102; 'Junius', *Life of Henry Clay*, New York, 1844, p. 5.

14. *Sketch of the Life of Major General William Henry Harrison*, 1836, p. 5; Henry J. Raymond, 'Life of Henry Clay', *The Whig Almanac and United States Register for 1843*, New York, p. 19, p. 28; Charles S. Todd and Benjamin Drake, *Sketches of the Civil and Military Services of William Henry Harrison*, Cincinnati, 1840, p. 160; *The Life of Gen. Frank. Pierce, The Granite Statesman*, 'by Hermitage', New York, 1852, p. 30.

15. Holland, *Life of Van Buren*, p. 362; [R. Hildreth], *The People's Presidential Candidate; or The Life of William Henry Harrison, of Ohio*, Boston 1839, p. 194; *Pol. Biography: Polk, Dallas, & Shunk*, p. 4; *A Brief Review of the Career, Character and Campaigns of Zachary Taylor*, Washington, 1848, p. 15.

16. Livermore quoted by Cunliffe, *Soldiers & Civilians*, p. 74.

17. *Life of Gen. Frank. Pierce*, 'by Hermitage', p. 45.

18. William Emmons, *Biography of Martin Van Buren, Vice President of the United States*, Washington, 1835, p. 38.

19. Holland, *Life of Van Buren*, pp. 13, 81, 199; Emmons, *Biography of Van Buren*, p. 13.

20. *Biographical Sketches of the Democratic Candidates*, [1844], p. 2; *Life and Public Services of Polk*, p. 7; *Pol. Biography: Polk, Dallas, & Shunk*, p. 4; 'A Brief Biography', *Young Hickory Banner*, 17 Aug. 1844, pp. 17–18.

21. *Biographical Sketch of Jackson*, p. 7; *Life and Public Services of Polk*, p. 3; *The Democratic Text-Book, containing the Life of Franklin Pierce . . .*, Philadelphia, 1852, p. 3.

22. Holland, *Life of Van Buren*, p. 28; *Biographical Sketches of the Democratic Candidates*, [1844], p. 1; *Life and Services of Cass*, p. 40; D. W. Bartlett, *The Life of Gen. Frank. Pierce, of New-Hampshire, the Democratic Candidate for President of the United States*, Auburn, 1852, p. 13; *Life of Gen. Frank. Pierce*, 'by Hermitage', p. 10; *Life and Public Services of Pierce*, p. 6.

23. Holland, *Life of Van Buren*, pp. 81, 358–9; *Pol. Biography: Polk, Dallas, & Shunk*, p. 4; *Life and Services of Cass*, p. 33; Hawthorne, *Life of Pierce*, p. 28.

24. Goodwin, *Biography of Jackson*, pp. 357, 386–414; Holland, *Life of Van Buren*, pp. 281–2, 285–97; *Life of Martin Van Buren* [1844], p. 13; *Life and Public Services of Polk*, p. 7; *Life and Services of Cass*, p. 29; *Life and Public Services of Pierce*, p. 10.

25. Holland, *Life of Van Buren*, pp. 51–3; Emmons, *Biography of Van Buren*, pp. 3–4; *Biographical Sketches of the Democratic Candidates*, [1844], p. 2; Hawthorne, *Life of Pierce*, pp. 139–40.

26. Holland, *Life of Van Buren*, p. 80; Emmons, *Biography of Van Buren*,

p. 41; *Life of Gen. Frank. Pierce*, 'by Hermitage', p. 17; *Life and Public Services of Polk*, p. 16.

27.  *Life of Gen. Frank. Pierce*, 'by Hermitage', p. 58.

28.  'Junius', *Life of Clay*, pp. 2, 4; Epes Sargent, *The Life and Public Services of Henry Clay*, New York, 1844, p. 3; Littell, *The Clay Minstrel*, p. 9.

29.  *Sketch of Life and Services of Taylor*, pp. 2, 21, 32; *Reasons Good and True for Supporting the Nomination of General Zachary Taylor*, [Washington, 1848], p. 3; Poore, *Life of Taylor*, p. 16.

30.  George Denison Prentice, *Biography of Henry Clay*, Hartford, Conn., 1831, p. 282; Raymond, 'Life of Clay', p. 36; *A Sketch of the Life and Public Services of William Henry Harrison*, New York, 1836, p. 31; *General Harrison in Congress*, [1840], p. 32; *Sketch of the Lives of Taylor and Fillmore*, Boston, 1848, p. 5; Edward D. Mansfield, *Life and Services of General Winfield Scott . . .*, New York, 1852, p. 344.

31.  *More than One Hundred Reasons Why William Henry Harrison Should and Will Have the Support of the Democracy, for President of the United States . . .*, 'By a Workingman', Boston, 1840, p. 14; Raymond, 'Life of Clay', p. 36; *The Presidency – Winfield Scott – Franklin Pierce*, p. 14.

32.  *Brief History of Services of Harrison*, p. 16; 'Junius', *Life of Clay* p. 3; 'Biographical Sketch of General Taylor', *The Taylor Text-Book, or Rough and Ready Reckoner*, Baltimore, 1848, p. 6; *Sketch of Life and Services of Taylor*, p. 30; *The Presidency – Winfield Scott – Franklin Pierce*, p. 14.

33.  Hall, *Memoir of Harrison*, pp. 151, 268–9; Sargent, *Life of Clay*, p. 7; Mansfield, *Life of Scott*, p. 344.

34.  *Brief History of Services of Harrison*, p. 6; [Hildreth], *People's Presidential Candidate*, p. 197; 'Junius', *Life of Clay*, p. 15; Poore, *Life of Taylor*, p. 9; Mansfield, *Life of Scott*, pp. 183, 185–8.

35.  *Sketch of Life and Services of Harrison*, p. 3; Littell, *The Clay Minstrel*, p. 9; *Sketch of the Lives of Taylor and Fillmore*, p. 3.

36.  Alexis de Tocqueville, *Democracy in America*, ed. Phillips Bradley, Vintage Books, 1945, i, pp. 185–6; Holland, *Life of Van Buren*, pp. 79–80; *Scioto Gazette* (Chillicothe, O.) 19 Dec. 1839.

37.  For other recent studies of party beliefs and values in this period see Rush Welter, *The Mind of America, 1820–1860*, Columbia U.P., 1975; John Ashworth, *'Agrarians' and Aristocrats': Party Political Ideology in the United States, 1837–1846*, Royal Historical Society Monographs [forthcoming], which emphasizes the radicalism of the Democrats and the conservatism of the Whigs; Marvin Meyers, *The Jacksonian Persuasion*, Standford U.P., 1957; Daniel Walker Howe, *The Political Culture of the American Whigs*, U. Chicago P., 1979.

## Chapter 9: The anti-image

1.  For discussions of 'negative reference group' activity and its part in the politics of this period see Lee Benson, *The Concept of Jacksonian Democracy: New York as a Test Case*, Princeton U.P., 1961, pp. 27–28, 284–6, 315–28; Michael F. Holt, *Forging a Majority: The Formation of the Republican Party in Pittsburg, 1848–1860*, Yale U.P., p. 81; Richard L.

McCormick, 'Ethno-Cultural Interpretations of Nineteenth-Century American Voting Behavior', *Political Science Quarterly*, No. 89 (June 1974), pp. 351–77.

2.  *Speech of Mr. Bartlett, at a Meeting of Citizens Opposed to the Re-election of Andrew Jackson, holden at Portsmouth, N.H. Oct. 15, 1832*, [Portsmouth, 1832], p. 10; *Johnny Q!* [n.p., n.d.], verse 9; *Letters addressed to John Sergeant, Manuel Eyre, Lawrence Lewis, Clement C. Biddle, and Joseph P. Norris, Esqrs. ....*, Philadelphia, 1828, p. 87; *A Brief Account of the Life and Political Opinions of Martin Van Buren, President of the U. States: from the Most Authentic Sources*, May 1840, p. 4; 'Speech of O. P. Baldwin, Esq.', in Miller, *The Great Convention*, 1840, p. 30; David Crockett, *The Life of Martin Van Buren, Heir-Apparent to the 'Government', and the Appointed Successor of General Andrew Jackson*, Philadelphia, 1837, pp. 27, 29; 'The Character of Mr. Clay', *Young Hickory Banner*, 7 Sept. 1844, p. 75; [Kendall's Expositor], *Life of Henry Clay*, [1844], pp. 81–3; *Prospect Before Us, or Locofoco Impositions Exposed*, 'Published by order of the Whig Congressional Executive Committee, at Washington', Washington, 1844, pp. 1–4; *Arguments in Favor of the Support of Taylor and Fillmore*, Washington, 1848, p. 2; 'The Opposition and Their Candidate', *Democratic Text Book 1852*, pp. 37, 40–1.

3.  *Our Country*, 26 July 1828; *Truth's Advocate and Monthly Anti-Jackson Expositor* (Cincinnatus), 1828, pp. 42–8, 183–91, 319; *A History of the Life and Public Services of Major General Andrew Jackson*, n.p., 1828, p. 9; *A Brief Inquiry into Some of the Objections Urged Against the Election of Andrew Jackson to the Office of President of the United States*, n.p., n.d., p. 7; *U.S. Telegraph Extra*, 1 March 1828; *The Claims of Martin Van Buren to the Presidency Fairly Represented, In a Sketch of the Chief Political Transactions of His Life*, [n.p., 1840], p. 9; *The Contrast: or, Plain Reasons why William Henry Harrison should be elected President of the United States, and Why Martin Van Buren Should not be re-elected*, 'By an Old Democrat', New York, 1840, p. 14; 'The Character of Mr. Clay', p. 75; 'Review of the Life and Services of Gen. Lewis Cass', *The Battery* (Washington), 6 July 1848, p. 4; 'General Scott's Pay and Allowances', *The Campaign* (Washington), 11 Sept. 1852, pp. 209–10.

4.  Crockett, *Life of Van Buren*, pp. 80, 180; Miller, *The Great Convention*, p. 31; *Prospect Before Us*, p. 25; 'Review of ... Cass', pp. 2–3, 5; *Great Speech of the Honourable James Buchanan, delivered at the Mass Meeting of the Democracy of Western Pennsylvania, At Greenburg, on Thursday, Oct. 7, 1852*, Philadelphia, 1852, pp. 6–7.

5.  *National Intelligencer*, 23 Oct. 1832; 'Granny Jackson's Lullaby to Little Martin', *U. S. Telegraph Extra*, 17 Sept. 1832, p. 33; *The Contrast*, p. 14; *A Brief Account of Life and Opinions of Van Buren*, p. 22; *Speech of Mr. Rathbun, of New York*, n.p., n.d., p. 7; *Young Hickory Banner*, 21 Sept. 1844, p. 106; *Papers for the People*, v, 24 July 1852, p. 91.

6.  *Politics for Plain Democrats*, [Philadelphia, 1836], p. 7; *The Conduct of the Administration*, Boston, 1832, pp. 21, 74; Sutherland, *Three Political Letters*, 1840, pp. 12, 19; 'Hamilton', *Address to the People of Rhode-Island*, 1844, p. 40; *American Whig Review*, Aug. 1852, p. 127; *Papers for the People*, v, 24 July 1852, p. 92; see also *Whig Testimony Against the Election of General Scott to the Presidency of the U.S.*, [1852], *passim*.

7. *U.S. Telegraph Extra*, 12 July 1828, pp. 275–6; *Pennsylvania Reporter* in *The Nose*, 7 Aug. 1828; Crockett, *Life of Van Buren*, p. 27; *The Contrast*, pp.10, 15; [Robert Mayo], *A Word in Season; or Review of the Political Life and Opinions of Martin Van Buren. Addressed to the Entire Democracy of the American People*, Washington, 1840, pp. 9–12; *Richmond Enquirer*, 16, 20 Sept. 1836; *Globe*, 7 July 1840; 'Review of... Cass', *The Battery*, 6 July 1848, p. 1.

8. *U.S. Telegraph Extra*, 12 July 1828, p. 278; *Conduct of the Administration*, p. 27; *U.S. Telegraph*, 7 Sept. 1836, in Erik McKinley Eriksson, 'Official Newspaper Organs and the Presidential Election of 1836', *Tennessee Historical Magazine*, ix (July 1925), p. 124; *Young Hickory Banner*, 17 Aug. 1844, p. 23; 'Review of... Cass', p. 5; *Arguments in Favor of the Support of Taylor and Fillmore*, [Washington, 1848], p. 2; *The Crisis* (Richmond), 21 Oct. 1840, p. 268.

9. *Conduct of the Administration*, p. 7.

10. 'The Character of Mr. Clay', *Young Hickory Banner*, 7 Sept. 1844, p. 75; *Speech of Rathbun*, p. 8; [Kendall's Expositor], *Life of Clay*, pp. 81–3, 86, 88; *Albany Argus*, 2, 4 Nov. 1844; 'Fifty Reasons Why Henry Clay Should Not Be President of the United States', *Young Hickory Banner*, 7 Sept. 1844, pp. 106–107; 'The "Embodiment"', *Lorrain Republican*, in *The Dollar Gobe*, 7 Aug. 1844, p. 114.

11. J. B. Mower to John McLean, 14 Nov. 1846, McLean Papers, Library of Congress; *Principles of the Two Parties. Speech of Hon. J. Thompson, of Pennsylvania, in the House of Representatives, Tuesday, June 27, 1848* ..., p. 5; see also *The Union*, 10 June 1848.

12. *Great Speech of Buchanan*, pp. 4–6; *Democratic Text Book 1852*, p. 37; Charles Winslow Elliott, *Winfield Scott: The Soldier and the Man*, Macmillan, 1937, pp. 429–31; *Richmond Enquirer*, 7 Sept. 1852; *Papers for the People*, v, 24 July 1852, pp. 91–2; *Whig Testimony Against Scott*, p. 1.

13. *Richmond Enquirer*, 16 Sept. 1836; *Young Hickory Banner*, 17 Aug. 1844, p. 23; *Papers for the People*, v, 24 July 1852, p. 91.

14. *Principles of the Two Parties*, pp. 5, p. 1; *Richmond Enquirer*, 16 Sept. 1836; *Young Hickory Banner*, 7 Sept. 1844, p. 106; *Papers for the People*, v, 24 July 1852, pp. 91–2.

15. *Globe*, 30 March 1840; *Great Speech of Buchanan*, p. 10; [Kendall's Expositor], *Life of Clay*, p. 86.

16. *Albany Argus*, 24 Oct. 1840; *Speech of Rathbun*, p. 5; *The Political Letters and Writings of General Scott, Reviewed, Discussed, and Compared*, [Washington, 1852], p. 14; *The Campaign*, 17 July 1852, p. 82; *Great Speech of Buchanan*, p. 9.

17. *Young Hickory Banner*, 21 Sept. 1844, p. 106; *Principles of the Two Parties*, p. 6; *Great Speech of Buchanan*, p. 8.

18. William Jagger, *A Book Addressed to the People of Suffolk County, Upon Some Important Points of National Policy*, [Brooklyn] 1836, pp. 28–9; Crockett, *Life of Van Buren*, pp. 13, 27 and *passim*; *Speech of Mr. Ogle, of Pennsylvania, on The Regal Splendor of the President's Palace*, n.p., n.d., p. 1; *The Claims of Martin Van Buren to the Presidency Fairly Represented*, p. 7; *The Contrast*, pp. 10, 13; *A Word in Season*, pp. 29, p. 21. See also Wallace, 'Ideology of Party', pp. 251–9.

19. *The Presidency – Winfield Scott – Franklin Pierce*, pp. 3, p. 1; 'Bela' in *New York Tribune*, 10 June 1852; 'The Democratic Nomination', *American Whig Review*, Aug. 1852, p. 133; *The Signal* (Washington), 1 July 1852.

20. 'The Hornet', *Political Primer*, 30 June 1828; *The Contrast*, p. 11; *Prospect Before Us*, pp. 23–4.

21. Crockett, *Life of Van Buren*, p. 13; *A Brief Account of Life and Opinions of Van Buren*, p. 21; 'Hamilton', *Address to the People of Rhode-Island*, p. 40; *Whig Text Book, or Democracy Unmasked. To the People of the United States*, Washington, 1844, p. 17; *The Presidency – Winfield Scott – Franklin Pierce*, p. 3; *The Battery*, 6 July 1848, p. 5.

22. *Politics for Plain Democrats*, p. 7; *Whig Text Book*, 1844, p. 2; *Arguments in Favor of the Support of Taylor and Fillmore*, p. 2; *American Whig Review*, Aug. 1852, p. 133; *A Brief Account of Life and Opinions of Van Buren*, p. 21; 'Hamilton', *Address to the People of Rhode-Island*, p. 40.

23. *A Brief Account of Life and Opinions of Van Buren*, p. 22; *A Word in Season*, pp. 16, 45; *The Contrast*, pp. 14, 16; *Speech of Hon. Andrew Stewart, of Penn., Delivered in the House of Representatives, U.S., August 3, 1848*, [Washington, 1848], p. 3; *American Whig Review*, Nov. 1852, p. 391.

24. *National Intelligencer*, 23 Oct. 1832; *The Contrast*, p. 14.

## Chapter 10: Conclusion: presidential campaigns and American political culture

1. *Address of the Democratic Hickory Club, for the City and County of Philadelphia, recommending Martin Van Buren As the Presidential Candidate for 1844*, [Philadelphia, 1843?], pp. 1–2.

2. James Bryce, *The American Commonwealth*, new edn, Macmillan, 1911, ii, p. 21.

3. Basil Hall in Clement Eaton (ed.), *The Leaven of Democracy*, George Braziller, 1963, p. 50; *Public Ledger* (Philadelphia) 15 Sept. 1836; Joseph G. Baldwin, *Party Leaders; Sketches of Thomas Jefferson, Alex'r Hamilton, Andrew Jackson, Henry Clay, John Randolph, of Roanoke, including Notices of Many Other Distinguished American Statesmen*, New York, 1855, p. 344.

4. *Niles' Register*, 9 Nov. 1844, p. 149.

5. *Journal of the Proceedings of the National Republican Convention, held at Worcester, October 11, 1832*, Boston, 1832, pp. 18–19 (see also *National Intelligencer*, 23 Oct. 1832, 8 Oct. 1844, *Richmond Enquirer*, 6 Nov. 1848, 29 Oct. 1852, *The Campaign*, 24 July 1852); *The Pennsylvanian*, 27 July 1836; *Richmond Whig*, 1 May 1840; A. E. Wing to Polk, 11 June 1844, Polk Papers; J. J. Crittenden to J. M. Clayton, 30 Aug. 1848, Clayton Papers, Library of Congress.

6. Seward in Heale, *Making of American Politics*, p. 162; Cass to A. Stevenson, 30 May 1848, *Niles' Register*, 5 July 1848, p. 7.

7. Jackson, 'First Annual Message', James D. Richardson (ed.), *A Compilation of the Messages and Papers of the Presidents, 1789–1897*, Government Printing Office, 1896, ii, p. 449; Marvin Meyers, *The Jacksonian Persuasion*, Standford U.P., 1957; see also James Roger Sharp, *The*

*Jacksonians versus the Banks*, Columbia U.P., 1970, and John Ashworth, *'Agrarians' and 'Aristocrats': Party Political Ideology in the United States, 1837–1846*, Royal Historical Society Monographs, [forthcoming].

8. 'Grattan', *The Globe*, 10 Oct. 1840.

9. *Richmond Whig*, 2 Jan. 1844.

10. Daniel Walker Howe, *The Political Culture of the American Whigs*, U. Chicago P., 1979, p. 236.

11. A. Logan to Van Buren, 12 Oct. 1836, Van Buren Papers; John Tyler to J. M. Clayton, 18 March 1840, Clayton Papers; Silas Wright to Harmanus Bleecker, [1842], Harriet L. P. Rice, *Harmanus Bleecker*, p. 148; E. Pettigreu to Henry Clay, 1 Jan. 1845, Colton (ed.), *Clay Corr.*, p. 518.

12. Brock, *Parties and Political Conscience*, p. 171; J. Mills Thornton III, *Politics and Power in a Slave Society: Alabama, 1800–1860*, Louisiana State U.P., 1978; Eric Foner, *Free Soil, Free Labor, Free Men: The Ideology of the Republican Party before the Civil War*, Oxford U.P., 1970. See also Michael F. Holt, *The Political Crisis of the 1850's*, Wiley, 1978.

13. John Campbell to J. J. Crittenden, 12 July 1839, in Kirwan, *John J. Crittenden*, p. 129; J. K. Kane to Polk, 30 May 1844, Polk Papers; W. C. Rives to Edmund Fontaine, 1 Jan. 1844, in *Richmond Whig*, quoted in *Springfield Republican*, 20 Jan. 1844.

14. Eric Foner, *Free Soil, Free Labor, Free Men*, pp. 8–9, discusses the notion that a stable democracy requires the major parties to share fundamental values, a condition which he believes obtained during the second party system but not in the political system of the 1850s.

15. Van Buren to A. Stevenson *et al.*, 23 May 1835, *Niles' Register*, 13 June 1835, p. 258.

# Index

in campaign of 1832, 86–91, 104,
109, 111, 218
in campaign of 1836, 93
in campaign of 1844, 99, 101
Democratic party forms around, 86
as Democratic patriarch, 173, 174–5
image of, 51, 53, 158, 159, 163–7,
170, 171, 173, 175
as military hero, 135, 138
as strong president, 150, 154
Van Buren visits, 97
Jackson administration
loses support in South, 113
National Republicans alarmed by, 109
Van Buren identifies self with, 92, 94
Jackson, Rachel, 71, 72
Jacksonians, the, 68, 86
and corrupt bargain charge, 65–6
and election of 1828, 73–4, 76–82,
189, 216
as nucleus of Democratic party, 83
Jefferson, Thomas, 1, 18, 23, 40, 41
in campaign of 1796, 3, 13–14, 16
in campaign of 1800, 16–17, 19, 39
death of, 24
distrust of government of, 6–7, 8
on Federalists, 15, 215
loses control of Congress, 22
on qualities of rulers, 9
re-elected, 24
reported comments of, on Jackson, 55
Jefferson administration, 18
Jefferson Day dinner, 1830, 87
Johnson, Cave, 100
Johnson, Richard M., 96, 98, 116, 144,
146

Kane, John K., 100
Kendall, Amos, 90, 97
Kennedy, John P., 60
Kentucky, 109
King, *see* Caesar, an American, and
monarchy
King, Rufus, 30
King, William R., 146, 199
Kitchen Cabinet, 194

Lafayette, Marquis de, 142, 175
Land Act, 1800, 159, 164, 181
Lane, Joseph, 146, 171
Latin America, 43, 46
Lee, Richard Henry, 14
legislative system

for choosing presidential electors, 21,
26
criticized, 28, 29
generally abandoned, 33
legislatures, state
political authority of, 20, 35
and presidential electors, 12, 25, 26,
33, 216
letter-writing, as campaign device
Jackson pioneers, 49, 72
popularised by Van Buren, 92–9, 104
used by Clay, 120, 122–4
used by Harrison, 114, 115, 117, 118,
120
used by Taylor, 125–7
used by Whigs, 107
used by White, 113
Lewis, William B., 77, 90
libertarian tradition
English origins of, 5, 6, 31, 58
in 18th century America, 8
in 1810s and 1820s, 30, 58, 77, 79, 80
in Jacksonian era, 152–3, 215, 224,
226–8
*Liberty Hall & Cincinnati Gazette*, 71
Liberty party, 122
Lincoln, Abraham, 149
Livermore, Abiel Abbott, 169
Locofocos, the, 94
Log Cabin campaign, 96, 106, 214 *see
also* campaign, presidential
election
Lowndes, William, 1, 66
luxury, corrupting influence of, 6, 8, 9,
24, 27, 28 *see also* Corruption

'Macbeth policy', the, 41–3
McCormick, Richard P., 34
McDuffie, George, 24, 28, 31
Mackay, Alexander, 147
Madison, James, 3, 4, 40
in campaigns of 1808 and 1812, 18, 24
as caucus candidate, 35
and Congress, 22
at constitutional convention, 1787,
11, 12
encourages Jefferson's candidacy, 14
on need for good rulers, 10
majority principle, 33, 94, 105, 187, 215,
227
Marcy, William L., 144, 146
Maryland, 27, 34, 59
Mason, George, 14
mass meetings, 106, 119